SAME GAME, DIFFERENT RULES

How to Get Ahead Without
Being a Bully Broad,
Ice Queen, or "Ms. Understood"

JEAN HOLLANDS

McGraw-Hill

New York   Chicago   San Francisco   Lisbon
London   Madrid   Mexico City   Milan
New Delhi   San Juan   Seoul   Singapore
Sydney   Toronto

McGraw-Hill

A Division of The McGraw·Hill Companies

2 3 4 5 6 7 8 9 10   DOC/DOC   0 9 8 7 6 5 4 3 2 1

ISBN 0-07-137967-3

This book was set in Bembo by Patricia Wallenburg.

Printed and bound by R.R. Donnelley & Sons.

McGraw-Hill books are available at special quantity discounts to use as premiums and sales promotions, or for use in corporate training programs. For more information, please write to the Director of Special Sales, Professional Publishing, McGraw-Hill, Two Penn Plaza, New York, NY 10121-2298. Or contact your local bookstore.

 This book is printed on recycled, acid-free paper containing a minimum of 50% recycled, de-inked fiber.

DEDICATION

I am a California girl, but my cousin's wedding brought me to New York City. Thank goodness. There I met my senior editor, Mary Glenn, and the wonderful Susan Clarey. They changed my life, and, I hope, yours. Others who helped were the special Dan Mandel, Joy Thisted, Nan Cascaddan, actually my whole staff, but especially Christina Syrett, Ellen Bona, Patricia Goss, Sandy Peterson, Jeanne Shizuru and the marvelous Sally Pera. Thanks, too, to Scott Amerman, Editing Supervisor, Maureen Harper, Production Supervisor, and the rest of the production team at McGraw-Hill.

Then there were those fabulous Bully Broads who teach me and inspire me and grow with me every night of our group, and every day when we can remember to be calm and demure while remaining our audacious and charming selves. Heidi, Helen, Francine and Suzann started it all.

Thanks always to the men in my life, my father, who was a great mentor for me; my husband, who loved me to his last breath, my brother, Ron Madsen, my sons, Glenn Hollands and Todd Hollands, and son of Thomas, James Hollands as well as my son-in-law and friend, Ron Steck. Lastly, Laura Hollands-Steck, who coached and studied these women and wrote with me, whose name is not on the title page, but whose inspiration and challenge made this book such a happy event.

CONTENTS

PREFACE

BULLY BROADS RUN IN THE FAMILY

Why did I write this book? I am from a long line of Bully Broads. With each generation, the trait diminishes a bit. My daughter, Laura, is less bullying than I, and I am less bullying than my mother, Helene. Well, what is this trait that is so readily identifiable?

We all act out on occasions when we are disappointed, rejected, or hurt. We quickly slap our disdain on the table and hope you are strong enough to take it. We've been known to say too much, too quickly, too loud, and too long. But, here's the rub: Despite the sometimes gruff and aggressive exterior we present, inside we are really mush balls who hate to hurt anyone and who are sensitive to slight and rejection.

If we teach what we ourselves need to learn, then undoubtedly my daughter and I became psychotherapists and corporate coaches who now work with executive women because we identify so strongly with Bully Broads. We want to help these intense, intimidating dynamos like ourselves who show anger or impatience but who feel compelled to hide pain and vulnerability.

Thousands of women referred by their premier Silicon Valley corporations to our executive coaching ranks can be classified as bullies, or the quieter Ice Queens. Time is usually their enemy and their excuse for acting abusive. Watching intimidating and aggressive women self-destruct is a painful and sobering experience. Ironically, these remarkably capable and talented women who aspire to power are handicapped by the very courage it took them to rise to the ranks of Director, Vice President, or CEO.

So we work with these women who sound and act like my Mom. (By the way, my mother was also a beautiful, generous, loving, and fun woman.) Sometimes they sound and act like my daughter and me. Sometimes they are all three of us in one body. However they manifest their Bully Broad attitudes and behavior, they are always in trouble. Yet the intimidators are often misunderstood and frequently used to buffer the timid manager who won't stand up to anyone. Bully Broads hardly notice that they are being used because their eyes, ears, body, and soul focus on the end result.

During the past twenty years, I have received countless calls from desperate, top-echelon corporate executives. The tone and content are remarkably similar: "Listen. I have to send Cecilia to you. I am finally at my wit's end. I can't protect her again. Being founder of this company doesn't give me enough leverage to help her anymore. She has no credibility left, and I am losing mine. The complaints outweigh the millions of dollars she brings to our company. She made this quarter happen, but I am losing good people. The trade-off is getting lopsided."

Cecilia recovered. She smoothed her edges, listened to others, softened the impact she made on others, and began to empower those around her. She joined our Bully Broads Group, which gave her the chance to be in the same room with other highly opinionated and intimidating women like herself. She learned to show vulnerability and to understand the negative effect of being sarcastic and abrupt. The edge disappeared.

When Cecilia reported back to us after several months, she said, "You guys saved my career. My boss thinks I've had a brain transplant, and my team thinks I've had a heart job. It was easy. I stopped thinking about myself and my own point of view all the time. I started disciplining myself. I held back sometimes. I smiled sometimes. I started showing the inside of me, and, surprisingly, nobody laughed. They called me brave. I can still get judgmental, but I know when to pick my battles, and I know how to mend fences if I go too far."

Many readers will identify with at least a few aspects of our Bully Broads' stories. You probably are also acquainted with someone like this. There seems to be one in every office. Just hearing the label, women say, "Oh, yeah, I used to work for one," or "My boss is one." Just as this book can give you rules for playing the game *without* becoming a Bully

Broad, it can also give you some tips for dealing with the Bully Broads and Ice Queens who are already in your life. Understanding the exceptional bully woman and then understanding yourself—your fears, your habits, and your working style—will start the journey.

But playing the game doesn't mean letting things slide, especially when you are faced with another Bully Broad. You will have to learn to stand up to someone who is just bluffing or to someone else who can be tamed with just a little courage from you. Are you a masochist who keeps taking it and turning the other cheek, or are you afraid to confront her issues? In learning how to handle your own Bully Broad tendencies, you will learn how to respond to a real Bully Broad who doesn't know the rules.

I want to thank the clients and organizations that support us and pay us to do our work and our research. I especially want to thank the Bully Broads who took a chance and trusted us to guide them through the minefield. These very special women allowed us to show them how to make life-altering changes, and I want them to know how profoundly grateful we are for the opportunity to have participated in the transformation process.

Finally, there is another population to worry about. It is you, the potential bully—those of you who will become our leaders, our heroines, our models. At the moment you may be doing everything right, you are credentialed, and so far you are conducting yourself with professional decorum. This book will prepare you, however, for the crisis moments you may experience. It will prompt you not to jump into the bully roles.

Our male leadership models have exercised their egos and treated us to their tirades over the years, some without punishment. Women can't seem to get away with it as well as men can. Stop moaning about that, and start equipping yourself with the soft touch, even in hard times. Your patience may wear thin over time. Only stress and changing rules and high drama could turn you into that bully. Plan on stress and changing rules and high drama. It will be part of your future. As a corporate salvage expert, my goal is to catch you before you trip the circuit breaker.

THE PURPOSE OF THIS BOOK

This book is designed to do three things:

1. Help every woman achieve psychological balance, integrating her emotions and intellect so that she becomes a whole, multidimensional woman.
2. Show Bully Broads how to channel the energy they now expend recklessly and randomly into more productive relationships and processes.
3. Provide tools to repair and enhance interpersonal relationships for all women at work.

Find your own favorite chapter. Find your own rule. Make something happen before you close the book. You cannot afford not to. Whether you are a Bully Broad, Ice Queen, or an Everywoman on the go, we have tasks for each of you. Women at work—that's us. To make it work; work it!

Jean A. Hollands
Mountain View, California

INTRODUCTION

This book is about women who pay a steep emotional price for winning in corporate America. It is also about the victims of these exceptional women.

In the game of ascending the corporate ladder, some men have succeeded by grabbing power with both hands and doing whatever it takes to hold on, using intimidation, impatience, and aggression as their tools. In short, they have been bullies. Maybe they are disliked by their subordinates and colleagues, but they can also be the darlings of management and richly rewarded for their behavior. On the other hand, very few women can succeed with such heavy-handed tactics.

The corporate bosses who call the male bullies among their subordinates "aggressive" and then promote them may have very different things to say about their female employees who are similarly hard-driven. The direct reports who will go no further than grumbling by the water cooler when faced with a merciless and unforgiving male boss seem to leave in droves when faced with a woman whose demands are no more over the top.

The sordid truth? No one likes a bully. Even so, in today's business climate, many men can get away with it. Women almost never can.

By the way, we are not talking about the schoolground bully who torments young adults into the hellish acts of this new century. We are not even talking about the psychotic employee who chooses to be physically abusive. We are talking about intimidating nuances and language which can worry someone into a nonproductive state.

This book, though, is not about why men can get away with some things that women can't. We know that may be true, but we don't care. We simply want to help women who seem to be so easily labeled with the "B" word. The truth is that a reputation for bullying can often damage a man's career, too, and men who are bullies can be helped by this book as much as any woman. I have even given much of the data already to intimidating men in our practice who want to change their image.

But in this new era of the executive leader, bullying behavior seems to have become a much bigger problem for women. Of the people who are referred to our twenty-one-year-old corporate coaching company, 28 percent are women—a figure that has risen from 15 percent in the last two years. Of these women, 95 percent are referred because of intimidating styles. For the 72 percent of referrals who are men, there is a whole range of reasons—presentation skills, delegation, withholding of information, stressors, team play, and so on. Few of the men referred are labeled bullies. Go figure.

Bully Broads are usually very high profile women. They are exceptional. You may know one or two, or be one of them yourself. If you are one of them, you spend the money, deal the deals, win the wars, sell the contracts, and run the institutions. You have emerged into the world to grow and build empires, and you are here to stay. You are the titans of the world, the successful and powerful alpha females, the women managers and executives who drive some of the premier New York Stock Exchange and Nasdaq corporations. You are the darlings of your bosses and customers. Companies love your work. Your drive and dedication enhance profits and production. Until you have a problem ...

We define Bully Broads as aggressive and driven women who are completely misunderstood by their friends and colleagues. Ice Queens are the more silent bully type who can appear to be judgmental without saying a word. Unfortunately, they are all also usually in the dark about the enormous impact they have on others. They don't believe there is another way to get the job done. They work long and hard, with intensity and aggressiveness tipping the scales if they are stressed or in a state of ambiguity, or when things are out of control. Exceptional women come in all forms, colors, and personalities. Bully Broads happen to be at the top of our lists of problem executive women. Those 95 percent of the women who are coached by our firm are known as intimidating, controlling, aggressive women, who are, at the same time, the cream of the corporate crop.

Everybody understands what we're talking about. This exceptional woman carries a very high profile. She disdains weakness. She is well known in any organization. Even her family knows she is rather exceptional. She is tacitly understood as the sibling who is in charge, the one who will take care of the elderly parents, or at least handle their affairs.

We are interested in the Bully Broad because she seems to be the woman with the most high-maintenance problems—but with the lowest amount of feedback about her behavior. Our program grew into executive coaching because we realized that the derailed executive or the new leader with enhanced responsibility is often in the dark about what he or she needs to do to win the support of management, colleagues, or subordinates.

Bosses seem to get away with just performance coaching—not interpersonal coaching. Most reviews are about tasks. Of course, tasks are easier to measure. Measuring rapport-building, team-building, and morale-building traits is much more sophisticated and requires a systems orientation in the evaluation. We teach executives how to listen, give and take critical feedback, and inspire those around them to achieve cooperative and efficient work methods. Those skills are difficult to measure and to coach.

In this new management era, however, collaboration is vital. Exceptional women, or Bully Broads, seem to be one-woman teams. But today we all have to know how to work at intertwining our talents and roles. When our company merges with another, we have to learn to navigate in a new culture and align with the former competition.

When Sun Microsystems and Netscape formed an alliance, we knew that this called for new interactive skills. The enemy became our sister or brother. Then America Online was added to the Sun-Netscape family alliance, and we had a mix of cultural temperaments, management styles, and corporate agendas. When Microsoft—with its confident and self-assured employees—merges or takes over a smaller company like Visio, we expect new challenges for the stars of yesterday.

These new pairings provide opportunities for emotional growth in all forms of leaders, but the blended families require leaders who are team players.

This book is written for the Bully Broad, but especially for those women who are in the earlier stages of their careers, and who need to learn how to exhibit the aggressive, go-get-'em attitude necessary for success, without crossing the line into a style of management that might be seen by others as abusive and coercive. It is written for high-tech, low-tech, and no-tech organizations that suffer the subliminal or the very obvious dysfunction of the woman who tries too hard, drives too hard, wants too much, and thinks she can do it all.

Not all of these intimidating women occupy high places. The Bully Broad can be found at the secretarial desk, the bank teller's cash box, or waiting on you at your nearest convenience store. She is some-one whose fierce determination outweighs her ability to understand the "people damage" around her. She may be controlling. She may demonstrate a fierce level of entitlement. You know the ones I mean. This book also includes tips and suggestions for dealing with these and other as yet unreformed Bully Broads around the office.

The goals we have for Bully Broads, their victims, and you are, first, psychological balance, integrating the emotions and the intellect. Second, we hope to channel the intellectual energy that some women expend recklessly and randomly. Third, we want to make you all more productive and efficient and less stressed. Last, we want to provide tools for personal interventions with others and repair kits for inter-personal relationships that go astray.

Many executive coaches will tell you stories of the Bully Broad. You might be married to her, mothered by her, or supervised by her. Others of you are simply trying to supervise her. We have conducted our form of executive coaching for the last decade—and the decade before that in the field of counseling—with leaders from all over the world taking our classes and accepting our advice. The Bully Broad has been one of our biggest challenges.

People don't like to give 360-degree feedback about a Bully Broad, even when it is collected confidentially. They still fear retaliation. The 360-degree evaluations are the most popular and sustaining evaluations that management consultants have been able to use for employees. Many companies have built their own instruments, asking people to evaluate an employee based on the company's values and the position's criteria. The 360-degree survey asks managers, peers, and subordinates to judge this employee based on an inventory of items predetermined for the employee. Our company has its own evaluation tool and there are probably thousands around. It gives the whole view of the employee, based on a circumference of individual views of the employee. It can be very illuminating, but it can also be very disappointing. Many a client has wept and groaned and felt very depressed over these 360s. The results are there in measurable black-and-white numbers, with a range of 1 to 5 (low to high ratings) average for each category.

Because the results of these tests seem to be so reliable and so visual, the Bully Broad may receive some startlingly eye-opening scores. Those who complete them for her seem afraid to tell the truth. Even though the inventories are confidential, the victims of her abuse are often afraid the system will break down and she will discover who has given her these scores. But we all must take the risk and start somewhere.

You are about to change your life. Get the medals, certificates, and trophies out. Either you are becoming the brave heart who can take on a bully or you are the falsely accused intimidator who is misunderstood. Most of you are probably a little of both. You will be making life-changing adjustments. Don't worry. Most of these changes are slight, and they will bring on big results. You will still be you, and you will not have to give up the best parts of yourself. You will still have your own integrity and principles. You will simply make some enhancements that will bring about a new view of you.

ABOUT THE PHRASE

We know the words *bully* and *broad* may be uncomplimentary and don't sit well with some people. We tested these words for eighteen months, and they are the only two words that seemed to evoke the primal response we were looking for. Everyone, even those who hated the words, knew what we were talking about.

When we conduct our programs, both managers and candidates for the program are asked to provide goals for the person who has been referred to us. Over the past ten years, nearly all managers and all Bully Broads have given us identical goals. Following is a typical list of goals.

From the boss:

1. Reduce the complaints about outbursts and offending behavior.
2. Improve relations with peers and subordinates who find you intimidating.
3. Learn how to respond appropriately in critical situations.
4. Repair working relationships damaged by aggressiveness.
5. Manage your own stress and the stress you cause in others.

At first, few hard-core Bully Broads believe these to be viable goals. They may actually have very different goals from their bosses or the company. In the first stages, their goals usually look more like this:

1. Find out how to get Phil (that incompetent) out of my department.
2. Get more resources for my group.
3. Convince management to screen out incapable colleagues.
4. Help the company to be more efficient.
5. Get Human Resources off my back.

The Bully Broad is misunderstood. She doesn't translate well, especially to the more formal, cautious, or timid employee. She works hard and often does not get the credit she deserves because she has angered so many people along the way. There is a high burnout rate among Bully Broads.

The attrition rate of her employees is usually equally scandalous. Over time, the complaints far outweigh the compliments, and the complaints are always the same: "She alienates people. Most folks are wary of her intimidation tactics. And nobody wants to tell her." But she may not realize that people feel this way. She believes that staying the course with a clenched fist will energize others and may propel them to get the job done. She has little patience for the wishy-washy tactics of those whom she calls manipulators. Bully Broads loathe deceit and cunning, and like it straight with no chaser.

Ironically, the majority of these heavy-handed women haven't a mean bone in their bodies. They are actually wonderful human beings, but their defense mechanisms can sometimes cover up the woman inside who hates to show weakness and is afraid of being hurt.

It is easier to be angry and gruff. Bully Broads feel better showing anger than pain. Ultimately, the strong opinions and results-driven style derail some women. They burn too many bridges and hurt too many people.

We will explore the bully/victim syndrome and give you solutions to change your spots. We will introduce the four types of Bully Broad: the *Sounding-Off Tyrant* (ST), the *Sarcastic Aggressive* (SA), the *Selectively Quiet* (SQ), and the *Silent Judge* (SJ).

Who is this Bully Broad? Despite her brusque and crusty manner, she is likely to be the person who:

- Is awarded more contracts than anyone else
- Contributes the most to the bottom line
- Is the top saleswoman
- Produces as much as 60 percent of the company's revenue
- Is the chief technologist on the product that defines her company
- Is the corporation's worldwide marketing guru
- Gets the job done

How do you explain this paradox? She is productive, successful, and, in many cases, even loving, but she doesn't appear so. She is an enigma to herself and others.

The list of counterproductive and self-sabotaging behavior that eventually undoes the Bully Broad is long. The eruptions of her worst traits happen in crisis. She seems to attract drama. Bully Broads tend to show working behaviors in the following list:

1. Tunneling in without attending to the people in the way
2. Leaving broken bodies strewn across the landscape
3. Hating incompetence and making no attempt to hide her displeasure
4. Disrespecting and sometimes stepping on those who seem afraid
5. Speaking her mind without judging the impact of her words
6. Failing to realize she is intimidating
7. Alienating colleagues, subordinates, and bosses
8. Being unable to express vulnerability
9. Hating to cry in public
10. Hating to cry at all

Bully Broads work hard and achieve credentials, degrees, and awards at high levels. They also tend to:

1. Fear weakness in themselves
2. Have high expectations of themselves and others
3. Be time-driven and time-deprived
4. Have few friends and few confidantes on the job
5. Be completely goal-driven
6. Deny their limitations in the fear they might appear weak
7. Be good-hearted, but express only toughness
8. Be fiercely competitive
9. Have little resilience when intimidation doesn't work

The intense bully can snap and turn into an ogre when the tension rises. Why are these women willing to be so abusive and strong-willed?

Many of these women:

1. Learned the debate style of argument in their early life.
2. Admire a particular family member or mentor who openly asserted and got what he or she wanted.
3. Have been successful with aggressive and forceful behavior learned early in their career.
4. Get depressed when thwarted or challenged.
5. Are often loved, praised, and promoted until they become a liability, and are, eventually, ostracized or dismissed.

Beneath the casehardened exterior, Bully Broads are rarely as ferocious and tough as the image they project. They are usually much kinder to their subordinates than to their peers. They can work better with their bosses and those in a superior position than they may with colleagues, whom they might perceive as competitors. However, they are known to put managers in their place whenever they think they deserve it. Fiercely competitive, these women take no prisoners.

Asking a Bully Broad to change is bound to trigger knee-jerk defensiveness. Some will immediately jump to the conclusion that they are being asked to forsake their finest quality—honesty. "I will not abandon my principles and become wishy-washy just to be political!" she may well proclaim self-righteously.

But women at work will need to be aware of the typical response to the very behaviors we learned from men. Bullies are rarely truly popular, but men have been able to pull off the bully routine in a way that women simply cannot. For whatever reason, realistically or not, women are expected to be fair, nurturing, and caring. When we don't appear so, the shock is huge and the punishment is often fatal to a career.

After having coached thousands of Bully Broads, we can attest that they are capable of making changes. The transformation process, however, is not easy. When we meet a Bully Broad in our work, she is probably already in trouble. Even when she self-refers, she often has an underlying fear, deeply tucked under her aggressive style. Her fear may be that she can't perform a particular task well, or that she is really not good enough, or—heaven forbid!—that she will be discovered. Her intimidating behavior has muddied the waters and she may be drowning in the riptide. Her working traits have now become entrenched habits that she may not know how to relinquish.

Once you, the exceptional woman, understand how you are behaving and you come to realize that you are imminently at risk of destroying your career, you have two choices: redefine yourself and alter your *modus operandus* or lose the new responsibility, position, or the job itself.

But playing the career game using women's rules isn't limited to curbing your own bully broad habits. If you work around, for or under one of these Ms. Understoods, your insights to their behavior can help you deal with other intimidators around the office, be they bosses, colleagues, or even your direct reports.

This book, then, is about change. You must change; she must change. We will give you tests and prepare you for the four stages of change—"No Clue," "Know It/Lose It," "Doing It," and "Got It!"

You, the reader, will meet exceptional women who have positively altered their lives. If you identify with these women, you have a golden opportunity to profit from what they have learned. If you also identify with the victims of Bully Broads, you must believe that walking the line between Bully Broad-ness and success can help turn even wimps into heroes. Managers can and do learn specific techniques for handling their aggressive intimidators more effectively. Only you can determine the necessity and the urgency for changing your life. If your intuition tells you that you must do something now, then keep reading!

The twenty-five rules spelled out in this book can apply to anyone. All of us can benefit from the reminders included throughout. Women intimidators, particularly, need these concentrated nudges.

This book is *not* written to turn women into ninnies. I love strong women and I want them to have a better chance to be heard, seen, and promoted. If you are a Bully Broad, your success will come from harnessing and controlling your talents and energy, not muzzling them. So, off we go!

THE BULLY BROADS GROUP

Jackie, Theresa, Sally, Serena, Pat, Alice, Pauline, Georgia, Cynthia, and many others, were charming and talented, and held mostly executive-level positions. All of these women had a great deal of responsibility. One participant was a president and several were vice presidents of some of the major national companies. They were sparkling jewels—representing the best of the best in Silicon Valley.

On the first night together, we asked each woman to introduce herself and then to tell the story of how she got to this place. The stories were strikingly similar. Their mouths fell open and their eyes widened when they heard each other describe the path they took to our group. Each woman talked about her job, her company, and her professional history. Each began with a saga that sounded something like this:

> I've been sent to this Distinguished Executive Program because my boss thinks I am intimidating to others, sometimes even with him. I can't understand what he is talking about. I've never had a problem before, although people always told me I was intense.
>
> I work around or for a group of wimps. The efficiency of our company is low. I have to endure some incompetent souls who should not be on the job. They should be in the soup line, or serving soup, or being served for soup.
>
> I just say what I mean and I am not afraid to say it. I am honest and direct. I don't believe in manipulation. Say what you mean and say it straight. If I want to know something, I ask. I don't beat around the bush. It is so frustrating to see people cower around me.
>
> I don't know what they are afraid of. I don't know how I intimidate; I'm just doing my job. I really am mad about this whole thing. Why was I singled out? I am the best worker our company has.

And, by the way, don't expect me to give up my principles. I am honest to a fault, but I am not going to go mealy-mouthing around trying to placate people. It is condescending to talk down to people and kiss up with nice phrases I don't mean. So don't make me say any.

Each of these women is highly respected in her company. They have been endowed with great stock packages and fabulous wages. They also have the requisite pedigrees and degrees. The average education level is MBA; many also have Ph.D.s.

These women do not look like bullies. The first few who arrived were petite, willowy, short, blond, blue-eyed, and very professional looking. They all had flirtatious styles and, of course, they were articulate and sophisticated.

The Bully Broads group is going on two years old—"the terrible twos"! The group now includes an average of fourteen women at any given time, some coming and some going as they graduate. Most want to stay in the group permanently. It is always wonderful fun to have a newcomer join the group because she reminds the others of the first-timers they all once were.

As an executive coach, I had become weary of saying the same things over and over to these individual women in their private coaching sessions. So we decided to try a sort of a class. I have twenty-five years of experience with group dynamics, and my assistants, including my daughter Laura, have been faithfully conducting groups weekly for twelve years. However, the Bully Broads Group was a new venture. This is really a voluntary group of people who want to learn about themselves. This came as a surprise to my colleagues. We were not sure which of the invited women would show up.

We originally asked eight women from our executive coaching program to join. "Join a group? Are you kidding?" they responded. Being diligent students, they came to the first session, but I can tell you that none were enthusiastic.

Eventually our group became integrated and varied. We were of different sizes, shapes, races, and creeds. What we seemed to have in common were our working styles. But every woman was accomplished and stunning. Every single one had won acclaim in her current working world. Every one had worked hard and persistently to get to her current career position, and every one of them had some of the following characteristics applied to her in person, in a review, or in a 360-degree evaluation:

Abrasive	Abrupt	Accusing	Aggravating	Blaming
Caustic	Clipped	Driven	Frightening	Impatient
Impudent	Intimidating	Irritable	Loud	Outrageous
Pushy	Rude	Sarcastic	Self-centered	
Sharp-tongued	Tough-minded	Tyrannical		

We initiated the Bully Broads Group at GLC by sending out a flyer to some of the participants in the Distinguished Executive Program as well as to some Human Resources people at various organizations. The flyer looked something like this:

Stress Management for Overconscientious, Successful Exceptional Women
Alias: The "Bully Broads" Group...

First Thursday of Every Month—4:30 p.m. to 6:30 p.m.

This special group will be made up of some great women who are confident and assertive, but sometimes have a difficult time showing vulnerability—which makes them pretty frightening. We will facilitate the group, to learn, share, get insight, laugh at ourselves, and grow a little. — *Jean Hollands and Laura Steck*

Bully broads have the following characteristics:

Very task-driven.
Do not show vulnerability easily.
Limit confidential information.
Limit intimate relationships.
Do not read their impact on others.
Have a "mush ball" inside.

We were afraid to call it what it really was at first, but it took only one meeting to get past that. As soon as these women sat down with each other and understood how much they had in common, they liked each other, and within minutes they also realized how much work they had to do together.

I also wrote a personal letter to a few special candidates. Others I just begged to come. Most of them replied, "Are you serious? Sit around with a bunch of women who are complaining because nobody understands them? Ugh!" Here's the actual letter:

Dear Friend and Colleague:

Thank you for being a woman—in the workplace—in a position of power—in our sphere of influence—and in the state of courage it takes to be an executive woman today.

Oh, I know. You don't all feel powerful at any given moment. Neither do I. But we need to stick together anyway and support our work even when it falls short of our own expectations.

Enclosed is our flyer about Stress Management Group, alias "Bully Broads"—women who are known as a little too aggressive sometimes. They are seen as intimidators on the job. The participants in this group will teach one another some political and business moves, given their styles. These are incredible, powerful, successful women who are having a great time together learning to soften their reputation a little.

This class will be harnessing and using the great, creative, intense energy of women who care. I believe it will change the tone and timbre of some working women in our Silicon Valley—no less the world. Thanks for listening. Call to check in with me.

With continued excitement,

Jean Hollands

FOUR CATEGORIES OF BULLIES

Type One: The Sounding-Off Tyrant (ST)

This is the aggressive woman who acts out with a crowd around her. She isn't shy about making a scene. She tends to throw tyrannical tantrums and is immune to those who work around her. She is loudly self-righteous and she frightens most of her audience when she is in her high gear. She is used to acting out and sometimes doesn't even mean much by it. If only frightened listeners knew to respond with humor, with a show of their own strength, or by limit setting, she wouldn't have reinforced her bully tendencies.

Type Two: The Sarcastic Aggressive (SA)

This woman is seen as a put-down artist. She has an edge. Her mocking tongue is sharp and she often disguises her anger with harsh sarcasm. She will claim she is being humorous, but others may get her point only too sharply.

She doesn't mean to sound so deadly. She enjoys a good laugh, is very thick-skinned, and doesn't mind it when others get right back at her. She doesn't realize that most people don't have her on-the-spot wit and don't see her dark humor for what it truly is—her way to relate.

Type Three: Selectively Quiet (SQ) but with High Expectations

This one sets the bar high. She is rational in her approach and can be very calm, but her colleagues whisper that she never lets up. She may seem to be someone who is always keeping score or waiting to catch others at mistakes. Her subordinates are never at rest when she is on.

But she is not as demanding as she would appear. Often all she has to do to smooth relations in her department is relieve her coworkers once in a while with lightness or personal insight, rather than what they perceive to be criticism.

Type Four: Silent, but Judging (SJ)

This is the Bully Broad who rarely bullies—at least, not openly. She is also our typical Ice Queen. Her insight is acute and her observations are sharp, but she rarely speaks. When she does it is profound and often pretty damaging. Because she is more discreet than most, her co-workers often feel that they don't know what she is thinking. They also claim that she usually has a set frown on her face when she is listening, thinking, or processing.

The Silent, but Judging Bully Broad is a classic Ms. Understood. Often her frown is a sign that she is just trying hard to understand, or is maybe a little distracted. If only she would speak up more, share more, and let out her human side, her colleagues would stop seeing her silences as ominous.

▷┼◈▸○◂◈┼◁

We have all four types in our group. They tend to have overlapping traits, and you will find this to be true, too. You may shift from type to type, depending on your surroundings and your temperament. Or you know or work with or for someone who shifts from type to type. The four types grow and contract from session to session. With insight, they calm some of the old habits. We even have some silent bullies who did not know they appeared to be sitting in judgment of others. We have graduated some group members. Isabel left her company with three years' pay and a wonderful consulting job. Marlene got a new job. She was one of the withholding types of bullies, always looking like she was interrogating you and expecting you to have the right answers. Well, she called me recently to tell me how she interviewed. Actually, this woman was an anomaly in our group. She was not overtly intimidating, but she held back her judgment so that everyone was always wondering what she was thinking. They politely labeled her "a black hole." She changed. Months went by and we heard from her after her job search. This is the message she sent to us from her interview: "I was amazing. I was wildly forthcoming. My old colleagues would never have recognized me. I was free and open and truly charming, and I spoke up without waiting to appraise the situation. The interviewers seemed at ease. I was too. I got the job!" She brought us each a dozen roses the next week.

Another Bully Broad, Joanne, had been placed on probation, but she will now be a managing partner in the organization. While she was on probation she made some automatic slips in behavior. The irony is that she didn't know what she was doing at the moment the slip was occurring. She couldn't stop herself in the middle of it, but she later realized what had happened. Of course, the group comforted her and reassured her that she was going to have some blips here and there, and that knowing it had happened made the difference.

Another wonderful woman, Trish, came in one night crying. "I'm on probation now and I've screwed up on the very first day!" she lamented. "I had a fit about someone. I didn't yell or scream, but I did impress on her that it was her fault. And I think my ears got red. I'll never make it. I'm just too bossy."

She passed the probation and was promoted. "I am having such a good time now. Of course, my year-end bonus will not be as big as it has been, but I am actually having fun and I think they like me now. Gads, I didn't even know I wanted to be liked."

A few months later another Bully Broad, Caitlin, took us all in a stretch limousine to San Francisco for an enormous dinner. She was thanking us for seeing her through the tough times. The tough times had nearly cost her health, her career, and her family. She is a big success now, but a quieter one!

CASE STUDY

Jackie is a client whose story illustrates the fundamental Bully Broad character with all its paradoxes, problems, and hope. Jackie is the number-one salesperson in her high-tech Fortune 1000 company. She has won all the awards, nationally and internationally. She gets the job done—sales in the millions, beating out 500 men and women in the last ten years. She is poised to be the VP of Sales. She looks good, has a professional demeanor, and her customers are addicted to her.

"Jackie, you know the company loves you," the CEO begins. "You've outsold everybody and John [the President] and I are in your debt. But we can't give you this job. Your reputation in the company is killing you. People think you're the most aggressive monster they've ever seen. Your own staff is terrified of you, and your peers want to see you fail. John and I like your numbers, but we distrust your style. We want you to calm down, slow up, rest up, and take off the boxing gloves."

"You mean, in spite of my sales, I don't deserve the job?" Jackie screamed. She couldn't believe her ears.

If it were just about sales, of course, Jackie would have the job. But she had created enemies at her home base, and she wasn't even aware of how frightening she was to people. She lived with the delusion that sales were enough. Sadly, they were not.

When Jackie decided to take a look at herself, we showed her the written evaluations from her bosses, co-workers, peers, and subordinates—complete with anecdotes that demonstrated how they'd come to their opinions about her. Jackie was appalled. This information was completely outside her reality, and it hurt.

Jackie went through all the stages of grief. First, she was outraged: "How dare you spy on me? How dare you take comments out of context? How dare those wimps complain about me when they never even hinted of any of this to my face?" Then she went into denial: "No, this is not happening. You're playing a foolish joke. You know what I mean to the company. You couldn't be keeping this promotion from me over some petty issues from petty employees!"

Depression and despair followed. "Well, I can see I am not appreciated here. I have to quit. It is a sad world when I kill myself for years and end up with this pile of garbage. I'm out of here." Grief often includes a bargaining phase. Jackie tried, "Why don't you just fire all my peers? I can make as many sales as all of them put together anyway. And I will terminate my 'nark' staff members who sabotaged me. They are not loyal and I don't need them."

The last step in grieving is acceptance. For Jackie, this happened two weeks later in our office. "I can't believe people really hate me. What hurts so much is that Janet and Lois were afraid of me and Bob and Bernie actually thought I was ruining their careers. I can't bear thinking they all hate me and want me out of there. I didn't know I had this hideous reputation."

Jackie cried for a very long time. "I don't want to hurt anyone," she said. "I am the kind who carries bugs out of my house in a spoon. I don't think of myself as a monster. What a way to get a job done. I am really a mess."

Ultimately, Jackie looked inside herself. She realized she had been driven internally by a mother's clock ("Hurry or you'll miss out"), a New York pace ("Stay on target and don't look around"), a rewarded style ("Boy, you sure get the sales"), and a head-down approach. She had been moving only toward the goal, and not toward the people around her. Jackie worked *results* rather than *relationships*. The only relationships she worked were with her customers, the people outside the company to whom she sold the product. She didn't realize that the colleagues around her were also customers.

Jackie recovered and became the new VP. Her boss said it was a miracle. Actually, it was an easy transition. Jackie listened to some new voices for a change. She was finally ready to believe the perceptions of others and not just her own sales pitch to herself. She made friends, listened to feedback, and began to trust the perceptions of others in addition to her own. She even admitted that she probably had some big blind spots about herself and would have to look at them on a regular basis. She knew her new allies could give her that mirror.

>—+·+>·+·O·+<+·+·<

What Jackie went through in reforming her Bully Broad tendencies is typical of most Bully Broads. The change from Bully Broad to success story usually occurs over four stages:

1. *The "No Clue" Stage: Unconscious Incompetence.* In this stage, we don't even know how aggressive and intimidating we are. Jackie had had no idea until it was too late that her reputation within her company was derailing her career.

2. *The "Know It Academically" Stage: Conscious Incompetence.* This stage occurs when we recognize what just happened, but we still can't pull it off. Academically we understand what we've done, but in practical terms we miss a lot. When Jackie was shown her evaluations and forced to accept that they saw her in a way she didn't like, she was appalled and grief-stricken, but she didn't yet know how to get her career back on track.

3. *The "Doing It" Stage: Unconscious Competence.* We're doing it and it feels great, but we're not exactly sure how or why it is happening. It's working, but we are not choreographing our delivery. Although Jackie's transition was fairly straightforward once she had accepted the way her actions had been affecting her staff, it took a little while to implement her new style. Fortunately, her new willingness to forge ties in her department gained her allies whom she was able to turn to for the occasional reality checks and feedback about whether her efforts were proving effective. Once colleagues realized that she was genuinely trying to turn herself around, they became supportive and encouraging.

4. *The "Got It!" Stage: Conscious Competence.* We know how to say what we really mean. We are aware of our receiver and our message and we confidently communicate what we mean with assurance. Although there are still times when Jackie has to fight hard against her frustration at colleagues, by the time she became VP she was able to control her impulses and begin to treat her coworkers as well as she treated her favorite customer.

The group practices these four stages by analyzing interaction with others during the week. They give each other feedback. Some of it hurts for a while.

One night Leila was very bewildered and hurt that the group still thought she was being sarcastic. We helped her to see that what she meant to be saying was still a little rough. In this group she feels acceptance from the others so she can take in feedback. The group is ongoing and people come and go, thus, the old participants have to teach the new participants how to assess their progress. The camaraderie of being with others who have been misunderstood for so long creates the bonding. The growth they see in each other is what glues this diverse group together. No one had ever attended anything like this, and now they claim they can't live without each other. They do, though—very well. We all stand up if anyone uses the bully words: *stupid*, *lazy*, *ignorant*, or *incompetent*.

These women have different backgrounds—some were only children, some are from huge families, some are married, some are young, some are new in business, and some are ready to retire. They know about each other's bosses and their families. They know where a Bully Broad goes when she doesn't get her way. They recognize her hurt when she isn't being heard and when she can't control her environment. They remind each other of the habits that are so hard to give up, such as the following:

- Having to be right
- Making excuses for bad behavior
- Applying the quick-response syndrome
- Using sarcasm
- Being judgmental
- Being unable to show vulnerability
- Having unrealistically high expectations

"I live for this group," piped up one woman who originally thought this was all poppycock. These women believe they are a sorority or a family, and they will always remember their first nights in the group. They are friends, colleagues, supporters, and mentors to each other, and some of them will probably start their own companies together some day. They have been through the valley together—not Silicon Valley, but the valley of humiliation, disappointment, and misunderstanding. They are all wading back to shore. They are happy and content, and they report that, finally, the people around them probably are happy, too.

I will describe these women in case studies adapted from the real women we have worked with over the years. The real group members will not be able to recognize themselves because we have mixed their profiles, histories, and symptoms. You, the reader, may recognize yourself in a story or two. If you do spot yourself, say hello, and make the changes these women made so vigorously.

1 Don't Tick Off the President, the CEO, or the Human Resources Person

CASE STUDY

Jane Montgomery, the Controller, stamped her beautiful shoe. As a senior player in a major computer company, she went by the rules. When conflicts arose about payroll or investment issues or stock bonus plans for the president, Jane could always recite proper procedure.

On the other hand, David, the Human Resources Vice President, understood the idiosyncrasies of the president and the company. He had grown up with this ever-evolving company and played to special circumstances whenever necessary. Additionally, David was much more ethereal and easygoing by nature. Sensitive and playful, dressed in casual clothes, David was a striking counterpoint to Jane in her black pin-striped suit and button-down collar.

Jane was quick and loud when she pointed out discrepancies in the system. She would lose patience with David's sympathetic ear for employees who Jane felt were "using" the company. Finally, Jane made her fatal move. She forgot that the CEO and David had worked together for twenty years and that they had a complementary relationship in which David patched things up when the CEO got out of line. It was a relationship that worked for them and for the company.

But Jane finally became fed up and complained bitterly to the CEO about the slipshod and preferential treatment David demonstrated. In doing so, she made a big mistake. She naively believed that the CEO would not report her complaints back to David. Bully broads are not always aware of loyalty issues, so they often take a very pragmatic and analytical approach without understanding the relationship nuances among other workers. Of course, when David heard about her tirade, Jane became his permanent enemy.

Subsequently, Jane was put on probation about another issue that previously had been hushed up and hidden. She was also sent to our coaching program. Although Jane rapidly got our message and began showing a softer persona to most of her staff, she remained angry with David. She would not agree to mend fences with him. Instead, she still made fun of him whenever she could. She also refused to acknowledge David when they passed in the hall. Not such a smart move for Jane. She knew that David was the right-hand guy to the CEO, but she could not bring herself to kiss up to him.

Soon after Jane was placed on probation even the smallest complaints about her landed on David's desk. Now was the time for David's revenge. Within a month Jane was given notice to leave. David, who had referred her to our program, never asked for feedback about Jane. In fact, David wrote off Jane permanently.

Jane left the company quickly, but she had learned her lesson. She is now CFO at an even larger and more prestigious company. Upon embarking on the new job, however, she made a conscious effort to meet and really understand the HR

Department. She stopped judging and did not take on the role of critic and management consultant the minute she hit the front door of the new company.

>-·+>·-O·-<+·-<

If you are already in charge, or you are on your way up, you may eventually have some difficulty with your HR Department. Be careful. Don't burn your bridges with the people arm of your company. Eventually they may have influence over your stock benefits, any harassment charges you might want to bring, your requisitions, new hires, or any significant moment in your career. Don't tread too heavily, especially if you don't really understand the responsibilities that have been given to these people and the impact they can have on you and your staff.

Many employees don't trust the Human Resources Department. Some executives think that HR staff members are intrusive, nosy, whiny, and always looking for problems. They harbor suspicions that HR people go sniveling to management, even when the discussion in question was confidential. This attitude of doubt will only land you on the wrong side of the table one day. Give HR administration the benefit of the doubt. They may be more sensitive, more touchy-feely, and more compassionate than you are, but they can be very helpful in a pinch—unless you have already pinched them so badly that they could not, in good faith, be on your side.

Just as it is wiser to make friends with than fight your HR people, it is imperative to stay on the good side of your CEO, President, or Chairman of the Board—or the whole darned board. Bully Broads are often frustrated by upper management's seeming ignorance or even incompetence. The key thing to remember with these powerful people is that you don't always know the big picture. You don't have to meet the expectations their performance package demands, and you don't have to cater to the investors, analysts, or the press. Even a CEO, who has to worry about all these things as well, still has to report to someone. So watch yourself—very few CEOs will forgive subordinates who keep them from fulfilling their own bosses' demands.

CASE STUDY

Pam Gossett was very judgmental about her CEO, Carl, because he was more of a marketing guru than a technical person. Having a law background, Pam fumed and fussed and took every opportunity to prove the CEO wrong at staff meetings. This fusser really believed that she was helping the company by keeping the CEO and the corporation out of trouble. Finally, Carl asked to have Pam excluded from his executive staff meetings. This chief executive officer could not tolerate Pam's devil's advocate approach to every new idea that he proposed. His creativity was often stifled by Pam's continual and severe censure, and he concluded that he couldn't perform at his best in the presence of this tormentor.

Pam was very hurt about being banished from the executive staff meetings, but she used that to add to her misgivings and judgments about the CEO. Not a great political move for Pam. She could not stop and look at the consequences of her judgments about the CEO. Pam steadfastly believed that she could convince the world that she was right and David was a misfit. Nobody listened. Even her legitimate complaints about David were discounted because of her personal reputation. She became the scapegoat for any of David's problems. She would not look at her part as an excuse for David's actions. She could not see her role. Ultimately, she was asked to leave the company.

>-!-<>-O-<>-!-<

Being more tactful may not come easily, and in the beginning you might feel as if you are being phony. However, with the amazing good strokes you begin to receive from your colleagues, you will eventually feel encouraged enough to keep trying. Remember that you don't have to agree with the HR person or the CEO, but you must let them know that you understand their perspectives and can honor their points of view.

Revere your Human eResources Department. They may understand something you don't, and they can be your greatest allies. Suspend judgment until you get to know the person's rationale for things you may not have fully comprehended. These people tend to be the morale barometers for your company and they have some important information for you.

As for the President, CEO, and other superior officers—give them a break, too. By virtue of their position, they must be responsive to everyone in the company; therefore, they often have secrets or concerns about the company to which you cannot possibly be privy. Listen before you leap. Learn to do reflective listening, repeating what the other person said but in your own words. You do not have to agree with their ideas, but you have to prove that you understand them. Learn to read the intent as well as the content, and try to match the emotion in which the message is delivered.

Some women to whom the title applies have not yet been labeled Bully Broads. They are just conscientious, talented, and ambitious women who are moving up the ladder. But with time, with crises that have to be handled, with responsibilities too burdensome for their years or their experience, they might revert to some of the styles and behaviors on which we are concentrating in this book. As the stress mounts and they find themselves coping with constant interruptions, as well as with moving targets and pressure from all sides, their patience subsides and the wild woman within them might rise up. If this sounds like you or someone with whom you work, we want to protect you from that consequence. So read on to temper yourself, to gain insight, and to learn about the people you alternately admire, hate, respect, and fear.

Important Note: This book is mainly focused on the Bully Broad. If you are an Ice Queen, or the victim of one, please keep reading. The Silent Bully, or the Bully Broad Type 4, is the Ice Queen. She is reserved and steely. People shy away from her because they expect her to judge them. She is often surprised by this behavior of others. The frown is just concentrated listening—not disdain. We can't always discern the icy look, and we interpret the frozen face to mean something negative.

Interpreting an Ice Queen's signals is difficult. Her behavior is hard to read, and the interpreter is often off the mark. We often misread the actions or signals of Bully Broads, Ice Queens, or other Ms. Understoods, often considering them to be much more negative than they actually are. Unless you can break through the wall around one of these Ms. Understoods, however, and get her to explain herself to you, you will never fully understand that person's behavior. So both the interpreter and the misunderstood person have to work at perceiving accurately—and then determining what the other person's intentions are. We usually give up long before the accurate intentions are determined. The task is too hard, too frightening, or too discouraging. Sometimes it's easier simply to give up on each other. The rewards for maintaining smooth interpersonal communication are infinite; setting a few seeds can begin the process. Creating toxic relationships on the job costs too much in terms of time, energy, money, promotions, and morale. Stop doing it!

APPLYING THE RULE

If You Are an Everywoman:

Be political.   Being politically smart will help you in every position in your career. Political intelligence is simply figuring out the power base in your organization. Being political does not mean playing dirty or being manipulative. Being political means understanding that having power for, and not over, people is best. It means being responsible and responsive. It means being a leader who is held in trust and who holds the employees in trust. Being political means being conscious of what is going on around you.

Figure out what you have to do to get her attention.   If you work around a Bully Broad or an Ice Queen or any other Ms. Understood, learn the dynamics between the two of you, and then learn what you have to do to change her, you, and the situation. You cannot protect yourself from the crossfire permanently. No matter what your position is in the war of aggression versus passivity, each of us has a responsibility to improve communication and offer insight on working-style differences when it is appropriate. Recognize the value of your CEO or highest officer. Understand the demands of the position and respond accordingly. Be aware of your Human Resources Department and the great asset they can be to any organization.

If You Are a Bully Broad:

Make friends with HR, silly. They can probably understand you and help you in ways you have never imagined. Be kind in your assessment of the boss. He or she may not possess certain qualities that you value. He or she may not be aggressive, directive, pragmatic, or charismatic. Too bad. Whatever traits a boss has, they are factors in what brought the person to this position, so reserve your judgment. Try actually complimenting the CEO, instead of calling attention to every piece that is missing in his or her design, strategy, or personality.

Often, a bully will be managed by a passive nonmanager who simply doesn't have the emotional stamina or the courage to address the bully's bad behavior. This dynamic only intensifies the problem. Although it is natural that a passive manager would want to shift the blame and the hot stuff to someone who can take it, it is also natural that a bully woman working for a bully boss might be spending too much time on power struggles. Moderation the middle of the road—that's what we strive for. Managers who manage by employing the overall working trait differences among their subordinates are still a little scarce.

Acknowledge your behavior. If you are a bully, regardless of whether you are receiving useful feedback or supervision, try defusing tense situations by saying: "Boy, I seemed to have had a tantrum just now." Or: "I really let out some old anger. I feel silly, and I know I messed this meeting up. I'm even a little humiliated." Later, if this doesn't work, you can add: "You didn't seem to want to hear what I was talking about, and the more I said, the more you seemed to go away. I couldn't get you back in the game."

Then start the problem-solving segment of your relationship. "Can we meet tomorrow to talk about my interpretation of your behavior and what we can do about it? I really want to work with you, and I'm afraid I have little tolerance left about you now, so let's change that."

Believe change can happen. Bully, you can change. You will feel better, look better, and be much more promotable if you are willing to examine yourself now. You may think you have it all—the perfect portfolio, the awards, your homework in your briefcase, wonderful new makeup, your favorite suit, and years of experience and achievement that bring you to this precise moment. But that still might not be enough. If you are not understood by your peers, subordinates, or manager, you are doomed.

Your best assets can trip you up. If your reputation for disruption and dissension precedes you and you're not aware of it, you are in trouble. In spite of all your good work, your intelligence, and your proven results, you may not be promoted or you might be turned down for that new job. The very traits that brought you to the top—the drive, the focus, the aggressive pursuit of goals—may now be working against you if you've forgotten that there are other people traveling the road along with you. If you've been running over those people and they aren't as effective when you're around, you may actually be costing your organization a great deal of money, even if you bring in millions of dollars!

You are high-profile women. You bullies really are the exceptional women. You spend the money, deal the deals, win the wars, sell the contracts, and run the institutions. You have emerged to build and grow empires, and you are here to stay. You are the new titans of the world, the successful and powerful alpha females, the women managers and executives who drive some of the premier New York Stock Exchange and Nasdaq corporations. You are the darlings of your bosses and customers alike. Companies love your work. Your drive and dedication enhance profits and production, at least initially.

Who wouldn't value a highly focused individual like you, who gets the job done without hesitation? Someone concerned about the bottom line, that's who. And someone concerned about his or her own sanity and the sanity of others in the organization. When you are that driven, focused power can turn strident, judgmental, opinionated, and insensitive to the needs and feelings of others. You stop being an asset and become a liability—to yourself and everyone around you. You are the cream of the corporate crop, but you might find yourself in a brown paper wrapping marked "Caution: Tough and Fragile. Handle with Care!" When we get an assertive and goal-driven woman in our office, we know we have a hot package. We also know there's an expiration date stamped on the wrapper. If you aren't refrigerated and cooled down, you might spoil and have to be discarded.

Our mission is to prevent that from happening. This book is for you, the Bully Broad, and also for the people at home and at work who have to deal with your intimidating style. It will give you the tools to channel all your wonderful energy into productive work and rewarding relationships so that everybody wins. It will also help the people in your life understand and work with you. You may pay a steep emotional price for winning in corporate America, but so do many others. Almost everyone I talk to seems to have been married to a Bully Broad, or worked for one, or had an employee who is one. For the benefit of all of you, we will first explore what happens when a Bully Broad appears on the scene. Then we will learn about the impact these behaviors have on individuals and companies. Finally, we will look at some solutions.

Listen for intentions, not just the contextual or content data in conversations. What is behind the surface meaning? "Oh, gosh," you might say, "that's too much work. What is this, a therapy office?" No, it is not. And, no, it is not too much work. It is actually more effective to test your translations as you are hearing things, than to attempt to do so weeks or months later when the misunderstanding eventually comes to light.

In our training programs, we ask executives to practice listening for those intentions. They are usually fairly weak at it at first, but practice makes perfect. When they finally try it at work, under duress and with great trepidation, they are amazed at how successfully it works. One manager came back with an astonishing revelation: "Darn. All old Bob wanted was for me to understand his predicament." Understand and articulate the predicament! That's all it takes.

If you are the aggressive type, even if this message about you is not being delivered intentionally, you might be in trouble. We have identified four types of bullies: the *Sounding-Off Tyrant*, the *Sarcastic Aggressive*, the *Selectively Quiet*, and the *Silent Judge*. Any one of these bullies can make any or all of the mistakes we have been talking about, depending on the situation. You don't carry around a book of translations, ready to hand to people who have to deal with you. So you get into deep water because you simply don't know how to get people to understand your needs, goals, or values. You lose patience. The task of getting people whom you might perceive as being stupid, incompetent, unmotivated, or shallow to trust your good intentions is too hard. Well, guess what? You are all in trouble—the sufferer, as well as the intimidator.

Give your boss and the Human Resources people a break. Most Bully Broads are convinced that they themselves are simply courageous, wonderful, and generous human beings who are put-upon by others. They forget about the human beings who play other roles in their organizations. Bullies believe they should be appreciated for saving the organization and producing product and profits beyond the company's wildest dreams. Of course, this kind of thinking can be delusional—but in many cases, it's accurate. The Bully Broad *has* played a key role in the organization's success. The problem is that the value of her contributions may now be eroding. She may, in fact, be damaging her company.

WHEN YOU WORK WITH A BULLY BROAD

When you work with a Bully Broad, keep the following points in mind.

She is not as frightening as she sounds.   If you are in the HR Department or you are the CEO, remember that her bark is worse than her bite. She may be afraid and just whistling in the dark. She has learned that intimidation works, but inside she is insecure. Or she may seem aggressive all the way through, but, of course, she is not. She is often very softhearted and can be a good friend, but she was inculcated early in life with the notion that she had to "take care of herself" because nobody else would. She is comfortable being intimidating. She has no idea how abusive she sounds and she can't imagine why anyone would call her strong voice a shout.

She thinks she has to have the last word.   If your bully grew up learning to debate, or if in graduate school she was heralded as the critical thinker and analytical wizard, she probably still longs for that acclaim. For heaven's sake, do not fear her. Just set some limits for her and try addressing some of the following topics with her:

- Calm down before entering your office.
- Don't send flame emails.
- Restrict emails to a single page.
- Refrain from picking on the Marketing Department (or the Engineering Department, or whatever her flavor of the month is).
- Concentrate more on her own inadequacies rather than on other people's flaws.

Name the problem.   You are doomed to failure with a Bully Broad if you are unwilling to figure out how to explain yourself to her. This is the first step in communication. Name the problem. Don't go on the attack. You can start with something like this: "Lynn, I am really feeling overwhelmed by your abusive language, loud voice, and apparent willingness to look and sound angry."

There—you named your response. Now name her behavior: "Lynn, it is inappropriate for you to swear about customers, scream at me, and stand there with your hands on your hips, glaring."

The bonus for speaking up to her will be the new respect she will show you for doing so. Bullies are contemptuous of passive behavior. When you stand up to a bully, her esteem for you will be elevated. She will listen better and see you more realistically—even if you stumble a bit with your first attempt at feedback to her.

2 "Listen Up" Until You Have to Throw Up!

CASE STUDY

Ruth Montgomery talks too much. Oh, she has plenty to say—much too much to say. She is a great orator, sales debater, and presenter. While those oratory skills are at graduate level, her listening skills are at kindergarten level. Because she is already an intimidator, and has already attained a megaphone-effect position (very senior officer) in the company, when she speaks, people must listen . . . and listen . . . and listen . . .

In Ruth's family of four brothers, everyone competed for the attention of the brilliant lawyers, Mom and Dad. Ruth learned the art of getting attention—with sarcasm, one-upmanship, and anything clever she could pull out of the hat.

"I get no cooperation around here," women like Ruth seem to believe. "You'd think I was a scrambling neophyte with the kind of respect I get!" she bellows and groans. When others speak, however, Ruth listens to the first few sentences, jumps to her conclusions, and begins again—right on top of the other speaker. She interrupts because she is passionate and impatient, and because she has not learned to discipline her impulsive wish to be the one talking.

Ruth believed she was well loved. Everyone came to her birthday parties, and no one missed lunch with her if she gave the invitation. But she was not a popular person on the job. Her evaluations revealed someone who never listened, was defensive when feedback was given, and could not participate in a collaborative conversation. She preached. She dictated. She had the last word.

Asking Ruth to listen was like asking her to cut out her tongue. She did not think she could do it. She also didn't think she knew what too much talking meant. It was only after attending our group and hearing recordings of every time she had anything to say that she finally awakened to the reality, and that was in the company of other aggressive women who didn't understand the concept of taking turns.

Ruth's wake-up call came when she was passed over for a wonderful new technical position in her company. It involved the sexiest and biggest product line in her company, and she knew she had the credentials. Her boss explained that she did not get the job because nobody—nobody!—wanted to work under her in the new position. She was devastated. Then she called us.

Ruth was motivated to change. She learned to bite her tongue, especially when she was mad, and most especially when she knew she was right. She learned that right was not as important as relationship. That was a hard lesson.

Ruth made the decision to submerge her initial response to things. Of course, the results of holding back were immediately noticed. Most people thought she was just sick or pouting or had lost her voice. After months, folks began to trust her, and Ruth learned the art of appreciating the views of others and not just her own. She learned to watch for clues in conversations, and within a year Ruth got the desired job. She was lucky. The first person appointed to the coveted position couldn't handle all the complexities, and by the time this was discovered, Ruth had asked her boss to take a census about her again.

>─┼◆>─○─<◆┼─<

Successful women have much to share, power to use, and directions to give. They can feel hurried and burdened. This is no excuse! When successful women learn to listen—for both content and intent—they become real winners. They get more done, don't have to backtrack, and can command the real attention they crave. Listen up until you are about to burst!

Be quiet. Shut up. Hold on. If you have to go back to your office and write down your thoughts, do that. But don't deliver that missive to others later. Writing is just a way to relieve your impulsive nature. Don't pass it around just to get closure for yourself. Closure is important to the bully, because she loves the last word. Give it up. If you can be patient, you will eventually find that your turn comes up.

When you feel you are about to burst, back into another room and take a deep breath. Most people who surround you know what you are going to say anyway. They are familiar with your opinions, biases, and trigger points. Finally, when you are about to turn blue from holding back, release some of the pressure with a few simple phrases such as:

- *I'd like to give you my translations now.*
- *I really need some time in this discussion.*
- *Perhaps we are going down the wrong track.*
- *Can I take up some of your time to discuss my ideas?*

At first you will feel manipulative speaking so softly. Others won't trust you either. They will think you are simply maneuvering them again. Be careful not to speak more than six or seven sentences at a time without asking for feedback. This is the limit that others can endure.

APPLYING THE RULE

If You Are an Everywoman:

Listen first.   Don't talk. Listen for content, listen for other people's intentions when they speak, and listen for the emotion behind the words. What are they really trying to say? Why did they say it? What did they want? How do they feel? Then respond with: "I think you are trying to tell me that . . ."

Even when you don't respect the style of a passive or indecisive colleague, or the aggressive noise of your bully friend, take it upon yourself to show these folks what you want from them. Sometimes you have to be quiet. Sometimes you have to speak up. Sometimes you have to be reflective.

If You Are a Bully Broad:

Endear yourself, dear.   Telling, preaching, and persuading come more naturally to you than actually listening for the other person's point of view. It's hard to keep your own position or bias out of the conversation. That's not to say that you should never express an opinion, or even that you have to curry favor in every conversation. Listening is not the same as playing up to someone—it is about being considerate, being respectful of colleagues, and holding back on your judgment until the moment is appropriate for comment. As things stand, you are probably asked to give feedback only rarely. People avoid asking for your feedback because you are too harsh, and you seem unable to see things from the other person's perspective. When your partner or colleagues believe you are really listening, they will indicate this, and then they will be willing to hear your reactions. Only then should you offer your perspective.

Exercise self-discipline.   You usually have a very hard time listening. You can seem full of yourself—some might think, too full. You know the answers, can give the solutions, and certainly have strong opinions about most matters. The key is to pick your battles. Don't indulge yourself by throwing in every label, diatribe, or rationale you can think of to justify your position. Discipline yourself, and open up to the challenge of really understanding what the other person is saying. Part of being a good listener is knowing when it isn't worth your while to disagree.

CONCRETE TIPS FOR SAVVY LISTENING

The following suggestions will help Bully Broads become better listeners.

Let others speak first. I know this is a novel idea, but if you can be sure that you will always have the opportunity to get your point across eventually, you may start letting others have the first turn at bat. When your conversational partners can get things off their chests first, they will listen more attentively to what you have to say. Many Bully Broads are also great debaters, so it won't matter when you speak because you can always remember what you had to say and you can always muster the enthusiasm to support your argument. If you always have to speak first, you can stifle good ideas or cut off some sound arguments that the other person really wants to offer.

Encourage others to dump on you. Imagine that. I am asking you to let your colleagues vent on you. You need to find out what they are really feeling. Don't interrupt and don't hurry them along. You will be amazed at how short their catharses will be if they believe you really want to hear what they have to say.

Listen for what people are not saying to you. If your peers don't talk to you at all, you are in trouble. If your subordinates make only perfunctory replies, you should begin to wonder whether they really do trust you, respect you, or want to cooperate with your ideas. If your boss doesn't talk to you, you are really in a pickle. This silence is your big enemy.

Suspend judgment. "But, they are not usually saying anything," you protest. You may be right, but discipline yourself anyway. There is often a kernel of truth hidden in even the most inane blather. It is up to you to look for it. Give yourself the opportunity to see whether you can understand the other person's position. The person will never really hear all of your pearls of wisdom anyway, unless you can demonstrate that he or she will be heard first. If you have a reputation for bulldozing, it will stifle the other person's potential for powerful responses. When he or she really believes you respect and will listen to an alternate point of view, the person will likewise listen to you. But don't talk too long or too loud, and don't get too aggressive if you are speaking to a timid soul. You'll only lose the person that way.

WHEN YOU WORK WITH A BULLY BROAD

When you work with a Bully Broad keep the following points in mind.

She appreciates straight feedback.   What keeps the Bully Broad going? What pushes her to keep working harder? She believes that staying the course with a clenched fist will energize herself and others, and may even propel her colleagues to get the job done. She has little patience for the wishy-washy tactics of those whom she may call manipulators. She loathes deceit and cunning, and likes it straight with no chaser.

At least that's how it looks on the outside to people who may not know her well. Ironically, most of these heavy-handed women don't have a mean bone in their bodies. They are actually wonderful human beings, with defense mechanisms that mask a fear of showing weakness or being hurt.

It is easier for a Bully Broad to be angry and gruff than it is for her to be soft or vulnerable. She feels better showing anger than pain. She is like a dog on a leash, growling to warn other dogs away—and her bark can be loud and scary, even when she doesn't want to hurt anybody. This alpha trait is primal in Bully Broads. I see similar alpha behavior in my Norwich terrier. She is a dominant dog in her world. When other dogs come around, no matter their size, she is in charge. Other dogs know to leave her alone. Even bigger, bolder, meaner dogs cut her a wide path.

She is a loving creature.   This is the paradox: the Bully Broad is loving, but she doesn't appear so. Beneath the hardened exterior, she is not as ferocious and tough as she looks. She might bring in bagels to the office and send flowers to a sick colleague. She is usually much kinder to her subordinates than to her peers, and she can work better with her bosses and those in superior positions than she can with colleagues whom she may perceive as competitors. She has been known to put her managers in their places if she thinks they deserve it—but the problem usually arises under stress. That's when she snaps and turns into an ogre. When tensions rise, she can use the crisis as an excuse to get ugly; and, fiercely competitive, she takes no prisoners.

Be the teacher.   Bullies have to be taught to listen, and you may have to be the teacher. Here's how you do it: "Sally, sit down. Now, be quiet for five minutes straight. Do not interrupt me. Do not sit there thinking about how you want to respond. Do not fade away. Stay with me."

When you have her attention, begin your sales pitch. "Andrew really wants the job. I know he lacks some of the skills needed, but we want him in this department. And I get uncomfortable when you yell, swear, or glare at me. Give Andrew and me a break. We can be a big help to you, but we can't if you make us so uncomfortable we can't think."

Ice Queens, on the other hand, do very little talking. They are afraid of revealing their real feelings because often they are perceived as being negative. Usually when they tried to open up before, people shied away and left them alone. Nobody likes to hear judgments. As with the Silent Bully, with the Ice Queen you will need to teach her ways to express herself. The best way to do that is to pay attention to the small nuances from her and then provide feedback to her:

"You look like you don't like what I just said."
"You seem to be pondering something."
"I am feeling a response from you, but I'm not hearing any-
    thing."
"Did I offend you?"
"Are you mad about something?"
"You look like you think I just did something wrong."

These statements and questions are teasers to get the Ice Queen talking. Even if she does say something, you will have to help her to the next sentence. The same thing applies to the noisier type of bully;

although you might find it difficult to get a word in, you have to teach her to express herself better, too.

So, now you also have to do some reflective listening. When bullies do interrupt or repeat their song, it is a signal that they don't feel they have been heard the first time. So if she starts to repeat herself, it's your turn for reflective listening. Do it for a limited period of time. Name the limits, then ask the bully to feed back to you in her own words exactly the points you are trying to make. She can do it. She will try to do it quickly so she can get back to her point. Reward her patience. You will need to have this kind of conversation a dozen times before she learns it. Be brave.

Remember that she hates to cry.   Bullies don't learn very well on their own. None of us really do. A mirror, a mentor, someone who sees what we can't see is the best teacher. But, as you are beginning to know, bullies hate criticism as much as the rest of us. Some of us just take it and slink away. Bullies prefer to bark a defense, hiding the fact that they are hurt. They surely can't cry or be vulnerable.

Criticism usually awakens the angry tiger—not the hurt child. Try not to be afraid of the tiger, because there is a child hiding in there somewhere. You may have to make several attempts. The number will depend on your tenacity and your courage. A first time is not usually enough.

Don't expect a reciprocal arrangement. Both of you may have to give a great deal more than you expect in the beginning. You will have to learn to be strong rather than fearful in front of her. The bully needs to learn to be vulnerable and open to criticism, but this advice is directed to you, the sufferer. Don't plan on getting back as much as you give in the early stages. Frankly, you have to work harder because you often suffer more than the Bully Broad. She may be unaware of her effect on you, while you are very aware of your impact on others. When you are hurt, with no avenue to relieve the hurt, you tend to take the pain inside, causing you the physical manifestations of stress. Start today. Talk to her!

RULE
3
Create Allies
(Lots of Them)

CASE STUDY

Teresa Giovanni loved her boss, Harry, and vice versa. Harry thought Teresa was his best asset, so he ignored her tantrums and turned away from her tirades. She was worth it. What would he do? How could they keep the manufacturing yield up without her? Sure, she was hard on people, but, by gosh, she got the product out the door.

Eventually, complaints about Teresa started piling up. The Human Resources people spotted her first. Next, some of the production managers whom she harassed started the rumor mill. The chant got louder, and finally, the boss was in trouble for not reprimanding her. Actually, Harry appreciated Teresa's aggression. He didn't like to cause scenes, but she did. It was a perfect fit: she had been doing his dirty work for a long time.

Because Harry was quite passive anyway, he preferred that Teresa take the heat. She is very thick skinned and seemed to thrive on controversy. She loves the pressure. When he finally called her in to timidly offer her the negative community feedback, Teresa was shocked, humiliated, and deflated. He, of course, was scared to death.

Without the boss to defend Teresa, she might be without allies. Since she is judgmental about people without power, she had a limited supply of applicants for the position of ally.

The inevitable happened for Teresa, when Harry was transferred across the country. She did not want to move her family, so she was stuck. Harry had put up with all of her antics. His solution had always been to just send her home when she was hard on people, and she always seemed to have a good excuse for her abusive outbursts. Then she would hurry in before the troops the next day, bringing bagels, and get things off to a good start with the boss. She got the job done, too.

Those bagels! I used to call them the "doughnut apologies." When people became a little more health conscious, these gestures became the "bagel apologies." I don't know what will be in vogue next. But whatever it is, the bully will try it. It is easier than saying "I'm sorry." It is especially easier than admitting you might have done something wrong or intemperate.

Teresa never recovered after Harry left. Of course, there was a line of folks waiting to get her the moment he was gone. Harry's replacement was new and from the outside, but colleagues bombarded his office with reports of the infamous Teresa.

"I knew I was over the top sometimes," she admitted, "but Harry seemed to appreciate me getting people shaped up and I knew just when to make a scene. Most of his workers were wimps who wouldn't fight back anyway. And all of these people were slow, incompetent, and lazy."

The new boss gave Teresa a fair chance. No one could explain Teresa, and no one stood up for her. She had not one ally left in the company. The new boss sensed that quite quickly. Then he gave up. Unfortunately, Teresa retired, never testing her power again or learning to undo the career damage she had caused herself. She had not learned a thing, and there's a good chance she is currently harassing her Parent-Teacher Association, her Homeowners Club, or the local City Council. She is excellent at pointing out what is wrong.

><-→>-○-<←->-<

The Teresas of this world usually do not have many friends on the job. A woman who takes on this role usually eats alone because she is too busy for social encounters and can't abide the small talk in the women's lounge. When she does become the goat in a focal review or ranking and rating discussions (which take place without her being in the room), her enemies speak up with big voices. Her supporters are usually as timid as the boss, so they are not likely to take her part in the face of such opposition. They think she works hard and gets the job done, but they will usually not speak up for her from their own minority position.

Why doesn't a women like Teresa acquire allies? She is usually a loner who doesn't want to reveal her inadequacies or concerns to anyone else. She believes that no one can do, invent, contract, or sell like she can, and she, therefore, would not invite support from others. The last thing our Bully Broad wants to do is look weak. That is a contemptible position for the independent bully who has never even heard of the cause for *interdependence*.

Bully Broads end up being judgmental of their friends, and then the friends feel betrayed. Allies represent confidantes to Teresa, and she is often afraid of revealing herself to anyone. She has probably been burned because she does not know how to be a true friend. The secrets slip out because the friend usually can't confront Teresa. Confronting a bully can be dangerous. The bully may lash out, hit below the belt, or change the rules on you. Bullies are great at deflecting and they can distract you from the subject. What might have been a problem for you can become a bigger, bolder, "badder" problem to poor Teresa when she gets finished with you. After all, Bully Broads are professionals at defending themselves.

If this Bully Broad does acquire a friend on the job, she often overuses her or him, and eventually wears the supporter out. She may also be possessive and jealous when the friend spends time with others. She can't widen her circle easily because that would mean showing vulnerability to the new people. In a one-on-one situation, the bully can be gentle, as she is adept at persuasion and usually wins her points. In a group situation, however, a bully like Teresa could lose some of her potency.

APPLYING THE RULE

If You Are an Everywoman:

Acquire allies.   Everyone needs allies. Keep track of yours. If you have mentors, agents, and supporters, count your blessings. If you don't, get some. It may start with your own advocacy for someone else. Eventually ask someone to help you with your point of view in the monthly meeting or the like. Take small steps toward trusting others, and then increase the size of those steps. Policies about not making friends on the job or not mixing business with pleasure won't supply you with the savvy needed for political relationships. Feedback is necessary and so is a safe place to vent. Everyone needs a confidential ear in order to gain some new perspective.

Learn how to enlist supporters.   If you are shy or can't ask for what you want, you will never get what you want. Asking someone to give you advice or to be your mentor can be very flattering to the recipient.

It is just like asking someone for a date. First, you have to find out if the person is really available. Then, whether the person likes you enough. And, finally, you drop the seed that you would really like to date this person.

So, in looking for an ally, try: "Maria, I know you are a busy person, and you may have many people you help or advise. But I so respect your judgment and would love to have some input from you some of the time. Would you consider being a mentor for me if I asked?"

You didn't really ask. You checked her out. "If I asked, would you consider it? If I were to ask you for lunch, would you possibly be willing? I need someone to help me stand up to Jack. Are you a candidate to help me do that?" These are ways of testing the waters.

Bully Broads usually respond to this idea by saying something like, "Oh, no. I wouldn't do that. It makes me too vulnerable. I would feel too pathetic!"

My answer to the bully is, "Well, you know, you really are in quite a jam, anyway, if you have no one on board who is an advocate for you." Making friends is hard for most people. We are universally afraid of being rejected. Most people make friends at work with people who sit within twelve feet of them. Familiarity, not selection by compatibility, seems to reign in a working environment. So, don't be so shy. Try sowing some seeds. The first few meetings may be awkward, but the second and third will feel better. I am quite busy myself, so I am always wary when someone approaches me, but I usually will try one brief meeting because I know every meeting is a two-way street. I also learn something for myself in the exchange. I'll bet you might have something to offer an ally, too.

If You Are a Bully Broad:

Practice asking for help.   Recognize that you may not be good at picking friends or allies at first. You may be used to wanting to compete with the woman who is as powerful as you are, or you want to show off to her. You certainly might not want to tell her that you need her help. Well, you need to do just that!

When Sun Microsystems and Netscape Communications formed an alliance, the international high-tech community understood that the merger would challenge the interactive and interpersonal skills of hundreds of key executives and thousands of frontline employees. Suddenly, people understood that a company that was the enemy yesterday could become an ally, or an employer, tomorrow. People would have to communicate and cooperate. Managers and executives would have to assimilate and motivate widely divergent personnel from different, often opposing, corporate cultures.

It is necessary to engage with others in our collaborative world.   Most Bully Broads know that the corporate landscape has changed radically, and that in the new management era, collaboration is a fact of organizational life. But in working with female managers and executives, we've seen that, although Bully Broads understand this idea intellectually, many simply do not grasp the notion of collaboration at a gut level. They pay it lip service, sometimes rolling their eyes as they do so, but they still think of themselves as a one-woman team.

In today's business environment, everyone has to intertwine talents and roles. Companies have to be capable of merging quickly with other companies. Databases have to be blended and operations coordinated. Managers may need to adjust rapidly to radically different corporate cultures, align with former competitors, and seamlessly integrate disparate operations and values. As intelligent and capable as they may be, some female dynamos don't always grasp how important relationship skills have become.

Check out someone you admire.   Watch the popular woman or the woman who garners the most respect. Watch what she does or says and how she handles conflict. Our true colors don't usually come out until we are in a conflict situation. Is she more diplomatic? Does she carefully pick her battles? Does she absolutely, positively, at all costs, refrain from publicly humiliating anyone? Is she politically aware? Can you be? Look at this as a political game. Where is the power, who wields it, and what do you need to do to be reelected?

Being political is not sleazy.   Bully Broads seem to confuse political moves with manipulation. I am not suggesting doing anything that will hurt someone else just to get what you want. Politics, with a small "p" is simply knowing what you need to do, within your principles, to acquire the support you need for your ideas. So many Bully Broads are allergic to the idea of being political on the job. Then they wonder why they don't get promoted or why one little pipsqueak can ultimately block their opportunity.

The list of counterproductive and self-sabotaging behaviors that eventually trip up Bully Broads is long. Their worst traits erupt during crisis—and they seem to attract crisis. When under pressure, Bully Broads are likely to be:

Abrupt	Accusing	Aggressive	Argumentative	Blaming
Brusque	Caustic	Frightening	Gruff	Harsh
Hostile	Impatient	Impudent	Irritable	Loud
Narcissistic	Outrageous	Pushy	Rude	Sarcastic
Self-centered	Sharp-tongued	Tedious	Time-focused	Tiring
Tyrannical	Uncompromising	Unrelenting		

The attrition rate among the employees of Bully Broads is usually scandalous. Over time, the complaints far outweigh the compliments, and the complaints are always the same: "She alienates people. Most folks are wary of her intimidation tactics. And nobody wants to tell her." That can be very expensive.

Focus on people.   Bully Broads focus on the goals and results, rather than on the people and relationships. They are usually in a hurry to get the job done and sometimes don't even notice when people get run over in the process. Bully Broads want to be friendly, but they don't have time to engage in frivolous or extraneous behavior. They often simply conclude that some people are too stupid, silly, incompetent, or noncompetitive to warrant their time.

Pay attention to your impact on people.   Bully Broads or Ice Queens are usually driven women who are completely unaware of their enormous impact on others. They just don't believe there's any other way to get the job done. They work long and hard, and their intensity and aggressiveness go off the top of the "Type A" personality chart.

How do Bully Broads get this way? They usually learned their style at a young age. Many of these women:

- Learned the debate style of argument in their early life
- Admire a particular family member or mentor who openly asserted and got what he or she wanted

- Have been successful with aggressive and forceful behavior learned early in their careers
- Get depressed when thwarted or challenged, but remain persistent
- Are often loved, praised, and promoted until they become a liability, and then are eventually ostracized or dismissed

Promotion or crisis will get you.   Bully Broads do very well until their habits and outbursts reach critical mass. Then the *Pricilla Principle* kicks in. (This is the female equivalent of the *Peter Principle*, in which a person rises to his level of incompetence.) At this juncture, their strong-willed determinism can undermine their success.

CASE STUDY

Essa demonstrates several of the aforementioned qualities. "Don't talk to me about attrition," she says. "It's about the economy, our place in the market—not about my management style. I know what I want, and I know how to get it. Don't bother me with your opinion. I have my eye on the goal, and I refuse to hear anything off the mark. I am not here to be popular. I am here to do a job."

Essa is an East Indian woman and the CEO of her own company. She is a big woman in physical stature. She is very successful, but has a hard time keeping assistants, secretaries, Human Resources people, and anyone else exposed to her harsh judgments. Very Americanized, Essa dresses in the latest styles, but her notion of managing others is authoritarian and punitive. She never talks about anything personal and does not show any vulnerability. Even when her parents died in an airplane crash, she made a strong point that no one was to talk about the death with her.

Essa spent many months exploring new behaviors in our Bully Broads Group, and she learned to receive the support first of others in the group, and then of the people around her at work. She is now a revered boss. She relinquished sarcasm altogether and started to take an interest in her employees. At first it was a real effort. Then it began to feel good, even natural. She mellowed so much that her board of directors gave her an amazing party on their third-year anniversary. She shyly admitted it was the first party of her life. "I never deserved one before."

><->-O-<-><

WHEN YOU WORK WITH A BULLY BROAD

When you work with a Bully Broad keep the following points in mind.

Get others to help you.   You already know the importance of having allies at the office. Well, they can help you with a Bully Broad situation too. Ask explicitly for help from your other colleagues. It is okay to admit that the bully scares you, if she does. She probably scares some of your colleagues, too. Standing up to a loudmouth is easier with support.

Find someone to help you help the bully.   And get some help for her. Ask someone who is politically savvy to mediate between the two of you, or ask that person to talk to the bully about how she is sabotaging herself. She may be unwilling to ask for help, or even to take it. This is because it is a new position for her. In my practice, I will say something like: "I am going to be your friend. I will help you in ways you can't imagine. You are very hard on yourself. You don't have enough people who are not afraid of you who can help you soften the edges. I will help you do that." At this point, the Bully Broad usually asks for the Kleenex box.

Being sensitive is not enough.   Those who work with Bully Broads often want their colleagues to listen to them vent about her. That may make you feel better, but it won't help the situation. Get allies to help you to see your part in the top dog/underdog system. Get someone to stand just outside the door while you make your first attempt to stand up to her. You may need a crutch at first. *This is not child's play.* You may be saying, "This sounds like junior high school. Aren't we all adults here?" The answer is no. After twenty-five years of listening and intervening for billion-dollar companies and their star officers, I guarantee you that the real business world includes little boys and girls who fall back into childish responses to crises or conflict situations.

Perhaps you don't want to be an ally of a Bully Broad. It will take a little work on your part. You will have to be courageous and tell the truth. Remember, she claims that she loves the truth. You will have to remind her of that—again and again. She will be a master at deflecting your feedback, of distracting attention from your complaints, and of making herself the winner of every argument. She has been training for years for dealing with you.

Ask for a handicap for yourself.   If you are concerned that the Bully Broad will bulldoze your attempts to reach her with her Bully-Broad debating style, ask for handicap scoring: "I know that I am not the debater you are, and I know that you like to get in the last word, but if you are going to be my friend, you are going to have to concede once in a while. Let me win, or at least pause, so I think I am winning some of the time. Give me the same handicap scores you would apply at your next golf game. I really need the extra points to be able to feel I can compete with you. Maybe I will get better, and then we can reduce my handicap. Until then, cut me some slack when we are having a heated discussion."

Many people, even Bully Broads, suffer from the compulsion of wanting to be liked. You may not win that kind of approval from your bully friends. So you need allies, too. Acquire the kind of supporters who will cheer you when you make inroads with a nemesis. You deserve reinforcement, especially if you are beginning to give up your need to be sweet, nice, or charming in every situation. Your courage will be a side benefit to you. Let your own allies enjoy that part of you, too.

4 Keep in Mind That 85 Percent of the Rest of the World Is Conflict-Avoidant

CASE STUDY

Terry Martin grew up in a home that relished conflict. Saturday nights meant debates at the dinner table, and put-downs were encouraged and applauded. "I'll take on anyone," she boasted.

When I suggested that every time she walked into a room, eight or more out of ten people would be terrified of her, she stopped short. I amplified that statistic with the fact that if others witnessed her tirades, even if they were not involved, they felt the battle fatigue.

This feedback was disappointing to Terry. Even though they all hate it, the members of our Bully Broads Group need to recite this statistic to each other at every meeting. "We want to be around people who can stand up and take it—and give it back," they groan. "There are only about 15 percent of those people around, you know," I chide.

"You are the minority," I remind them. "You are the big and loud and courageous and unpopular minority."

Women like Terry constitute the first type of Bully Broad: the Sounding-Off Tyrant (ST). They act out, speak out, and will handle themselves in any disagreement. They seem to thrive on conflict and they never shrink from a confrontation. They tend to make a lot of noise about almost anything. They certainly never remember that most people will be afraid of them. Sounding-Off Tyrants seem oblivious to the reactions of others.

If you are the flaming, aggressive bully who has more energy than you know what to do with, take your aggressions to the tennis or racquetball court. Knead bread, hammer abalone, or beat a rug, but use your excess energy productively. Very aggressive bullies can have three severe disadvantages when asked to take their energies outside:

1. Some are not physically active and prefer verbal combat.
2. They are very competitive, so in a team sport, they want to win. Then they can be just as unrelenting in a game as in a problem-solving conversation.
3. They don't like to be beginners at anything, so if an endeavor is new, they will pull away from it

We ask our Bully Broads to practice, in groups, reducing the conflict-appearing persona. Sometimes we ask them to wear pink or embroidered daisies, or something rather soft and lacy, just to show the softer side. They usually laugh and hate those suggestions. One night, however, we asked everyone to dress "out of power." This meant no power suits or imposing colors. One woman forgot. The contrast between her outfit and all the others was startling and revealing.

Nowadays, we don't ask people to change their wardrobes but to just take a look at the message being sent. If you are 5 feet, 11 inches and you wear power red with epaulets, you may appear imposing. You cannot take the inches off your height, but sometimes you can choose to compensate a little in the other direction.

When you realize how fearful of conflict even a CEO can be, you might believe it could be worth the effort to make some adjustments. Terry the tiger was a good example. She was a wild woman. She made scenes wherever she went. She was also the most valuable technical trainer in the entire company. The boss sent her all over the world when new products were introduced. She was a marvelous public speaker and great at closing sales. She was known far and wide within her billion-dollar company. She was also known farther and wider for her intimidating style.

Terry came to our company with flaring nostrils and arms folded. We convinced her in the first session, however, that she could apply some of these tools to her unsuccessful personal relationships off the job as well as on the job.

We learned early why Terry had made no progress in her thirteen years with the company. She had been known as a bully from her first year. Her boss was a complete wimp, and so was his boss. Each admitted to me in my office that they were terrified of conflict and that neither could confront Terry about her behavior. Of course, they had confronted her in subtle ways and in written evaluations. They then pushed her bad reviews to the Human Resources staff. But to her face, in the many years they had all worked together, the two passive managers had avoided telling Terry the real truth. Even with bad evaluations, she always received fat raises because, in truth, she was very valuable to the company.

Terry had three rounds of coaching with us. Each round takes at least three months. After nearly a year, Terry is a happy and productive woman. She is also engaged to be married. She learned a lot, but guess what made the big difference? Her two bosses also went through our program. They learned how to confront issues, how to face anger and conflict, and to set limits and boundaries for Terry. They also learned to talk about consequences with each assignment.

They even had to face the initial threats that Terry would leave the company. After having passed all the tests, these gentlemen were able to apply the appropriate leverage to keep Terry in line. By the way, both bosses have been promoted, which reinforces the lesson that there is power in telling the truth and getting what you want as a result.

Why are so many people afraid of conflict? In my long career, I have conducted more than 300 anger workshops, working with everyone from accountants at major corporations to heart surgeons at a nearby hospital. In every group there are three or four people who have had a lifetime of experience in expressing anger. They are good at it. They need to have receptacles for their anger. They are used to venting their feelings and seem to be addicted to making wild scenes.

The rest of the people in the group are completely and utterly terrified in the presence of the Bully Broad's anger. I have seen huge, musclebound men shiver with fear in the presence of an angry woman. I have seen people shake and cry at the prospect that someone in the room might attempt to answer that nasty human being who shouted and ranted and raved. People who are that frightened become children again. Their primal response can often be traced to a chaotic scene in their past in which they had no power. Being in that victimized state, they remained paralyzed with fear, unable to protect themselves.

The loud and agitated comments of a Bully Broad can actually induce this same paralyzed state in those around her. She can render adults, no matter their authority or rank, helpless and fearful with just her raving. Her boss may not actually admit this to her. The big wiseguy hero might not act like he is nervous, but there's a good chance that he is. I have seen people walk a lot of miles to avoid a confrontation. Here are some examples:

A medical officer cancelled a 2000-person conference to avoid meeting up with a man whom he had argued with earlier.

A woman left her job rather than face the boss who accused her
of some intricate manipulation.

A long-term employee left stock options on the table rather
than defend himself.

Another employee refused a raise because he did not want to
address a certain coworker.

There are many such stories. Companies lose contracts, profits,
credibility, and good employees when people fear having a confrontation with a coworker. How do some people become so conflict
avoidant and others so conflict prone?

Look back at your mother and father figures. Did Mom get her
way in spite of being abusive and intimidating? If so, you may choose
not to be like her. Did Dad remain gentle and sweet and noncon-
trontational and yet seem to win friends and have what he wanted
anyway? Then you may choose to use Dad's technique to get what
you want. You may regard the overbearing blowhard as a powerful figure, and the milquetoast as a passive figure who is afraid of everything.
We tend to select one parental role model on which to base our own
self-image. Being like one of your parents is like having an instruction
book. You can always recall what Mom or Dad would do in a particular circumstance as a guide for your own behavior. However, if you
wish to be unlike either of your parental role models, then you have
no such instruction book to help you.

Many well-known heroes of industry have had a traumatic experience in their childhoods, one that they have pushed down so far that
they cannot tempt themselves to show anger again. Therefore, they
have to be wary of anger in others, and they will walk a long way to
avoid a conflict. This situation is often hard to believe, especially when
you see this same captain of industry talking the big talk. Catch him
behind the curtain, however, and he will cleverly manipulate any situation to get out of a heavy scene. These tough guys don't admit their
fears. They simply avoid any possibility of having to witness a drama.

Of course, there are well-known tyrants who pride themselves in
their emotional courage and ability to scare an audience. Their voices

are loud and clear. But what major corporate giant would admit to being afraid of his assistant's tirades at him? Trust me, dear Ms. Understoods, conflict is a frightening event for most of your colleagues.

APPLYING THE RULE

If You Are an Everywoman:

Think conflict resolution.   You may be one of the 85 percent of the troops who will stay away from conflict. But remember that sometimes the resentment leaks out inappropriately anyway. Check yourself. Do you need to say something about the elephant in the room? Or do you need to ask others whether they think you may have started something or appear to want to be starting something? Check out conflict. Conflict resolution is a popular service request directed to our company. It is difficult to achieve with two subjective parties. Bringing in an outsider can help. All of us need new perspectives sometimes. If you have a team made up of those who fear real conflict, it is likely that feedback loops don't work. Convince your team to plan on disagreements, and then plan to process the elements of the difference. In the process of uncovering the differences, you may actually come to a win-win conclusion.

Recently, I was a keynote speaker for a world conference of 200 YMCA leaders in Mexico City. When my presentation time arrived, I realized that I was a minor player in a house full of actual world leaders, since the YMCA sends mediators all over the world and has headquarters in Geneva, as well as a position at the United Nations in New York. Suddenly I felt terribly inadequate and insecure.

So I started my talk with these statements: "I am not an attorney, a negotiator, a mediator, or a United Nations participant. I didn't even know the Y had 88 countries represented and had international arms and legs all over the universe. So all I know is how to help you personally deal with your own personal fears of conflict and styles for disagreement."

Participants told me that they had expected just one more series of mediation rules. Instead, they got to check their guts and their hearts in some interactive exercises. I made up one role-playing exercise on the spot for those 200 people: to tell their assigned partner that his job was being eliminated and then see if he could really hear why. The results were quite startling.

We think that people can concentrate after bad news, but they often can't.   In this group of YMCA leaders, one individual, even within the role-playing situation, seemed startled by the fact that his position as Regional President could possibly be terminated. People need time to digest a shock. Interestingly, most Bully Broads react quickly. They seem to have internal survival skills. Some others take much more time. That evening at dinner, some of the participants, even if they had registered that the whole thing was just a simulation, still felt edgy about the possibility of being replaced. Be aware of this common response.

Lay groundwork for difficult discussions.   Conflict, bad news, and crises are all hard to take. Most people don't fight back. They hurry away—far away. If you have something controversial to present, you can do some setup work to help people get used to the idea. For example, you might approach them thus: "Gang, I know this subject is a hot one. The Tom team loves product A, and the Ben team loves product B. Let's see if we can list the advantages of each and weigh the consequences if we don't select your product. This is not going to be easy, but I think we can begin to use objective data to sort out some of the differences. Please don't shout or slam the table. I want us to have a calm discussion.

If You Are a Bully Broad:

Keep that 85 percent statistic in mind.   I think the figure might actually be higher, but I am using a sampling drawn from 150 anger management workshops as well as from the groups we conduct and our 6000 clients. Many people become process introverted when the argument gets personal or heated. That means they direct their thinking inward and cannot choke out retaliating words. They blanch.

They stutter. Don't take advantage of this. Recognize that you have gone too far. You will not have a viable recipient. Quit for now.

Build in some reminders for yourself.   Do what you have to do to compensate for your native style. Loosen up a little, or try conducting a meeting in which you do not interrupt, say something sarcastic, or confront anyone with a cutting edge. One of our clients has learned to say "um" as she talks. She says that gives others a chance to listen to her with the time to digest her words and not be so afraid. She also changed the way she answered the phone, from "Smith here, what?" to the more congenial and social greeting, "Hello, Helen Smith here. I hope you are having a good day." At first, she gagged, but she got so many compliments immediately that she never changed it. "It's not really me," Helen remarks, "but it is closer to what I want to be. I am tired of barking and very tired of having people shrivel around me."

Tell people that you are comfortable with conflict, but you realize that others may not be.   When things get rough, explain yourself. Try saying, "You all know that I am the kind of a person who loves to jump in right now and start this battle raging. But I am not going to do this. Let's try articulating each other's point of view first, so we can come from a place of understanding." Then all your colleagues faint.

Be patient with others.   Sometimes it won't take long to change people's perceptions of you. We actually want to think the best of each other. That is our human nature—to hope you will like me and that we can be friends. But noticing change in others is not always easy. Most of us are unabashedly preoccupied with our own lives. Everyone seems concerned with his or her own translations of the moment. So you be the one to make the healing move.

Feelings are chemical.   What you feel can churn in your body, pulsate in your blood canals, and rev up electricity in your brain. Adrenalin gets released and pupils dilate. In order to pump energy into our muscles, we have to divert energy away from its normal destination, our stomachs. Then we get upset stomachs. Or we get terrified and send energy to our muscles, so we can shake with fear or flee, instead of sending the energy to our brains so that we can think and use good judgment. Tension will strain every muscle in your body.

When an emotional response is triggered, there is no shutdown button. You are stuck with the response running its full course. Certain thoughts—for example, remembering a criticism—can actually evoke the same response as that of someone who has been physically threatened.

WHEN YOU WORK WITH A BULLY BROAD

So you work with one of those 15 percenters, and maybe in her presence you start to feel like one of the 85 percent. So, what if you are one of the 85 percenters? Perhaps you loathe fighting. You saw enough when you were a kid. You heard enough to last you a lifetime. Listening to fighting or abusive parents without the ability to protect yourself or your parent can bring on emotional paralysis.

Or you might have grown up in a very serene and gentle household. Your first boss might even have whispered. You are not used to being with a boisterous human being. The following are some techniques you can use when confronting the unrecovered Bully.

Remind yourself that other people are not always afraid of disagreement. They welcome it. First, try to understand your Bully Broad. She is addicted to conflict. Loves it. Knows it. Welcomes it. Begs for it. She is not allergic to drama. But she is not a bad person. The battles stir her adrenaline and give her the excitement she needs.

Describe yourself to the bully. Explain yourself to her. Let her know some of your background or your lack of experience in combat. Don't make excuses. Just present the facts. "I have never encountered the likes of you. You will probably be a good test for me. I am new at standing up to someone who is as demanding as you seem to be."

Ask your bully broad to help you set some limits.   She can hear these when she starts up. Ask her to give you some boxing-glove maneuvers that you can tolerate. Come up with the signals to stop, delay, and move to the next subject. Insist on helping her monitor her approach to conflict and get her to help you become acclimated to the more confrontational style. You can do it, you know. As soon as you begin to look inside the Bully Broad and realize why she does what she does and when she does it, you will relax and be able to breathe in her presence.

RULE

5 Learn That People Will Sabotage You If They Can't Confront You

CASE STUDY

Sally Yee prides herself on talking straight. "I don't mess around with syrupy talk. I am honest. I always have been, and I always will be. Don't you try to get me to sweet-talk these folks. People know what I mean, and they know I mean what I say. And, by the way, I am not working to win a popularity contest. I don't actually give a hoot about what other people think of me. I want my colleagues to respect me, not necessarily to like me."

We have heard that little sermon from every Bully Broad who has been referred to us for being intimidating. She doesn't seem to realize that her straight talk feels like mean talk to many of her constituents, and she is unaware of her impact.

If you are a Bully Broad starting up the ladder of success, you may have watched your boss or another successful inspirational person get what he or she wanted by speaking the

41

preceding sermon. You may have even given it yourself, and maybe you have been giving it all your life. Well, I am asking you to change it just a little. Being abrupt is not necessarily being honest. Sometimes it is just being rude. You may only have the perception that you are being honest. Unless you are telling the big picture, from all sides, your straight line may be a little shortsighted.

Sally represents another Bully Broad type: the Sarcastic Aggressive (SA). She is not a comedian as some Bully Broads are, but she is fast on the uptake. She is definitely aggressive, although she would never throw a knockdown tantrum. She has her pride, after all.

Sally is a pretty good team player. She just has a low emotional quotient. This is a measurement of emotional intelligence, or the ability to know yourself and recognize and understand your impact on others. Sally might have earned a Phi Beta Kappa key, but her relationship knowledge was weak. Her IQ doesn't match her EQ (Emotional Quotient).

When Sally learned the facts about herself, she was completely disheartened that people did not really want to work with her. Their reasons for abandoning her and omitting her from special meetings were vague. The best explanation any of her colleagues could offer her was, "I am uncomfortable when you are around."

When an opportunity arose for some of the employees to participate in a trip that meant a lot to the company and to the prestige of the participants, Sally was voted off the traveling team. She questioned every member of the team, but no one would confess to blackballing her. Interestingly enough, this reminded Sally of her sorority days, and she became furious. Of course, the fury didn't help; it only cemented the feelings of the others, who were relieved that she was not accompanying them on the trip. Getting mad doesn't help, but it is the first response from someone who does not easily show disappointment, hurt, or sadness.

No, you are not competing for Miss America, not even Ms. Congeniality or Ms. Biz. Surprisingly, however, those who seem well liked by their colleagues often get an awful lot done. It is possible that you are substituting fear for respect. Your colleagues may fear you, but they do not necessarily respect you. They may not even like you, either.

If people are afraid of you or are unwilling to confront your blunt talk, they may also harbor some deserved resentments toward you. With no place to direct their anger because they fear you will strike back in some disturbing way—a form of behavior for which you are renowned—they hide their resentment toward you. Eventually, however, they find a way to express it.

Following are some of the maneuvers commonly used by those who work under a Bully Broad to ultimately sabotage her:

- They simply fail to complete an assignment.
- They make excuses for this failure, claiming that they forgot, were sick, lost it, never heard it.
- They claim they didn't understand the assignment.
- If they can get you in trouble over it, they will happily observe your discomfort. (Of course, their satisfaction won't show.)
- They will misinterpret the assignment.
- They will turn it over to someone else.
- They will not speak up in meetings when an important explanation or intervention could have helped matters.
- They will leave you in the lurch, move, transfer, get food poisoning, or quit.
- They will complain to the Human Resources Department.
- They will hint to your boss, write a note, send email, leave a voice mail, or use anonymous 360-degree feedback surveys to convey their message about you.
- They will get you . . .
- They will not show up at your farewell party—not many people will.

Whose perception counts? In the corporate world, the perceptions of the people around you are of critical importance. These perceptions can be as significant as—or even more significant than—your actual skills or intelligence in determining your future.

When your staff sees you in a positive light, they will do more for you. If they are convinced that you are competent, fair, and effective, they will support you actively and voluntarily. If they believe you can lead them toward shared goals, they will follow you with enthusiasm. If they understand that your advancement will benefit them, they will work diligently on your behalf. They will see themselves as part of a team, with you as the coach. They will know that you are concerned not only about yourself and your own best interests, but also about them and their best interests.

If they don't perceive you in a positive light, their behavior may be just the opposite. Good intentions don't always count. What counts is what people perceive. Even a first-rate mind and impeccable skills don't count if you intentionally or unwittingly trigger knee-jerk reactions of dislike, distrust, and fear every time you interact with your staff or colleagues.

The perceptions that count are those that people see today. It doesn't matter whether your previous company, boss, or mentor appreciated you. It doesn't matter that you don't appreciate your company's corporate culture or that you think some of their policies are stupid. Your job may not be to appraise the company or your fellow workers. You may be having a problem that others want changed. A working style that served you well in the past may now be ineffective. Values have shifted significantly in corporate America over the past ten years. Unfortunately for Bully Broads, this shift has been in the direction of relationships and cooperation—precisely the areas in which Ice Queens and Bully Broads need the most work. Your style may be outdated. If your current company, colleagues, or boss doesn't approve of your habits, you're in trouble.

Before an exceptional woman can change, she needs to be made aware of the way people might be perceiving her. This is the hard part, because nobody wants to be the one to tell her. Your colleagues may opt to fight back at you by being passive–aggressive and just not doing the work or by complaining behind your back. This is what I call sabotage.

If you know that your strident behavior has had a negative effect on your staff, you may begin to realize that this can also affect their efficiency and efficacy, as well as the bottom line. Only when you understand the potential importance of every worker within your purview can you move forward. When you are capable of examining honestly your own counterproductive behavior, you have a chance for success.

New behavior takes practice. There will be plenty of slipping and sliding. Don't give up, though, when the sabotaging behavior does not cease overnight. People won't trust the new you immediately. You must allow them time to digest the differences in you, and then to believe in them. Figure out where your enemies are, and start your campaign to get them to switch sides.

APPLYING THE RULE

If You Are an Everywoman:

Gather your own feedback.   Sniff out resentment. If you are not sure about yourself, ask for feedback. "How was I at the quarterly meeting? Do you think I put Hank on the spot? Was I hard on you? Am I being too domineering now? Did I micromanage that project? Can you help me understand what was really going on in there?"

The responses you get could make you feel bad. Sometimes it hurts to get feedback. It is easier to stay in the comfortable dark. But it's time to wake up, get up, go outside into the sunshine.

To complicate matters, if you appear to be delicate, you may not get straight answers from those whose feedback you seek. Assure your colleagues that you can take it. Make a bargain: "I'll let you know when I see you slipping up on something if you can tell me how you see me in meetings with Charles."

A Bully Broad who appears vulnerable is a major worry for her timid coworkers. If she looks like she is easily hurt, most people will fear that she will roar up and really attack. At first, then, you may not get much feedback. After all, you are probably not so good at asking.

When you can assure folks that you can take a little honest information about yourself, you will start getting more feedback.

If You Are a Bully Broad:

Ask multiple-choice questions.   Learn to take feedback. Because you appear so strong, and because you may have been defensive, some folks are reluctant to give feedback to you. Help them out by asking multiple-choice questions. Slip them some possibilities that they are probably really thinking about anyway. In my experience, they won't even answer your multiple-choice questions at first. You may have to give them another round. You may even have to say the words for them. "Yes, I bet you really do find my voice too loud when I am showing vigor about something."

A session using multiple-choice questions might go something like this: Marilyn believes that Ralph thinks she is too abrasive. Ralph is very timid, but as Senior Vice President he is two levels higher than she is. He seems very wary of conflict. Marilyn is an Information Technology Manager whose troops have been complaining about her. She is trying to stop the bleeding. She really is being attentive to her staff so the attrition rate goes down. She plies Ralph by saying, "Ralph, you know that I am trying to be less aggressive with my staff. I would like some feedback. Have you noticed that

   a. I am not publicly incriminating any staff member at the staff meetings,
   b. I am talking more quietly and slowly,
   c. I am accentuating the positive whenever I see it, or
   d. I am much more lenient about reports arriving at 8 a.m. on Tuesdays?"

Say that Ralph chooses answer " b." Marilyn will then give him another set of choices:

   a. Is this a noticeable improvement,
   b. Am I still abusive in meetings,

   c. Are you hopeful this is a permanent change, or

   d. Do you think I am just faking it?

We hope that Ralph answers one of the above, but he may not volunteer anything. You, the bully, have to do all the work.

Let others defend you.   As a Bully Broad, you are most likely an independent type who is not used to having others defend you. You usually don't use experts or help from the Human Resources Department or supporters, and, of course, you think you don't need comforters. In actuality, you probably need those comforters more than others do, but you won't ask. You likewise won't ask someone to mentor you—unless she is your idol and someone who you believe has made it. You need mentors of all kinds, but be careful whom you choose as a mentor. The tough-minded woman who is just like you might only encourage your abusive style and not help you with the necessary softening. Some bullies simply can't help each other. Some people who have taken our classes and asked for a mentor have ended up being mentors themselves. That's okay.

Expect that if you hurt people, they will bleed. If they cannot safely reveal the hurt to you, they will allow the blood to leak out, often inappropriately. The weak bladder will probably not even get your attention. Sometimes the retaliation is so mild that you will not even notice. The exceptional women often have very thick skin, and it takes a lot to touch them.

Your safety net is to directly ask people to tell you if they believe you have been abusive. Some people will not be able to tell you, however. You must come to realize that even when people are quiet, say "yes ma'am," or even seem happy about what you have said to them, you might not always be perceiving their responses accurately, or, more important, your victims might not always be giving you an honest response. Be prepared to get it back in some other form—at a later date, in another venue, under other circumstances. Victims don't forget. If they are passive, they really become your enemy because you never know when they will strike. Long memories seem to accompany patience in the timid.

WHEN YOU WORK WITH A BULLY BROAD

Say it. If you believe you have suffered at the hands of a Bully Broad, don't hold in your upset feelings. Talk to someone—although, in the early stages, perhaps not the bully herself. You may want to practice a little with someone else first. However, once you muster the courage, attempt to tell her that you were put off by what she said or did. Disarm her by saying, "I know you must not have intended to attack me," or, "I really caught you on an off day, and I'd like to give you a chance to explain."

Try to see the bully's side of the situation. Giving the aggressor the benefit of the doubt will set in motion some gentler responses. This may be hard to do when she has been such a brat; however, her defense mechanisms will not kick in when you appear to be understanding of her dilemma. Remember that all of us believe we have reasons for feeling or doing what we do. Give the bully a chance to present her rationalizations. Ask her to give you a chance to express your reactions to her attack.

Don't wait. If you hold on, waiting to sabotage or retaliate, you have created a cold war. Express to the bully your response as quickly as you possibly can. It is not fair to let the situation fester. The buildup will be overwhelming to her later—and to you if you keep fanning the flame with resentment.

Don't be passive-aggressive. You can hurt her eventually. You can go underground and try to sabotage her indirectly. You can even go to others and let them get her. Or you can wait for the right moment to turn her in. If you confront her early, you will prevent the buildup of toxic resentment inside you. Try to let your Bully Broad know in small ways that you are unhappy. You can always start out with disarming her by saying, "You know, I am not so good at this. But I really want you to understand the impact you are having on me (this project or whatever). I usually prefer to be well liked and not confrontational, but I will make a try at this today."

6 Give Up Words Like *Stupid, Incompetent, Ignorant,* and *Lazy*

When we conduct our Bully Broads Group, we have a rule that everyone stands up if someone says a word like *stupid, incompetent, ignorant,* or *lazy.* This quickly broke all of us of the habit. When a new person, already identified as having intimidating qualities, joins the group, we anticipate with glee how often she will mouth those words. It seems instinctive for some of us to judge others.

Successful women are heavy achievers. They listen to instructions, work hard, and get the job done. Chances are, they grew up with parents who taught them a strong work ethic and abhorred slackers. They have high expectations for themselves as well as for others. As a result, they become labelers—quick to name the qualities they despise in others. They easily detect underachievers, but they don't understand them. They can't figure out why people don't do their best at all times. They have trouble empathizing with those who have learning disabilities, attention-deficit disorder, hyperactivity, or just plain old depression, which can stifle some people's ability to even think.

CASE STUDY

Serena Smith was good at being funny and sarcastic when someone would mess up an assignment. She'd roll her eyes, toss her hair, and question how someone could have been so s-t-u-p-i-d! Serena is cute and sassy, and most people enjoy her cleverness—until it is aimed at them. Serena didn't think she was doing anything wrong, until the CEO of her company told her she could either undergo coaching or be "laterally transferred" to a position with much lower visibility and prestige than the one she had.

Serena joined the Bully Broads Group. When she would exercise her wit at another member's expense, we would make a point of it for her, even though the sarcastic remark would sometimes go right over the recipient's head. After all, these Bully Broads had thick skin—they could usually take it as well as give it!

>─┤─◆>─O─<◆─┤─<

Surprisingly, though, they couldn't always take it. Giving and taking critical feedback is one of the lowest marks recorded in the category of management traits for anyone who is an intimidator. No one wants to give these people feedback, and when they try, the intimidator is often unreceptive or unpleasant. A Bully Broad's level of sensitivity is often clustered around her own feelings, rather than the feelings of others. She might say, "I'm really very sensitive, you know." (We know.)

Type A high-stress women are those classic hurry-worry folks who think that judgmental statements are more direct and efficient than quieter, equivocating words. Such hyperactive types don't know how to relax. They think they have to do several things at once and that being busy means being productive. Because they are in such a hurry, they usually don't recognize when they have been insensitive. Sometimes it takes all of ten seconds more to gently explain the situation.

Watch out for "attack" statements, such as the following:

He started the blaze.
I could have killed him.
Let's hammer that department under.
I think they ambushed us.
Get that fink!
I'm gunning for him.

Attack words only add to your negative reputation. So does swearing. You would be amazed at the number of people referred to us because of their habit of swearing. It is only a symptom of the overall intimidation they perpetrate, but it surely is a ready and observable demonstration of aggression.

Clean up your language, especially in print or on voice mail. Those notes or calls can plague you forever.

If you are a woman in the higher echelons, you no doubt have won your position by being discriminating. In graduate school, you learned to select the good works and grade the poor ones. In your early career, you were singled out and promoted for being honest, upright, and discerning.

I teach at Stanford University's Technical Ventures School in the Business Engineering Department. These special entrepreneurially minded Mayfield Fellows who are my students are quick to find flaws in others. (Mayfield is a venture capital firm that sponsors these twelve whiz kids.) As prospective CEOs, they are always eager to proclaim in their papers how they will weed out the incompetent or uninspired early in the process of whatever they plan to design, build, or sell.

Think of yourself as a teacher. It is always quite inspirational to teach a class of gifted students. To teach the underdeveloped, limited, or creatively impaired kids is hard work. As you progress up your organizational ladder, whether it is at a major corporation or the seminary, you will find colleagues and subordinates who are not as bright or as quick as you are. Your challenge is to motivate difficult employees, colleagues, managers, or even your own boss. The smart ones are easy to handle. With the unmotivated, you have your work cut out for you.

Many supervisors want to slough off this work, complaining that underachievers don't belong on the team. Even after you reach the highest levels, you will discover that there are still incompetent people, no matter what rung of the ladder they sit upon. Most of your colleagues will have blind spots in particular areas. Maybe your boss has a learning disability in some form. For example, she might be dyslexic and thus always wary about writing her own memos. Or perhaps a subordinate employee has a learning block about math and becomes anxious if he has to do simple computations in public. On the other hand, the problem might be that you simply stifle the other person's creativity with your pointed interrogations or intimidating presence. It's possible that you remind the passive person you may not respect of someone in his or her life. You may appear to be like their big sister or first boss—the person of another bully from a different time in his or her life. Again, watch your language; it adds to your already strong reputation. And watch your printed word. Sarcastic and abusive emails or voice mails can be repeated or copied, and you do not need that kind of data distributed about you. Flaming notes tend to plague us much later.

APPLYING THE RULE

If You Are an Everywoman:

Even you have slipped now and again.   You use a judgmental statement about someone. We all have our little pet peeves. When someone you really disdain seems to be getting your goat, take a deep look within. Why is this person eliciting such a strong response from you? Whom does he or she remind you of? What can you learn from this person? Why can't you give him or her a chance?

If your first instinct is to label someone, you have the problem. It may have come from years of living with or working with a discerner—the person who is always looking to rule someone in or rule someone out. Try a different approach.

You are the coach.   Think of yourself as an important coach. The good coach not only talks about the long-range goals, like winning the game, but also helps his player tactically by showing him how to move his hands up or down the bat. In the workplace, the coach needs to infuse confidence while walking the employee through his or her own valley of fear. It takes a little longer to listen and understand before you demand—it might take four more hours in the first six months. But the payoff is exponential and incredible. Labeling your colleagues brands them, but it also brands you. "I wonder what she says about me behind my back," they may think.

Using words that ascribe handicaps to other people is a bad habit. When you catch your bully colleague doing so, or when you catch yourself doing it, make a loud noise about it. We all say things we don't literally mean. Help put a stop to it.

Watch your opinions—especially the monstrous ones! For example, whether you believe in working mothers, are one, never have been, or think you can do it all, the debate about the topic can be delicate, and it has been for thirty years. Some Bully Broads don't seem to be aware of the delicate subjects when they are giving their monologues. What subject matter is chosen, and how it is handled, depends on the audience and what type of reactions could be expected from the opinions expressed.

Labels hurt, but they also enable some preconceived notions to persist that can continue to keep populations separated. Labels can be a useful device. They help us to categorize our world and distinguish such things as fruits from vegetables. When we use labels to disenfranchise others, however, we are moving into dangerous territory.

If You Are a Bully Broad:

Give up judgmental words about your colleagues and everybody.   Your blaming and attack words tend to emphasize *your* worst traits, and, of course, you are then highly quotable! Don't put extraordinary expectations on people and then act disappointed when they don't fulfill them. Plan on the fact that some folks will become dumb with fright in your presence. Some of your victims may actually revert to a kind of preverbal state—unable to speak—when you read them the riot act. Rapid-fire questions and interrogation tactics make people feel even more ignorant and paralyzed. Don't do it. Give up using all judgmental words. Your reputation cannot afford it.

"He's too stupid for that job" reverberated throughout the department and landed in my office with a stunned, red-faced perpetrator feeling dreadful. She was sorry she had ever had the conversation. The interesting part is that those were not her actual words. They were taken out of context, but her colleagues could believe she had said them. Once a Bully Broad acquires a reputation for being vicious, whether or not it's justified, people may assume she has said even worse things than she really has.

If you are already known as a bully, any damaging words that you use will only intensify your negative standing. Your self-perception is, of course, quite different. You see yourself as a wonderful, kind, caring human being. Well, that may show up only in your own mirror. The minute you start talking about the popcorn boy at the theater and how stupid he was, you have made an impression on your listener. Those around you will always be wondering whether you might be thinking about them in such terms as well.

RESEARCH ON TRUSTWORTHINESS AND GENUINENESS

GLC conducted a research project based on the 2000 employees sent to our consulting service over the last few years. From that sample, 281 were randomly selected. The goal was to look for correlations between leadership qualities as identified by the 360-degree evaluations and the traits and values that the participants were reported to possess.

We were surprised that the ability to set limits, time management skills, vision, and other traits did not always match up with those who were identified as strong leaders. Only two characteristics, as reported by peers, subordinates, and managers, outweighed all others when correlating strong values with the reported desirable leadership qualities: *trustworthiness* and *genuineness*.

It would appear then, that if a Bully Broad can be trustworthy and genuine at all levels of interaction, she will also be considered a good leader. This could apply to all of us, but it is especially important to the woman whose reputation may be a little soured already.

The Bully Broads that we are dealing with all had weak scores on these two prime characteristics. You cannot present yourself as being trustworthy when you surprise your colleagues with "temper events" or publicly pass judgment on them.

Nor will you acquire a reputation for being genuine if you show only your complaining, whining, and self-centered side. The scores for being genuine were higher across the board than those for trust because bullies are often seen as being honest and direct. It's just that their honesty and directness can be hurtful, and coworkers are much less willing to trust someone they know may verbally attack them. That direct approach is not always delivered with the tact, poise, and political correctness needed for it to be accepted by listeners.

Armed with this research, the Costimators (an analysis of the actual time loss, and thus, money from abusive behaviors that inhibit other workers), and the 360-degree feedback, we are able to wear down some of our bullies. They experience an initial period of remorse, pain, and depression. They groan, "I didn't know I was this bad. If I'd thought I was hurting somebody, I would have stopped. I feel so awful that people see me as being so hard and ruthless. I wouldn't hurt a fly. And to think I've hurt all these guys."

Remember that you are not alone. The depression and sorrow that accompany these revelations about a Bully Broad usually last until she has her first meeting with the other Bully Broads. There she learns that her counterparts are also good and dear women whose delivery may simply be flawed. These women learn together to become aware of the impact they are having on others.

At first, they are wary. Sometimes they retreat to the far end of timidity, trying not to offend anyone or take a stand on anything. This does not last very long. It is hard to pull off, it feels phony, and they don't even get any reinforcing compliments for the extreme position.

So our recovering intimidators start back up the other side of the mountain, practicing balance and equivocating when they believe they have been overdefinite. We have discovered that most Bully Broads seem to love to use the overdefinite kinds of words— "*absolutely, positively, of course!*" They have to give up using words like *always* and *never*, and they avoid taking extreme positions, all of which have earmarked their behavior in the past. In the early stages, they wonder if they are sounding too wishy–washy. They miss their absolute proclamations.

Show your soft side once in a while. No, of course, you don't have to cry unnecessarily. You don't have to be all gooey and sad when you're really feeling revved up and ready to go. The dilemma for some women is that they cannot show their delicate selves. They have trained themselves to show strength, courage, and honesty, and it is difficult for such women to reorient their approach. When we can convince them that they are not giving up these traits, but merely modifying them somewhat, they will begin the process of change. We ultimately persuade these Bully Broads that it is much more courageous to talk about their concerns and fears than to charge ahead with no reservations.

The honest woman tells the whole truth. She can talk about being angry, but always with the reminder that anger can be masking hurt or disappointment, so she must be honest and strong enough to talk about that side, too. This distinguishes the successful and exceptional woman from the rest of the pack. You will know her when you see her, feel her presence, and hear her.

Acknowledge your reputation. Take ownership of the reputation you have acquired and then have the guts to change it. When you have established yourself as a judgmental human being in the minds of others, they fear what you might say about them if you ever get into a stressful situation with them. Ask people to remind you when you sound harsh or abusive. Convince them that you care and want to change. This will go a long way toward opening people's minds to you again. Intention counts. It even helps to admit to your peers that you don't think you will be able to give up your habit of labeling so easily. Set them up as monitors for you and ask them to be patient with your progress. It is amazing how indulgent your colleagues will be of you if they believe you want to change.

Don't worry about becoming a softie. You will not turn into a shriveling little mouse. Relinquishing sarcasm will be easier if you learn to direct it at yourself and refrain from any sardonic moves toward others. Don't give up your marvelous sense of humor; just turn it into a positive by lightly reframing it. There is no way that your no-nonsense, results-oriented personality is going to suddenly morph into that of a person who sits around exposing her neurosis to the world and expecting sympathy. By exposing some of your vulnerability, you open yourself to being more authentic and thus more respected by your colleagues.

WHEN YOU WORK WITH A BULLY BROAD

When you work with a Bully Broad keep the following points in mind.

Don't take her words personally. If she calls you incompetent, stop and think about how foolish she is being. Give yourself the edge by reminding yourself that bullies take advantage of situations in order to exercise primal control over others. Why do they have to do this? That is the million-dollar question. Because they are afraid themselves, because they are insecure, because they crave attention, or perhaps because they thrive on confrontation.

Confrontation seems to raise the endorphin level in a bully. It is both easy and fun for her. It makes her blood circulate—it's exciting. When you recognize the reasons behind the behavior, you can actually call the Bully Broad on one of these hypotheses if you dare. This puts *you* in the commanding position. Of course, she will not admit that you are right. She may laugh or ridicule you all the more; nevertheless, the seed has been planted. Watch for next time. Your Bully Broad will be easier to handle, and you will be stronger.

Name the attack words for her. This is going to be hard. But as either a witness to her bullying or as the victim of it, you must call the Bully Broad on her use of attack words. You also need to get her attention. A retaliatory attack won't work. She will just up the ante. Try sitting her down and asking her directly the underlying premise for her negative labeling of you. You can even try disarming her: "Yes, I really feel stupid when you glare at me and throw papers around. I get into one of those preverbal stages and can't think or talk rationally. It doesn't inspire me to help you either. Can you give up calling me stupid and help me to bring my best self to the task at hand?"

Adopt a rational approach to her attacks. When you can take a rational approach to dealing with the labels your bully applies when she attacks people, you will be strong enough to confront her. Whenever I speak publicly I take the opportunity to remind people that we all have learning disabilities of some sort. Each of us has some area in which we are more limited than others. From members of Congress to CEOs, everyone has to deal with some form of inadequacy, be it an attention deficit or hyperactivity, a fear of taking tests or of public speaking—each one of us is coping with something which prevents us from being the very best we can be. Remind your bully of this next time you feel that she is attacking you. Most Bully Broads hate to be known as the source of another's frustration. They would not want to be perceived as the cause of anyone's breakdown. They would prefer that you be independent and want no part of directly injuring you. Remind them of this.

7 Don't Cry Like a Man

CASE STUDY

Pat Browning, General Manager of one of the largest semi-conductor companies in the world, was responsible for a reduction in force of 2000 people. Although other officers shared the responsibility, she felt as if these employees were her family members. Since Pat had no family of her own, she regarded the production leads, supervisors, and line people who were subordinate to her as her children. Her counterparts in other areas of the company were like siblings to her. And, of course, the CEO, for whom she had worked for twenty years, was Dad.

Pat's tear ducts had dried up in public years ago. She could still cry over Hallmark commercials and during some sad movies, but in her work she was as tough as her product. A combination of two types, the *Sounding-Off Tyrant* (ST) and the *Sarcastic Aggressive* (SA), Pat made no bones about things. She dressed like a man, she swore like a pro, and, most important, she cried like a man.

>─┤◆├─○─┤◆├─<

What does "crying like a man" mean? On the job, you don't see it very often. Oh, a few of the more labile men weep easily, even over good numbers or the birth of a colleague's baby. However, we are talking here about the normal, average, typical man, who does not let the tears slip out easily.

Here's how a man cries: He begins to tighten up in the throat. Then he turns his head away and starts to cough. He will say "excuse me" nearly every time he tightens up.

Then he clears his throat and starts to talk. There are no notice-able tears a this point. He is still fiercely holding back. He may be wincing. His face may be getting red, his throat is tightening up, and he is pursing his lips. He might actually mumble that he is afraid he is going to have to stop. He really feels like he may faint or scream. He is exceedingly uncomfortable. In a public forum, he will look away and start to speak again. If he cannot say anything, he will stand there mute, trying to gain control before going on. Still, few tears fall.

The handkerchief is a man's only support tool in these situations. He uses it frequently. He blows his nose. This takes time and so allows him a chance to regain some composure. Women rarely carry handker-chiefs. They use tissues, but they don't carry them in their back pockets. They are not a piece of their wardrobe, as the handkerchief is for a man.

Finally, our hero starts once again to talk. His voice cracks. He says a few words. The tears flow. The brow wrinkles. He blows his nose again. His breathing is irregular. He may look like he is about to have a heart attack. His voice cracks again.

The next few lines are critical. He squeaks out a word or two. He may blow his nose again. He apologizes again. He turns his head away again. Then he walks away, whispering his apologies on the way out the door.

Bully broads cry in the same way. They behave like men who walk away rather than show their emotions, Such men don't want to show their vulnerability. They want to be strong. They hate being weak. They hate sounding like a woman! They apologize, they look away, they squeak out something. They wince and croak. They may not blow their noses, but they do frown and cloud up and turn red. Sometimes their ears turn purple. They excuse themselves. Then they walk away.

What's the matter with this behavior? If a Bully Broad speaking in public steps away to avoid continuing, her job is left undone. Somebody else has to stand up there and finish the task. Or she has to write a memo instead, or email her thoughts. Contrary to what she believes, she does not look strong by ducking out. She reminds everyone that she wants to look superhuman, not an average human being who is legitimately feeling bad about something.

Why do the men and the bullies duck out? They cannot stand the discomfort of the discomfort. It is awkward and frightening to be looking so nervous. They are not used to this kind of stress. They probably had very little practice with this kind of exposure. They enjoy feeling powerful, and yielding to emotions feels weak.

One day I took my grandsons to the gym and to child care while my daughter and I worked out. When we went to pick them up, four little girls were sitting at a table, coloring. The three boys were climbing things, throwing things, and rattling things. What a contrast. But in the car, they whined and cried and did not want their drinks, or they did; or they did not want their fruit, or they did. I caught myself saying, "Stop crying. You may not cry in my car!"

Oh, dear, what kind of men am I building? Will those little boys hear my words some day, when they receive the Nobel Prize, or terminate the employment of thousands, or wed their dearly beloved? Of course, little boys receive those "don't be a crybaby" messages and they probably internalize them. My clients will report, "I never saw my Dad cry," or "My Dad only cried when my grandmother died." Men also remember being taunted with accusations of "crybaby" from kindergarten through high school.

For Bully Broads and women with Bully Broad talents, crying in public is hard. Ice Queens rarely cry. Of course, they rarely laugh either. But crying is the worst sin for the woman who wants to be in control at all times. Do it anyway. In some form, a Bully Broad received the same message as her male counterparts. She learned to be uncomfortable with tears. By the way, no woman likes to cry in front of a man at work. We are inculcated with the belief that women are already known for being too emotional, and to prove we are as good as any man, we cannot show that emotional side at work.

It is certainly a bad idea to cry often at work. But today's driven women and those who are Bully Broads and Ice Queens have the opposite problem: they hide their tears completely. Don't go through all those gyrations to avoid the possibility of tears. For Bully Broads, it is even more important to show the whole range of feelings. Why? Because Bully Broads have a difficult time showing anything beyond anger or frustration. If they can show their more delicate sides, their colleagues will realize they are human beings after all. This is not intended to be flippant. Most associates of Bully Broads do not really see them as human beings with the same concerns, emotions, and fears that they themselves have. So if you are a Bully Broad, let the delicate feelings out whenever you can.

My message, then, is to do the following.

Say what you were going to say—shout, talk, explain, describe, wince, hesitate, but answer, talk, and explain, right through those tears.   Don't stop crying. Talk right through the tears. Some women have to talk louder when they are crying. They feel like they are shouting. But you will look and sound more courageous if you can appear to be focused and steady, and the tears are just those little nonsense things running down your face. You will really make an impression when you finish, in spite of your watering eyes.

Don't make excuses.   Please, oh, please, do not apologize for the human response of weeping. This only means that you are capable of having a strong reaction—that you care, that you are committed, that you are passionate about the situation, that you are dedicated, and that you are not afraid of showing a pure emotion.

Women are usually terrified that they will cry when they are asking for a raise or some recognition. In my office, when practicing the request, they worry about what would happen if they broke down. I advise them to go ahead and cry, but to talk right through those tears. When you find yourself in such a position, ask for the raise or promotion, explaining why you deserve it. Stress your successes, show off your star qualities, and describe your assets. Show how strong you are, and don't acknowledge the tears. Just accentuate the moves you want to make.

By not acknowledging the tears, I'm not saying that you have to hide them or act like they are not happening. But, like sweating or knocking knees, the tears are only a by-product of the tension. Try the following explanation: "This is important to me. That may be why I am crying. But don't see these tears as weakness. They are tears of passion, strength, devotion, and a commitment to excellence!"

When Pat Browning had to lay off thousands of her "family members," she stood at the podium and made a speech. She thanked her colleagues, her direct reports, her workers, and her boss, and wished them all well. She took care of things. She talked about the severance package, the alternatives, and the condition of the company. She reassured the remaining employees who would be the survivors. She did the job she had to do, even though the tears fell like waterfalls down her cheeks. She never apologized; she simply gave her speech. She did not clear her throat, wince, or blow her nose. The audience was transfixed—and grateful. She was a heroine.

APPLYING THE RULE

If You Are an Everywoman:

When you have the opportunity to show some authentic feelings, do it. Don't worry about being a woman, looking weak, or showing too much emotion. Just talk through the tears. This is a more courageous act than your male counterparts may be capable of. In many ways, they have had a longer, harder journey, filled with many more years of inculcated acts of presumed bravery. Women have a shorter history in the workforce, and if we can remember not to use the male model in every situation, we can begin to build our own culture of what is appropriate and what is not.

Let the feelings out. This does not mean you are too emotional for your professional position. As long as you are courageous about your feelings, and you can let your feelings out with articulate strength, you will become an authentic leader and team player. We know you have a history to overcome. Could a woman with mood cycles become president? Is it appropriate for a woman to express sadness by weeping in her president's chair? Interestingly enough, scientists have discovered that men have mood swings and also weep now and then. They do it differently. They do not do it better. In fact, they are usually not coherent at all while they are trying to compose themselves and blow their noses. Your actions should match your words. Men can learn the same lesson. Some have, and perhaps, after reading this, more will.

If You Are a Bully Broad:

Tear down the tightly constructed protective wall. You will have an opportunity to demolish the wall whenever something tragic, frightening, or touching happens. It is okay to show that you are a human being. In fact, for Bully Broads, it is the fastest way to earn respect and trust.

Most likely, you will not want to believe this. You will just have to test it for yourself to find out. Try uttering just one little sentence that reveals your vulnerability with someone safe, and you will be amazed at the response. Give yourself a chance to show the whole range of your emotions.

Upon the assassination of her husband, President John Kennedy, Jacqueline Kennedy represented the epitome of the stoic and grieving widow. The world admired and respected Jackie for this. Perhaps she was in shock. Perhaps crying did not fit her own image of herself. Perhaps we missed her tearful moments. I believe, however, that, although the world revered Mrs. Kennedy from those moments on, she conveyed a message to all women enduring similar moments of grief: be strong, keep your chin up, don't yield. So most Bully Broads take this stoic behavior to heart. Role models, men, and Jackie Kennedy all show you how to behave under stress. I am reversing the trend by asking you to show some tears if you have to. I am not advocating big emotional breakdowns. I am asking you to be congruent. Say on the outside what you feel on the inside. If you feel sad or discouraged, it will be all right to show it one or two times a year! Not everyday, not everywhere. But when it is appropriate, show what you feel.

"Isn't that ironic?" you muse. "I have to show my weakness to gain respect and confidence." True, it may seem paradoxical. Show your tears and you will look brave. What a concept! Being brave enough to let your feelings flow is a sign of a real leader. In our Bully Broads Group, we ask people over and over to express the hard stuff, the disappointments, the dark moments. What they discover from each other is that they actually respect the crises they each went through, and they are impressed by their comrades' ability to express their own disappointment or despair.

When that sharing is completed, we ask whether they could have presented the same story in another setting. They say no. I say, "Well, then do it." That is the homework for the next session.

Alice will call her brother-in-law. One participant called a college roommate she had not talked to in twenty years. Another woman practiced by writing a letter that honestly described her disheveled work life. Each woman promised she would share some vulnerable moments with someone. Amazingly, they all did it, and each returned session after session with more revelations they had had by sharing their true feelings.

Don't worry about becoming too soft. You will never turn into a shriveling little mouse. When you turn your sarcasm in on yourself instead of on the rest of the world, and when you can show your delicate side some of the time, you become a part of the human race. Don't give up your marvelous sense of humor. Don't give up your rational approach to issues. Don't change your personality. Simply add in the vulnerable qualities when they are appropriate. The opportunity for displaying them might come only once a year or once a quarter. Remember, crying is good for the tear ducts now and then. You won't have to buy those Artificial Tears eye drops as often, and you will be respected for showing the authentic You. Don't apologize for tears when they appear. In fact, congratulate yourself for performing the very uncomfortable and brave act of crying.

Tears aren't the only way to show your human side. You can discuss areas about which you feel passionate. Or you can bring your nephew's picture in to the office. When we suggest that these Bully Broads wear softer looking clothes every now and then, they belly-laugh. But when these women get in a jam, have to face a harassment discussion, want a raise from their timid bosses, or wish to make a different kind of impression, they finally try it. One woman actually gave up her stiff-colored wardrobe permanently. When our group got used to the different look, they could spot her in a crowd immediately. Some women wanted to change, and didn't need to. Others decided they would have the softer look when they felt they might be apt to come on too strong. Many of them thought the whole idea was silly, but every one understood the concept of compensating for a dominant stance. They watched how they sat, or sat forward, or walked, or moved toward someone. We know that body language counts. These Bully Broads had the great advantage of seeing firsthand the striking difference in perception that is created by the change of presentation.

WHEN YOU WORK WITH A BULLY BROAD

You may know she is about to cry. You feel her pain. You want to help. She will probably reject you. She is embarrassed. She wants to hide or run away. Don't give up on her and don't let her off the hook. If she tries to stop and apologize and get out of the moment, go and stand next to her, if you dare, and show her some support. Ask her to continue. Don't let her leave. Keep asking questions and prompting the conversation, just as though you weren't aware of the constricted throat, the wincing, the looking away, or the strained voice.

If you are uncomfortable with the emotionality of these scenes, discover what might be triggering your own reaction. Then decide if that reaction is legitimate or rational. Even though watching the temporary disintegration of a tough woman might be difficult, it is important for her to know that she can show her fragile side for a change. Everyone wants a balanced and grounded colleague, but in extreme moments of stress, we also want to believe that that colleague can have the normal response to horrific situations. Watching her can be a growing opportunity for you. It may just be the breakthrough strategy you need to look like a brave supporter of your Bully Broad, instead of her victim. Tears can be signs of great passion and commitment to excellence!

8 Beware of Jealousy

CASE STUDY

Pauline Smith was a vivacious, tall, stunning woman. Her husband Stanley was Vice President of Sales and she was Vice President of Marketing at a privately held company, where they had both worked for ten years. Everyone knew that Pauline was an intimidating bully, but they put up with her because of her brilliant marketing strategies. The company was very successful, the staff were highly rewarded, and things were going smoothly—until Ms. Trouble entered in the form of Cheri, a giggly, petite blond who loved to cup her chin in her little hand and roll her eyes up at anyone—particularly Stanley.

Stanley was the innocent, but oblivious, man who enjoyed the attention from Cheri. He loved to help her with all the domestic and professional problems she brought to him. She worked directly for Stan, so they had to go on a few sales trips together.

At first, Pauline was unaware of the interplay between the helpless female and the hero. Cheri was a very good salesperson and she made Stan's life easier, so he didn't mind the little favors she asked of him. He rather enjoyed Cheri's dependence on him. She seemed to worship him and told him regularly what a wonderful mentor and model he had become for her. She could listen to his stories forever, and she soon learned that he could point her in the direction of some wonderful leads, often sacrificing his own potential in order to throw business her way.

The drama erupted when Cheri sent Stan red roses as a thank-you gesture. Pauline, a *Sounding-Off Tyrant* (ST), jumped into action. These tyrants can't stand ambiguity, so instead of worrying herself over whether or not this could be trouble, she immediately started checking Stan's emails and credit cards for evidence to support her suspicions. There wasn't much. While Stan enjoyed Cheri's flattery and praise, he was quite unmindful to Cheri's flirting. He was offended when his wife accused him of letting his ego yield to the wily Ms. Cheri. The more Stan denied his involvement, the more Pauline went rabid.

Stanley could not remember that underneath Pauline's anger was hurt. He also forgot how reluctant she was about expressing dependency and rejection. All he could feel was her bitter accusations. All he wanted to do was get away from them—the accusations, that is—not his wife.

The play was interrupted when Pauline convinced the CEO to fire Cheri. Of course, they found very good reasons to do so. The truth is that Cheri had been leaning on Stanley for a year, she never did her own paperwork, and the company was beginning to hear complaints from customers about her. These customers only wanted to talk to Stan. Even when Cheri made some sales quotas, the atmosphere around her was contaminated by Pauline's negative interpretations of Cheri's actions.

But firing Cheri did not put an end to the problem. Stan really missed the person who idolized him. He wanted the glow of feeling admired and all he got from his wife was sar-castic abuse about how egotistical he was that he could not even see through Cheri's facade. Work was tense, but their home life was worse. Because of Pauline's and Stan's positions in the company structure, the whole company suffered. The office was tense, and sales dropped off. Finally, the boss asked that either Stan or Pauline take some time off. Everyone in the office was beginning to feel the tension, and the sales were beginning to drop off.

Pauline took a trip east, visiting with old friends, who assured her of Stan's loyalty. She finally returned, asking for forgiveness.

While Stan may have made the first move by allowing Cheri to become so dependent on him, Pauline was the one who created a huge problem with her undisciplined accusa-tions and public tirades. She is the one who had to become contrite and apologize to Stan as well as the rest of the team. So Pauline decided to drop the Bully Broad act. She used the opportunity to show her own vulnerability. Everyone liked that. She even got some sympathy when she calmed down. Some of the other women shared their envy over misplaced attention. Still others were angry with Stan, and Pauline liked that.

Ultimately, Pauline had to express her remorse to the whole team. She asked for help, and she was amazed at the supportive response.

>-⤙⤚-O-⤙⤚-⤙

A Bully Broad may have a fragile ego. This fact is often difficult to remember. When her ego or self-esteem is tested or threatened, she does not turn into a mouse; she turns into a lion. She roars and threat-ens and seeks action. The resulting attack stories are amazing. When a bully is cornered or worried or feels envy or jealousy, she can be ruth-less. She will throw a rock through a window, send a nude picture of herself, write a provocative letter, hire a private investigator, tell some-one's mother, enlist the children, or muddy her opponent's reputation in the neighborhood and on the job. If she is not reassured in the ways she needs, the tirade continues. She is seeking reassurance, but she is behaving so badly that no one wants to offer that reassurance.

Bullies can interpret events very personally if they feel frightened. They can translate innocent gestures into something suspect or they will read drama into situations where there is none. They can create their own perception of an event in order to support and justify their anger.

The Bully Broad in a jealous heat needs a calm voice to reassure her. Unfortunately, if she has acted suspiciously and threatened her mate or made him look ridiculous, he will balk. He is not going to want to restore her confidence in herself at the price of his integrity or his ego. Instead, he just wants to get away. This erodes the self-esteem of someone like Pauline even more. And, of course, the lowered self-esteem results in a louder voice. It is easier to be angry than to be vulnerable for a Pauline.

The contrasting dilemma for someone like Pauline is that there is always a someone like Cheri, who can show her vulnerability. It actually comes naturally to her. Then the bully can look like the bad guy. When Cheri felt falsely accused, she believed she was doubly victimized. She could then slip into a very dependent place—the perfect, but sometimes appealing, martyred position.

In this case, the tragic play was interrupted when Pauline convinced the CEO to fire Cheri. They found good reasons to do so. Cheri had been leaning on Stanley for a year, never did her own paper work, and customers were beginning to complain about Cheri's actions. Stan missed the glow he felt over Cheri's idolization of him. Stanley's major mistake was not recognizing that his wife's tirades were really about her insecurity and her hurt, and he enjoyed the attention from someone other than her. When he came to realize that the other side of anger is hurt, he began to notice the fragile side of Pauline. At that point, their relationship began to flourish.

Everyone experiences jealousy at one time or another. It is a very human feeling. It is not safe, however, to express it with rage and to create a hostile environment for colleagues. Not only can a toxic reaction to jealousy damage personal relationships, it can wreak havoc with a career. Both Pauline and Stan got lucky at their company. If they had not had their successful track records and allies around the office, one or both of them might have been fired. As for Cheri, she wasn't so lucky. Both Everywomen and Bully Broads need to be cautious not only of their own jealous reactions, but of those of other Bully Broads.

Pauline's case study describes a situation where jealousy was about a relationship, but jealousy isn't limited to loved ones or personal situations. Often we don't call it jealousy. We call it *concern*. For example: "I am concerned that Cindy seems to go to all the special account meetings." Or: "We are concerned that you were handed those options and the rest of us were not." Or: "I am concerned that you meet with Cecelia twice a week and you barely have time for a ten-minute phone call with me."

Harold was jealous because the boss picked Steve to travel with. Margie felt jealous because Ruth was always included in the meetings. Bob hated Luis because Luis seemed to make John laugh. Elizabeth was green over the way Tom was treated by Charles. Charles seemed to delight in Tom's working style and manner, while Elizabeth was chastised for being different. Any of these situations has the potential to explode into office conflict if the jealous party lets his or her feelings get out of hand. Bully Broads and Everywomen need to be savvy about how they respond to on-the-job jealousy.

The following list contrasts jealous reactions with their reasonable counterparts:

Jealous	Reasonable
Imagines the worst	Thinks positively
Worries obsessive-compulsively	Stays calm; thinks before she reacts
Feels love or loyalty is limited	Knows there is enough
Wants retribution	Forgives and moves on
Points outside of herself	Looks at her part in the situation
Is oppressive	Gives some room
Gives to get	Does not look for unrealistic reciprocity
Fears others are better	Knows she is good at what she does

Jealous	Reasonable
Is past oriented	Lives in the moment
Fears change	Welcomes change—or at least accepts it

APPLYING THE RULE

If You Are an Everywoman:

If you tend toward jealousy or envy, and you are an intimidator, watch your step.   Your imagination or your passion can poison you. You may not be conscious of the fact that jealousy and envy is a piece of your personality, but check yourself out. Sometimes just an old psychological tape that your mind keeps running can trigger feelings of inadequacy. Were you the favored one until your baby sibling came along? Did you feel that others got favors you didn't? Did you think teachers picked others for pets over you? Did you think things were not fair? Did your first boss play favorites and you were not one of them? If you have a predisposition toward being rejected, the green-eyed monster, jealousy, will appear.

If you are playing a Cheri role, watch your step.   Be aware that your actions do not occur in a vacuum, and be savvy about how others are responding to a sudden improvement in your status or closeness with a senior executive. Bully Broads like Pauline will take action if they feel you are threatening something of theirs—be it their sales territory or their husband. Cheri, who depended on Stan to protect her, was flabbergasted when Pauline went on the attack. But if she'd been smarter she would have taken care to position herself with a stronger record and more allies so she could have withstood Pauline's rage.

If You Are a Bully Broad:

Look for insight, not clues.   When you have some strong jealous feelings that seem out of proportion, look inside yourself and try to understand what may have triggered your response. Sometimes our colleagues or loved ones are unfair and unfaithful, but try to make the first step be one of introspection. Determine whether your suspicions are justified before you start looking for proof.

Remember the reality test. Talk to others, including the offending party. See if you can understand what might be happening *before* making a formal accusation. A wrong accusation can damage not only the offender's career, but also your own. Try giving the benefit of the doubt until the other party is proven guilty.

Watch your outbursts. This may be a very difficult time for you. You are tortured with doubt and you are not very stable in this frightening situation. Give yourself some support. Ask for help from others who will comfort you. Forget who is right and who is wrong. Urge others just to see your pain and to support you while you try to dig yourself out of a wild drama or deep depression.

Most often, the person you need the most reassurance from is the very person you have accused of disloyalty. Whether your accusations were rational or not, your victim may feel frustrated by you and under the gun to reassure you at the same time. It is an impossible job. He or she is mad at you for accusing, humiliating, or abusing him. He sees you as a vicious tiger and just wants to get away. This is a precarious time for all of you.

Get another opinion. Try to get your comfort from objective bystanders. If they agree that your fears are unfounded, they probably are.

If you have let jealousy take control, apologize. Approach your victim with a speech like the following:

> Dave, I have been a monster. I was so green with envy that I lost sight of the real facts. Now I am better, and I want your forgiveness. I will still slip and show that green-eyed monster now and again. I don't want to. I want to give you the benefit of the doubt. And I want you to give me the benefit of the doubt, too. I will make all of this up to you one day. You are patient with me now and I appreciate it. I will be patient one day when you need me. I hope it will not be on the same subject, but I owe you one!

Thank you for trying to understand. A terrible hunger gripped me. I longed for your loyalty and I did not know how to get it. So I raged—probably the worst thing I could have done. I am ashamed. I am also humiliated about my bizarre actions and hope you can forgive me.

Bully Broads don't apologize well. They are better on offense than on defense. Others already know this, but it is sanity-producing to be able to express your feelings to them. They all want to know that you do read yourself and that you know when you are being or have been unreasonable.

Know what triggers a jealous response in you.   If you begin to feel resentful of a colleague's expanding role in the company, or of a new friend that your loved one has made, remind yourself that the situation might simply have pushed one of your temper buttons. If you allow yourself to become the temper tantrum bully before you investigate the situation, you are liable to embarrass yourself. Pause. Think reasonably. Ask for help. Be rational. Don't act. Don't react. Your passion for action will tend to send you on some wild goose chase, or set you off on a tangent that could mean trouble. Restrain yourself.

Use a signal system.   When you are feeling insecure, you may need to remind your colleague, your boss, or your loved one to reassure you with some kind words, a reminder about how important you are, or a gesture that is meant just for you. I had an assistant who would eventually feel angry with me because I was taking so many different people to lunch and ignoring her. She could take about six weeks of neglect, and then she would desperately need some of my time or attention. I knew that when she suggested we should lunch at my Rotary club it was a signal that she needed some time with me, so I would almost always agree. We would take a rather long drive first, during which we would have time alone to rehash business matters and clear the air of any misunderstandings. Then we would enjoy the wonderful catered luncheon.

If you are feeling out of sorts and watching others get the attention you desire, instead of making a scene and causing enough commotion to get the negative attention, ask for it straight out. "John, I'm feeling left out. Can we have an hour together in the next few days? Terry has that great new project and I am not even on the team, so I feel like the kid who didn't get to go on the bus."

WHEN YOU WORK WITH A BULLY BROAD

When you work with a Bully Broad keep the following points in mind.

When you run up against a Bully Broad who feels jealous, beware! She is being tested on one of the primal areas of her personality. She will not cower and cry in the corner. She will rampage and call for action. She will point out the flaws in the system. She will attach negative labels to the person who is purportedly leaving her out and the person who is garnering the special attention. She will make fun of the person who is getting the rewards and she will belittle the colleague who is ignoring her. She will not take it well.

Whatever role you play, you will be in her way. If you are the recipient of the attention your Bully Broad really wants from the other party, you are really in trouble. Your job is to console her, give her some rational grounds for understanding the situation, and alert the third party to remember to attend to her. The triangle can be made up of innocent players, but a Bully Broad who can't express dependency or disappointment will simply go into a rage. Sometimes we confuse attention with caring. Sometimes we just don't understand what is going on with an intimidating bully. She may be like a caged animal to you. She is uncomfortable with the murky ambiguity of the situation. Either she is looking for evidence that she is right and someone is being disloyal, or she is looking to being reassured.

A Bully Broad is prone to action—even if the action is fatal. If she can't be reassured, probably because she is being so obnoxious that no one wants to be near her, she will simply continue the quest. Instead of berating her or hurrying away, try comforting her. That means you have to stick your hand in the lion's cage. Remind her that this is a frightening move for you. Ask her to treat you gently.

Try something like this: "Look, Louise, you are behaving like a kid. I can't help it that Sam and I are working so well together right now. I want to work with you, too. But you have been so edgy lately and you are no fun to be with. I'm going to ask Sam to meet with you and me so we can plan the trade show presentation. I know you want to be talking to Sam. I'll try to give you some time alone with him. But get off my case, will you? You have to relax and decide that we are going to be good working colleagues. I can't take your abuse. I don't deserve it, and it is not helping your cause."

RULE

9 Take the High Road—It's Faster

CASE STUDY

Georgia Matson went all the way, and she reached her highest aspiration. She is now a County Supervisor, but she had to work every angle to get there. From a conscientious and naïve young upstart, she has evolved into the pragmatic stateswoman who has been burned, scorned, and falsely accused because she did what she thought was right. She is wiser now—much wiser.

Earlier in Georgia's career, she worked with an incompetent colleague whose lack of judgment and ability cost taxpayers a significant amount in wasted public funds. The colleague's mistakes tarred his whole office, and Georgia, with her Bully Broad drive to succeed, resented having her good work smeared by association with his disastrous activities. So when the story of his misdeeds began to emerge and she had the opportunity to burn him by name in public and

77

later in the press, she did so. It felt wonderful. She was right, too. She certainly didn't make up the facts, and she didn't even initiate the story. But it ruined her political career.

When she was later asked about her reasons for speaking out, she explained that her resentment had bubbled up and the facts just spilled out. They did indeed; she had gone far beyond what she should have said. When jealousy spilled into the need for retribution, Georgia created one big mess. The public was angry; however, her colleagues on the Board of Supervisors and supporters all over the county, and then the state, soon realized that her viciousness was generated more by malice than in support of the truth—and they were furious. Georgia lost friends, votes, her reputation, and her self-confidence.

>——◇——○——◇——<

Take the high road. Don't succumb to the wiles of that small-minded girl inside who just wants to hit back.

There will be times in your career when you have legitimate grievances. You may have learned the harsh reality about who makes decisions and who doesn't. You might have discovered the limits of your subordinates' loyalty and the extent of your boss's endorsements. You may be bitter. An ambitious colleague may trample you in his rush to the top. A client may mislead you, and an assistant may let you down. Like Georgia, you can't make it as far as you want to go without making enemies. Someone out there may still harbor lingering resentments about you, and that is part of the world of business.

When you get the chance to strike back at these people, don't retaliate! It sounds like so much fun. You can really undercut Doug's achievements. You can show up your boss, Claire, for what she really is. Don't! Like some drugs or chocolate, public revenge feels good in the moment, but you may not feel so good about yourself five minutes later! More to the point, people have long memories. Doug and Claire may have been in a position to assist you at a later time despite past tensions; you can bet they won't if you humiliate them. Other colleagues will also remember, and whether or not they know the story behind your frustration, they will see your reaction as a sign that you are at worst a backstabber and at best someone they cannot depend on for support.

How do you move on then? How do you forget when someone takes advantage of you or disappoints you? Plan on disappointments some of the time. In the natural state of human affairs, someone will eventually misrepresent you or misinterpret you. You need to scuttle your reactionary desires and move on to the next event. Each malicious thought is poison. Each regret or resentment will take up a negative place in your psyche. These thoughts don't move you forward. They hold you back. Regrets are wasteful and resentment is poison. Stay healthy. At times, it is tough to take the high road, so bring your crutches along. You will need a friend or colleague to explain your predicament and to applaud you when you do show virtuous discipline.

APPLYING THE RULE

If You Are an Everywoman:

Acknowledge the sabotage.   If you are going to take the high road, you will need to believe that retribution doesn't really work. When you feel disappointed or depressed about the actions of another, do what you can to dislodge the hurt. Talk to friends who will not reveal your confidences. Think about possible positive outcomes. Reframe the situation when you can. Don't act on the urge to retaliate against your tormentor on the job. Set limits and look at your part in the dilemma, too.

The high road is faster and less bumpy.   Although it may be tempting to take the road of revenge or retaliation, you will usually pay in the long run. Don't talk about your nemesis behind her back. Don't be passive-aggressive—saying one thing and doing another. Even if you feel she does not deserve it, approach the situation with dignity. Try understanding her dilemma from her point of view.

If You Are a Bully Broad:

Try the right road.   Believe that what goes around comes around—but you don't have to be the one doing the spin! The high road is sometimes circuitous, lonely, and without immediate rewards. It can be cold and discouraging, while others may be having a pleasant, easy walk. As a Bully Broad, you are probably quite used to chaos and conflict. You rather like it, but keep your own faith that doing the right thing is the way to go.

Integrity is being congruent by being and doing what you say you are.   Practice what you preach. As always, check yourself against others to make sure that you are not just rationalizing your approach. You probably talk the high road, but do you walk it, too? You know what is right and what is wrong and you make decisions about that on a regular basis. You are conscientious about your virtue.

Watch out for your own hypocrisy!   Your ego or pride can pull you into some ugly decisions if you can't practice what you preach. Because you are so in touch with your own values, you often convince yourself about what is right, even when it goes against your better judgment. Check with others—especially others who do not think the way you think. Then do what you believe is right, regardless of your pride or your ego.

Reward yourself with personal satisfactions, such as buying yourself a new outfit or taking a trip. Again, you may get upon your own high horse and say, "I am just doing my job, so I don't need to reward myself." The truth is, we are asking you to discern between when you authentically take the high road and when you just go through the motions. You will need to know the difference between the two actions; when you can successfully differentiate between the two, and when you have actually and consciously acted from good spirit, you may want to thank yourself in some way. You are usually not so great at rewarding yourself. You don't believe in indulging yourself because your standards of judgment are very high, even for you. When you can, at least thank yourself for being noble. It can be discouraging when your noble acts go unrecognized. If you can let others know without bragging, do so. But watch your step. You may not be good at appraising your own gestures. Check them out, again and again!

WHEN YOU WORK WITH A BULLY BROAD

When you work with a Bully Broad keep the following points in mind.

Call her on her own principles.   If you are a victim of bully tactics, your Bully Broad will listen when you can call her on her own principles. She is respectful of her values and does not want to be incongruent with them. She may rationalize in self-defense, and that can end up sending mixed messages and leading to some wrong conclusions. Help her. Remind her of her high-road intentions and appeal to her good and fair nature. Even if you are not sure she can make the leap, assume she can and give her a chance!

Watch your own walk.   Are you walking your talk? Is your integrity intact? It is very easy to focus on outside pressures—that is, on your Bully Broad. After all, she carries a pretty dramatic profile and is prone to acting out and causing scenes. She seems to enjoy the attention—or else her system of rationalization is so strong that she can make excuses for her every act. She is a wonderful straight person for you.

If you are going to take the high road, however, you will want to examine your own path to success. Are you always honest, or do you use that magic excuse of not wanting to hurt someone's feelings so you withhold your real feelings? Do you take the back door because the front door is crowded with people who will quote you? Do you duck out of responsibility because you don't like the heat? Do you get out of assignments by acting like you didn't hear them, understand them, or believe them?

Bully Broads are great targets. They are often notorious for "putting foot in mouth." You may love the idea of putting her in her place, but she may just be misunderstood. Try to see things from her point of view. Then discipline yourself to seek the honorable route. If you walked in her shoes, danced her dance, and answered to her boss, would you be having some of the same feelings?

10 Don't Burn Bridges—Ever

CASE STUDY

Although Mary Ramsey had earned the promotion with her blood, sweat, and tears, it went to Cynthia. Then, due to company machinations and reorganizations, Mary ended up working for Cynthia. Mary quit in a huff and moved to another state. She wrote Cynthia a scathing letter and made sure most people knew why she was leaving. Goodbye, good riddance.

Seven years later, Mary walked into her new Vice President's office. She had heard the new executive was from out of state, but Mary had been on sabbatical and had no idea who her new marketing boss would be.

Of course, it was Cynthia. Now Cynthia did hold a grudge, she did want retribution, and Mary did not have a chance. It was a hard and sad meeting. Most executives with high profiles ultimately end up reporting to one of those bad guys with petty instincts and long memories. Many of us have had a similar meeting. It is part of being in business—the hard part. Mary suffered through many years with Cynthia. In this case, her stock options motivated her to stay with the company, in spite of the circumstances of having to deal with Cynthia.

Good news: Cynthia ended up receiving leadership training. She recounted the story of her conflict with Mary and the resentment each carried. We invited both to the office for conflict resolution. Each needed a great deal of persuasion to appear. "What have you got to lose?" we suggested. "Plenty," Mary replied. "A repeat performance," Cynthia replied.

In our office, we did some fancy footwork to get them to remain in the same room. Our coaches actually spoke for each of them as though they were not in the room.

Cynthia's coach began: "Mary, I know you felt passed over seven years ago. It really wasn't exactly fair. I was lucky. But you hurt me deeply with your resignation and your letters and the buzz around the office. It took me years to live it down, and every time someone left the company, I worried that it was my fault again. I was quite paranoid. I couldn't believe it when you walked into my office last month. Ugh."

Mary's coach went on to make the conciliating remarks for her: "Yeah, Cynthia, I know. It was a mess. I reacted like a spoiled kid and I really left quite a mess. I want to apologize, but it took me a long time to realize that you didn't take my job. Somebody else chose you over me. Politically, we were both pawns. It is hard to say that. I still want to blame you, but that would be pointless."

It took several meetings and lots of patience to get these two women on the same page. An interesting event occurred a short time later. They were both sent to Asia for a very long and involved trip. They called and asked for one more clearing session before they left. When they returned from the trip, they each called in with glowing words about their new relationship. Mary was promoted and they are now peers again,

prepared for being allies when things get rough for either one
of them.

>-+-<>--O--<+-+-<

Bully Broads tend to burn bridges. You may actually crave finality and
hate ambiguity. You might prefer a harsh ending over no conversation
at all. Or you cut people off. "I don't need her," you say. "Who needs
Chester?" you assert. But Chester is your boss, and the other person is
your bridge to the information you need. Someone in Chester's position sometimes returns to haunt you.

Burning bridges is impractical for anyone. You may be cutting off
a future power supply, or creating ill will that can stifle your career.
There are two kinds of power: *personal power* and *positional power*. Personal power belongs to the individual who simply oozes confidence.
This colleague is known for her decisiveness. She may use it regardless of her position. People want to defer to her and know she will
take responsibility for her acts.

The second power base is positional power, which is elusive and
much less predictable. Positional power is not as dangerous to you in
the long run as personal power. When you are burning a bridge,
watch the colleague with personal power. She can help or hinder your
career. Find a way to maintain a good connection with her.

Imagine that Emily just informed you that she does not need you
on her task force. Try saying, "Emily, I know this was a hard decision
for you. Of course, I am disappointed. I do respect your analysis of the
situation, and I hope I will have the opportunity to work again with
you in the future."

Positional power is still a serious factor in your failure or success.
When you are considering telling off someone whom you do not
respect but who wields that positional power, I would use great caution. Questions to ask yourself are: Will my farewell speech change
this person? Will he like me more? Will my approach simply trigger
his defenses? Could he translate me negatively to others? Will he ever
forget my outburst? What will I gain from the kiss-off? You might
answer these questions as follows: I had to do it. I got it off my chest.

Now I can leave with integrity. I am worthy of self-respect. He deserved it.

These answers may not enhance your career. You should not sacrifice your principles. Don't say anything that compromises your values. It may be better to say nothing at all. As you face temptations such as those mentioned above, before you vent your frustrations, tell yourself the following:

- I can discipline myself about this.
- That speech will not foster my career.
- He will not hear me anyway.
- His defense mechanisms could translate my words negatively.
- I have something to lose here.
- I can express my frustration in safer places.

Many of us want instant gratification, but in the long run, discipline must prevail. If you are already in crisis with someone or you simply don't understand each other, instead of a farewell scene, let the difference alone. Walk away without a closing speech. That speech could come back to haunt you in the long run.

APPLYING THE RULE

If You Are an Everywoman:

Pride can be dangerous.   Don't let pride run your career. If your child needed surgery from the only surgeon in town, whom you had earlier dismissed, you might choose to retrench and beg for the surgery. Sometimes your career is disabled or broken and you may need surgery from the very person whose bridge you burned. Be practical, not childish. Try to see the other person's point of view, and even if he or she was selfish and conniving, you may want to make an allowance for your own small-mindedness some day. We are not human doings. We are human beings.

Maybe you will want to make a list of your grudge people. Are they still holding a grudge, or are you still holding a grudge against them? If it is possible, make an appointment to clear the air. You can start out with something like this.

> This may seem out of the blue, but I have been holding something against you for a long time. It may seem ridiculous, and you may not even be guilty, so it's time I talked about it. If we can repair this, I'd like to. So please indulge me as I tell you the story about that trip we made to Beijing together. It was a while back, but I am still stuck about something. I bet you can shed some light on it for me.

A short time ago my daughter revealed that one of her colleagues had felt slighted by me at a wedding ten years ago. She recited the phrase I was alleged to have said, and I could not even remember saying it, nor could I have put it in some context to understand it. But I believe I said it. I will see this woman at a gathering in a few months and I will apologize. Of course, I will ask for her understanding of the event, but that is not as important as the fact that she chose to feel bad about me for ten years. Knowing that I am sometimes flip and can be processing out loud—a favorite trait of Bully Broads, I wonder how many others I have offended over time without even knowing it. I wish the woman had come to me instead of avoiding me. I would have made amends with her if I had realized there was a problem. I just thought she was rather cold, and perhaps shy, around me.

Bully Broads tend to feel confident about themselves. They do not introspectively delve into how they could have hurt someone else's feelings. Having thick, protective skin enables them to disavow the possibility of wrongdoing, unless it is very obvious. They also have a strong sense of entitlement, so when someone else feels that a slight has occurred, the Bully Broads simply believe that the offended person owes them an explanation of the predicament. They don't realize that it may be too painful for some people to bring up or discuss such an uncomfortable event.

If you feel that you have been accused, don't waste time denying it. Do spend a good deal of time, however, exploring why a person might want to attribute a cause to the act. Bully Broads may not want to acknowledge something negative about themselves. Given that the Bully Broad's colleagues or friends or family might be reluctant to talk about abusive behavior, everybody ends up in the dark. Two or more people being in the dark about each other is not grounding for an authentic relationship.

If You Are a Bully Broad:

Being right is not always good enough.   When you look back at your career, can you recall some horrible exchanges that took place just because you wanted to be right? Was being right worth making an enemy? Do you remember now what you were right about? Watch out for ego traps that tempt you into making a scene, as well as for issues that become bigger than they need to be.

Because you are such a high-profile person, people rarely forget you. Nor will they forget your tirades, your tantrums, and your direct approach. So beware of bridge burning. You can't afford as much of it as your colleagues can.

Fix it.   Repair work is hard for Bully Broads. They have to admit something and make themselves vulnerable. Then they think they have to beg. Admit, show vulnerability, beg—ugh! But you have to be honest. You have to recognize your part in any conflict. You may have to admit that you can be a challenge for some people some of the time. You may even have to admit that you are a little intimidating.

When you can admit that you might have had a part in the misunderstanding, you have committed a glorious act. It is not easy for you to want to own any of the bad news. Quickly explain that your intentions were honorable, but don't try to slip out of the fact that you might have been holding on to something not true. Most of our projections onto each other are not irreversible.

The reward for giving up a grudge is that others see you as brave, fair, and interested in them after all. Who wouldn't like to have such motives attributed to them?

Misunderstandings usually are the foundations for disagreements. Translations of events, as well as of words, usually depend on your frame of reference. Don't employ selective listening about the person you are mad at. Put in a new hearing aid or don some new glasses to wear with that person.

Walk in that person's shoes so that you can take a peek at yourself. You might guess why the other person feels badly about himself around you. Colleagues worry about things you may never have thought about. Managers may want something from you that you have never considered. Some people will be very wary about telling you anything that could set you into a temper or even just a sour mood. Subordinates may feel offended by something you meant as a compliment. You hope they would not give up on you. Turn the tables, and give them another chance. Make a list of the people about whom you have been holding something—give them a chance to get on your good side again.

WHEN YOU WORK WITH A BULLY BROAD

When you work with a Bully Broad keep the following points in mind.

Give her another chance.   Much as you'd love to slam the door on her, you can't burn bridges either. First, you may meet her again. Second, and most important, you are infecting yourself with resentment and rage, and neither is good for you. This does not mean that you have to play up to her. Rather, do what you can to minimize the damage and don't take her judgmental ways personally. The verbally abusive person can't really hurt you if you let her words go in one ear and out the other. If she never manages to mend her ways, you do want to give her a wide berth. A compromise statement could be something like this: "I know that we don't understand each other. I feel concern about you and your behavior and your words about me. I don't want it to end this way. I would like to forgive you and ask you to forgive me for what you may consider to be harmful."

Practice forgiveness.   Remember that saying "I would like to forgive you" does not mean you are actually forgiving her. You might think this is hedging, but it is actually a starting point for mending. It may mean you wish you could forgive. It is saying that your intention is to try to fix things. It is not a promise to do so.

You will actually feel better if you can make a move toward relieving the tension between the two of you. It does not matter who is holding the grudge. The second person usually feels the coldness, the quiet aggression, but she or he is often busy with other issues and would rather not take you on anyway. That person may believe that the risks of talking to you are too great. What if he is wrong? What if you laugh at her for bringing up old business? What if you dismiss the idea and tell the person you think the whole thing is ridiculous?

Get back on the right foot—you will move faster. When you can clear up an old grudge, you can move faster and more freely. Carrying bad feelings is the kind of weight that stifles your creativity in your enemy's presence. It also depresses the other people because, even though they doesn't know why you are upset, they can never feel good about themselves in your presence. Open the door. You will be surprised at the good news that will blow in.

11 Wait for Apologies, but Don't Wait to Make Some!

CASE STUDY

Debra Markham, the star of the training department, was the impatient type. She tapped her foot while waiting in line and hung up on phone operators who took too long. She was a "sentence finisher" for other people, which is a strong Type A trait. You can hurry people along by finishing their thoughts for them.

Debra was very impatient about her training assignments. She began to notice that Sue, her colleague, wasn't giving her training assignments. Sue was the top saleswoman for her company and usually she made recommendations for the training assignments that she sold. Sue seemed to be friendly with Debra, but she never gave her any business.

When Debra realized what was going on, she decided that she needed to talk to Sue. Being the Bully Broad that her reputation labeled her, Debra went straight to Sue to confront the issues. "Why wasn't I getting assigned any business? Haven't I proved my credibility? How long do I have to wait before you make recommendations for me? What is enough?"

Debra was using all of the typical "what about me?" questions. Nothing seemed to get through to Sue, who denied the accusations and simply made excuses for the assignments. Debra huffed and puffed and basically reprimanded Sue for being so stingy with assignments.

Months later, Debra was growing impatient. "What's with that woman?" she would demand from anyone who would talk about it. "She is basically withholding my income and stifling my career growth," Debra screamed. Still no assignments.

Sue remained steadfast in her lack of trust in Debra. She watched her in staff meetings and convinced herself that Debra would be just like that with the customers she had cultivated—angry, belligerent, and impatient.

In the next several years, Debra mellowed and began to get some training assignments from Sue. Finally, they addressed the issue, nearly four years later. "I wanted an apology from you four years ago, Sue. You just about killed my career. How could you have done that? I've been waiting for an apology all this time."

Sue was not aware of the length of the waiting period. She believed she gave assignments when she thought Debra was ready. She did not feel obliged to apologize, and she surely wasn't going to apologize now, especially after Debra had raised the roof again.

"Well, if you felt that way back then, why didn't you tell me?" demanded Debra again. "You owed me that!"

"No, I didn't," Sue answered. "If you could not have figured yourself out then, I wasn't about to teach you. You were intimidating and abusive. You were demanding then and you still are."

That analysis—that she needed to wait for another person to evaluate her—was very hard for Debra to accept. So she campaigned. The combined effect of the campaigning, the complaining to others, and the intimidating interrogation did not endear Debra to Sue.

When Debra realized she wasn't getting anywhere with Sue, she decided to use a different approach. She backed off. This took discipline, which was not Debra's long suit. She finally decided to give up on the apology and just figure out why she didn't get assignments in the first place.

It was only when Debra was coached to accept her own responsibility for what happened that Sue loosened up enough to say, "I wish it had been different for you."

Although Debra wanted more, that was all she was going to get. Don't negate the value of something like this pseudo message by demanding more.

>—+—◆>—O—<◆—+—<

A Bully Broad always yearns for an apology if she feels she has been wronged. Even if she thinks she deserves one, she still needs to go through the motions of discovering whether she has provided the opportunity for the other person to want to apologize.

Sometimes you will get an apology. Sometimes you won't. Why not?

The answer to that question is that a Bully Broad does not provide the atmosphere wherein someone may want to be humble. She is usually not a receptor that accepts such a gesture kindly and thanks the messenger. Instead, she may get offended and up the ante with more offensive comments, such as "Well, it's about time" or "Is that all you can say?"

The entitlement issues that a Bully Broad has may push her into believing she deserves an apology for a perceived slight. Usually she is so belligerent that she will not invite a sincere apology. People do not regret injuring her if her claws are out again and ready to scratch.

Debra hadn't understood herself and she surely didn't understand Sue. In fact, she never gave Sue a chance. She only considered Sue in relation to her own needs.

Why didn't Sue just give Debra the vital feedback she needed to help her play on the team? Because many people don't believe that someone like Debra can change. Others do not want to go through the headache and heartache of the accusations and exasperations of another's reactions.

This may be why many male high-level managers do not take on these kinds of issues. They tend to think, "I'll do it sometime, someday, maybe when I have more energy and less pressure." They tend to do a better job of protecting themselves in these settings than do Bully Broads. Bully Broads want action; they want to do something. They will not discipline themselves to simply stand by and wait.

Interestingly, the Bully Broad and the Ice Queen are always sure when they deserve the apology but rarely remember when it is their turn to apologize. Asking the forgiveness from another person is quite an event for someone as self-serving and independent as our exceptional women. They believe, then, that having to apologize is a weak act. They choose to express regret very carefully. It is not easy; doesn't roll off the tongue. After all, being wrong is quite a dreadful event for the perfectionist, hard-driving woman who wants to be right most of the time.

APPLYING THE RULE

If You Are an Everywoman:

If your excuse is "I don't apologize," give it up.   Everyone needs to learn to be contrite sometimes. If you are around a Bully Broad, she will absolutely want your apology if she believes you were wrong. Even if she is not good at apologizing herself, she wants you to be good at it.

Trust is based on telling the truth.   Don't lie about your situation. If you feel no remorse, don't conjure up some. There are some appropriate middle-ground statements that you can try—for example, "I am sorry this is happening to us." This assumes no blame. It assigns no blame. It acknowledges that a problem has intervened between the two of you. I like to draw the analogy of California being a no–fault state in divorce cases. Although this law took effect nearly 30 years ago, couples still always try to assign blame.

If you are not willing to accept blame, acknowledge the predicament you are both in.   If you can just admit that you are caught in a ticklish situation, that each of you is in a catch-22 event, or that you are sorry that things are so confusing, you will have made the preliminary moves.

A third party can help.   Sometimes you just need another voice or another point of view to intervene between two people who are polarized. Just knowing the conversation is being monitored by an objective person heightens the chances for communication success.

If You Are a Bully Broad:

Be patient.   Being patient could offset your forceful personality. You may have to lower your profile by not confronting every issue you deem important. Rate the importance of an issue. Track how often you are pushing your own ideas or goals. Are you upset when you talk about the issues? If you are upset, unable to see a lighter perspective, and without the point of view of the other person, you are not going to be a good listener. Build in a sense of humor about yourself and the issues. ("Oh sure," griped Debra. "Relax! Just when my career is at stake!")

Listen for buying signs.   Don't proceed with your point of view without an agreement to begin to understand each other. Do others sense your disapproval? Do you have the kind of rapport with this person that would predispose him or her to apologize? Your waiting style might actually appear offensive. Only you lose the points for sounding and acting critical. Can you try to imagine how hard you are to approach when someone is experiencing that righteous indignation?

Apologize first, if warranted, but don't expect a reciprocal apology.   Sometimes the bully can apologize. Sometimes it is easier for her than the person who doesn't play fast and loose like she does.

Someday, when your colleagues feel you are humble enough, changed enough, safe enough, they might forgive you and reach out. But they will not apologize just because you have offered your own apology. Don't expect a reciprocal arrangement just because you are good at giving apologies. I recall my own staff member saying to me, "Jean, I don't want another of your apologies. I just want you to change. Your apologies come too easily for you. I want a promise that it won't happen again."

Wait a long time.   Patience is not a Bully Broad's long suit. My own mother waited seventy-two years for her sister to apologize over a Christmas gift misunderstanding when she and her sister were six and eight years old, respectively. When they finally started talking about it, her sister could not recall the incident. Poor Mom. Seventy-two years of waiting, and no satisfaction possible.

Keep yourself busy.   Don't obsess. Some apologies may never be forthcoming. Distract yourself. Keeping score is not good for you. Spend your time on positive aspects of your life. Don't waste time or energy waiting. The other person may believe that you are not worth his or her time.

Be gracious.   If you do get the desired apology, be grateful. Say something like this: "This might have been hard for you to say. I am not the easiest person to approach in these moments. I have not been receptive all the time. I want to change this perception of me. Thank you so much for apologizing now. It feels great. I won't use it to retaliate, either. I want you to begin to trust me."

WHEN YOU WORK WITH A BULLY BROAD

Here's the good *news*: the universe often pays back. Whatever someone did to you or your team can be a life's lesson. You may not always see the final justification for the wrong you felt you received. You may simply have to act on faith that some people eventually get the message. If your Bully Broad demands an apology from you, try giving it. Bully Broads, with their short fuses, often trip themselves up. If you have never been able to see the contrite bully, you may decide to wait to see it. Don't worry. Eventually Bully Broads slip and fall. They usually have a lot of pride and a lot at stake, and they hit hard on the way down. If you can see below their surface, you might conjure up some sympathy. Then again, maybe you won't.

Understand the bully's strong defense system.   Bullies don't allow themselves to let their hair down and show their sadness, embarrassment, or despair. They secretly wish to see or experience the tender parts in others, but they are loath to share their own. If they do ask for forgiveness, it can be a big deal for a bully. They want your immediate and positive response. Immediacy junkies, they yearn for a quick reward.

Toughen up!   If you feel like a victim, you will need to toughen your skin so that an apology from your bully becomes a possibility. If she wants one from you and you are squeamish, you can set the limits. "I am willing to accept my part in our original problem, Debra, but I don't want you pouncing on me now if I show a little vulnerability. You are so aggressive that I don't really want to apologize because I think you will just use the information and try to one-up me."

12 Stop Worrying About Getting the Job Done— Get People Done

CASE STUDY

Dianna Ferguson was a workhorse. As the Project Manager in Marketing for a large competitor in the computer market, Dianna loved to be productive. She didn't mind working long and hard. She often picked up her colleague's responsibilities because she knew they were probably not doing a good enough job. She could always see what was needed in her Marketing Department. She despised people who worked slower than she did and she started resenting that her boss was forgetful. She began voicing some of her criticisms directly to her boss and she would speak her mind to anyone around. Sometimes she helped other departments with major projects. She always chose to get involved in making decisions. She seemed to be able to do everything.

Except that Dianna could not build rapport with her colleagues. She was simply unable to establish congenial working relationships with them. Dianna just didn't understand office politics. "I won't do office politics," she sneered. She didn't grasp that coping with office politics is as fundamental as breathing. You need to do it and understand it, if you want to function there.

Dianna did not feel beholden to anyone. She was the workhorse, and others seemed to be slackers as far as she was concerned. She made the political mistake of naming her own boss as part of the problem. She exposed his shortcomings publicly. Dianna didn't think she needed to "make nice" as long as she was right. She felt that she knew what the company needed and she proceeded to get the work done. Following her first long vacation of her tenure, Dianna was asked to leave the company. Restructuring and the need to combine business teams were the official excuse. A downturn in business was a wonderful reason to reorganize. Dianna was not able to comprehend the decision.

Dianna was not aware of the temper trails she had been leaving. She didn't know that people were keeping score on her disloyal acts. She didn't realize that the stinging emails she sent to her boss were adding up. Insulting the performance of other departments without any regard to the personalities involved finally closed her deal. Even though Dianna was productive, she had violated her colleagues' sense of harmony. Her constant pessimism was contaminating the work environment.

>·|·◆>··O··<◆·|·<

Bully Broads often concentrate on the tasks of the job, and not on the people of the job. Thousands of people have been heard to say, "I don't know what they are complaining about. I never missed a quarter." They never see the bodies strewn in the aisles or the morale degrading right in front of their noses.

Getting the job done, the tasks, is fun. It is measurable. It is rewarding. Getting the people done is more ambiguous, more dangerous, and much more confounding. For the clumsy manager, doing the task himself is just easier than teaching someone to do it right. After all, people are unpredictable, not easy to interpret, and seemingly incapable of naturally doing do things your way. "What's all this consensus junk anyway?" such a manager might shout. Or, "c'mon, this talking about process is getting us nowhere." The employee who has not learned to be political, read nuances, or check for discomfort in others, is handicapped. That person can't get the ultimate cooperation of her colleagues. "I'll just do it myself and then I know it will get done," she muses.

In the end, it is easier and wiser to use people to help you to get the production done. When those without people skills perform well, their demise takes longer. The glowing production results can stave off other complaints, but not forever.

If a company can find an easy, noncontroversial means of exit for a complainer, and they can rationalize the production loss, the company will usually take the easy way out. That means taking the troublemaker out. Companies don't automatically teach people to "read" other people. They don't give out "How to Be Political" manuals. The smart people know this to begin with, or they take outside classes, or they watch the successful person do it, or they simply stop and take a look at how hard they are working and still not getting the cooperation of their colleagues.

But companies and individuals alike get seduced by the worker who seems to produce more than anybody else. They are often the stars, so it is difficult to find fault with the star just because people are complaining all around her.

Structure-bound and results-oriented employees like Dianna want to concentrate on output, procedures, rules, and policies. They have no patience for exceptions. They also show very little finesse when they observe colleagues who don't play by the rules. If Bully Broads like her try holding in their complaints, they often leak out anyway in some pretty messy spills. She may sound something like this: "Well, we have a new form to fill out, boys and girls, because nobody has been keeping up on the data sheets. I am giving you another chance, but I just know that I'm wasting my time."

The theories from Daniel Golman's book, *Emotional Intelligence*, introduced new tools for workers who have never put much credence into coaching or cooperating with others. Bullies always have their favorites—certain colleagues they might work with—but the majority of staff members were to be ignored, omitted from participation, or maligned. Emotional intelligence is the art and science of understanding your impact on others and being able to cooperate with the human frailties and subtleties of other human beings. It is also about disciplining yourself to give feedback to others who do not seem to care.

The TV show *Survivor* is quite popular these days. While watching the second series of shows, I was dumbstruck to see a Bully Broad kicked off the first evening.

Debb, a *Silent Judge* (SJ) Bully Broad, was a good, creative, team member. A former corrections officer, she seemed like the perfect match for her team, who had to compete with another group for their survival. This woman seemed like a good bet. She was strong and innovative, and she appeared to enjoy the challenge of the Australian outback, where the competition was set.

A single sentence, however, possibly resulted in her getting tossed out of the tribe. It was spoken one cold night, when, without food, the troops huddled together, trying to comfort and amuse one another. This was only the second night together. The conversation seemed to get a little colorful and sometimes sexual, and that was when Debb did herself in. She made the following judgmental statement to her team: "I don't think this is appropriate talk for this night."

Her team voted her off the island on the third day. She was the first of this series to be voted off. My analysis is that she set herself up to be an outsider who seemed to indict all of her teammates at that one critical moment. She was a worker, not a rapport builder. She did not understand the impact of her statement.

In our consulting company, we have heard countless versions of this statement that says so much to those around you. Debb's critical and self-righteous style cost her the program.

Here are some translations of Debb's offputting remark:

I can control you with my judgment.
I know better than you what we should be talking about.
You are not choosing well.
I know better than you.
I am judging you.
I don't approve of you.
Your behavior is out of line.
You are childish, silly, and stupid.
I am disappointed in your value system.
I am sorry I have to be subjected to this tripe.
I don't want you to have this freedom.
You are low-life folks who don't know how to be.

Before you call out your verdict, think about your audience, your colleagues, and the situation, and anticipate the response you may receive if you stick your neck out. Could the responses be something like this?

Who does she think she is?
She makes us feel small and childish.
Why can't she just be a good sport and join in?
She makes me feel foolish.
I am sad that we can't play anymore.
I feel bad about myself and the group.
She is making me want to have her away from us.
She is a wet blanket.

APPLYING THE RULE

If You Are an Everywoman:

Work the relationships all around you.   Incorporate the belief that morale counts and can make or break a company. Bullies usually choose to work with a limited number of colleagues in their own departments. They are selective and don't excuse incompetence or what they label stupidity. They have little interest in the morale around the people upon whom they depend. "Just shut up and get the job done" is what they would like to say. Don't get caught in their trap.

It is not enough to love your own people.   Look up, down, and sideways for allegiance. Actually taking feedback can endear you to some of your potential friends. Burning bridges is not politically smart. If you are a Bully Broad, you are high profile, whether you like it or not. Your people skills can serve you well when different factions are thrown together eventually.

If You Are a Bully Broad:

Relationships, relationships, relationships!   Don't let "R" stand for *right*. Let your "R" stand for *relationships*. Give up some other "R"s, too. *Rational, reasonable*, and *right* are the killer "R"s for a bully.

Rapport building is the work you need to do. You may not like it at first. You might feel silly and pathetic. You will think you are just manipulating and you hate that kind of behavior. But think of this as retraining yourself to begin to consider rapport before results. This is temporary training. You don't have to do this forever. You are shaping your behavior, adding to your repertoire. The enhancements to your working style will not constitute a complete transformation. In fact, you can still be a hard worker who is results oriented. You are only adding some people skills to your skill box. Do you take time to nurture the people who need it? Can you find compassion for some of your colleagues' deficiencies? Can you compliment smaller achievements in the work of others? Can you speak optimistically about someone, even if the person is not accomplished yet?

WHEN YOU WORK WITH A BULLY BROAD

It is so easy to be angry with a Bully Broad who doesn't have people skills. She is easy to judge, to laugh at, and to sabotage. Instead, try coaching her. She is not educated in the science of understanding herself, her interactions with others, or the impact of her proclamations on others.

Teach the woman about you.   Give her a chance to know you. "Lucy, you have been ignoring me, but you need me to get the shipment out the door. Sit right down here and listen to my story for five minutes, and see if you can muster some respect for what I do around here." Let her know some of the personal qualities, traits, and values you like about yourself. Humanize yourself to her. That will be awkward, because she will never invite a personal history. But give it to her anyway, as you teach her to really see *you*.

Ask her, "Do you know that I am..."

Smart	Loyal	Experienced	A critical thinker
A professional athlete	An artist	A dancer	Creative
A good thinker	Rational	Fun	
A fly-fisherman	Experienced in management		

This revelation means you have to speak up to the bully. If she is challenged when it comes to relationships, she will wonder why you are talking this way. You are trying to teach her that you are a human being.

If she is wounded and mistrusting about relationships, you will have to give her an opportunity to trust again. This may take a little time. It may be worth it. If you are her boss, reward her for taking the beginning steps toward people management, not just the measurable production results. If the launch happens on time, compliment her, if you can, on the positive morale in her organization that accompanied the wonderful results. Just imagine this fabulous worker who gets the job done but can also add some tact, poise, empathy, and collaborative thinking!

13 Perfectionism Kills

CASE STUDY

Toby Marshall wasn't on trial, but sometimes she felt like she was the perpetrator. Coming from a good family, cooperating in her neighborhood, and serving soup in a soup kitchen, Toby's dragon lady reputation was quite a contrast to her actual values. "What's the matter with me that people hate working around me?" she demanded.

Toby's small department had lost twenty-five employees over the last five years just because Toby couldn't give up the last detail. Being in the editing field didn't help. It was her job. She was senior editor in the Public Relations Department of the largest publicly held corporation in the area. She knew she was good. She proudly told me about a magazine she formerly worked for that had not had a single typo discovered in a stretch of a dozen years. She wanted the same for her department.

Here was her problem. The CEO, Charlie, was a nimble fellow who changed his mind about what was hot from moment to moment. Each event was subject to new priorities. He would cut a story and then demand a new one within hours. The industry, the economy, her immediate boss could all toss changes at Toby's department at the same time. Toby believed that she was the goalie and that she could not allow one puck, or one mistake, to get past her. When the company won its case against its largest competitor, Toby stayed at work all night. She insisted that half of her staff stay there also.

When some mistakes were made in a resource list of computer speeds for a twelve-year period, she insisted the team spend the night checking the list. This was not a lead story. Mistakes in this project would not have affected her company. The list was to be a small sidebar in one of their weekly in-house journals, but she treated the information in the same way that her headline press releases had been handled. She was livid when someone suggested that it might be a trivial matter. Toby felt her job was at stake. Good old "no-mistakes Toby" even believed her career was at stake. She fired the person who called it trivial.

"Get a life, Toby," they all whispered behind her back. To her face, they saluted, followed her instructions, and went on spending an inordinate amount of time on every detail of every project that left the office. Her group produced an in-house paper, newsletters, all press materials, some brochures, some data sheets, extra information requested by the CEO, and any special projects Toby could snag.

Unfortunately, Toby had no life outside of her work. Divorced and embittered, childless, and impatient with others who had children, Toby's highest priority was work. She believed that people used their children as excuses for shoddy work. She believed that no excuses were acceptable. Toby would not even have a dog to comfort her. No, her comfort was her scrapbook of clippings and the occasional note from her immediate boss or the CEO saying "what would we do without you?"

Perfectionists have no discernment software programmed into their heads. Everything and everyone has to be lined up, in order, right, straight, correct, and complete. Their motto is "If you can't do it right, don't do it!" Trying to distinguish what is important or urgent from the rest of the work is just frustrating and time consuming. It feels better to perfectionists just to do everything well. So they make a list of twenty things, start at the top, and do them all. Please don't ask these folks to take a day-planning course—they already have! They usually have elaborate systems for planning and plotting out what is important. They have the books on setting priorities. Intellectually, they get it. They can plan it. They just can't do it.

We asked Toby how she got this way. "Oh, I remember my mother teaching me how to make a perfect bed. It was fun. She loved it. So did I. We practiced over and over. Now I even come in and make over some hotel beds as soon as I arrive. I can't help it. It is still kind of fun to me.

"My Dad was a chief accountant and he believed that there were no frivolous numbers. I was adding up the grocery bills in first grade. If I found an overcharge or an item not in the bag, I would get the amount of the item. I had quite a bank account by age eight.

"My dad also paid me for any errors I could find in Christmas card letters mailed to us from others or from newspaper articles Dad would choose for me. I was happily grading papers for my teachers by age ten. I was not too popular with my classmates, but I was getting perfect grades myself."

Toby's perfect academic background led to her scholarships. Being indirectly assigned to the CEO felt like more honor roll grades. Eileen, the boss between Toby and the CEO, was often chagrined that Toby would be called in for certain tasks. When the CEO ordered them in at 5 p.m., Eileen knew she did not want to work all night to have the story ready by dawn, so Toby got the assignment. When she could do the task alone, she was fine. When Toby needed help and had to ask research people, copy editors, or the Legal Department folks to jump in, she would find herself yelling and screaming all the perfectionist's themes.

Perfectionists are likely to say some of the following:

Hey, it was not a big job.
Why can't you get one thing right?
Don't give me excuses.
I said "perfect"!
I meant every piece!
I meant every word!
I mean double-check.
Don't blame them. You did it.
Did you look it up?
Did you check?
It might have only taken five more minutes.
What's the matter with you?
Where's your pride?

The perfectionist knows how to rub it in. She is poison for the half-hearted, and she is a killer if you don't show the same passion for accuracy that she feels. You might get away with a few mistakes if you show a regretful response about them and rush feverishly to fix them.

The Bully Broad who adds perfectionism to her persona is boldly accentuating her bully liabilities. She will always push one little step too far and cause someone around her to give up. Her subordinates complain, "I can't live this way—always worrying, always wondering what I left out, and always feeling under the super eye of super Toby who wants nothing but the best."

At last, Toby's own boss, Eileen, blew the whistle. She had to blow it over and over again, though. Remember, the CEO loved Toby because she got the job done accurately—on his time line. When Eileen described how many good people the company was losing, the CEO decided he had to transfer Toby. He scrambled for a solution. What could he do to keep this worker bee without disturbing the rest of the team?

He decided that she could have an individual contributor job as a right-hand media expert to him. Everyone was thrilled with this solution. The CEO was satisfied, the Human Resources staff were relieved, her subordinates were gloriously grateful, and her boss was happy to release her. Those evaluations with Toby had always been excruciatingly hard on Eileen. Toby picked everything apart. Goodbye, evaluations. Goodbye, Toby. Hello, new world!

Toby lasted only 30 days with her new boss, the CEO. Subconsciously, she was always grading him. Her dad had loved that and had trained her to correct him whenever she could do so.

Toby was indiscriminate with her corrections, constantly pointing out the errors and omissions of others. She corrected the CEO's handwritten memos; she reminded him about double negatives and the proper use of semicolons. She fussed about his speech material, sending a speech back for revision again and again. She criticized everyone's work and she was a gloom-and-doom personality, which did not suit the CEO's positive nature.

"Get her away from me," he barked at Human Resources. "She is a human spell-check and grammar-check, and I am sick of her fault-finding. I liked it from afar, but when she took my diplomas off the wall and sent them back, after twenty years, to have the spelling corrected…well, she just went too far!"

Toby could not take the pain and humiliation of going back to work as senior editor. Eileen did not want her anyway. She left her twelve-year employment to do consulting jobs. She is great on her own, with no subordinates to berate or debate. She doesn't mind doing it all—because she is so careful, so accurate, and so reliable.

Her only problem has been her personal interactions with customers. Her judgmental tone eventually slips out. "I can certainly upgrade your annual report. It has many holes and doesn't seem to be as sophisticated as your company purports to be." Toby soon realized she needed the buffer of Eileen, the woman who had been the middle person between the CEO and Toby. Unwilling to hire anyone from her former company, and, more accurately, fearing they would all laugh at any offer from her, she worked alone. The last I heard, she was having surgery for a perforated ulcer. She finally wounded herself.

>–I–◆>–○–◆I–<

APPLYING THE RULE

If You Are an Everywoman:

My company is paid handsomely to tell company employees not to work so hard. No, we are not heretics. We believe that balanced employees who pace themselves will not wear out in the long run. If you worry about every single piece of data in your life, you will eventually overload yourself. You can take only so much. I personally have bargained for more memory packs for my brain, but the order is never filled. In fact, I believe I have experienced some recalls for some of my storage units. We don't seem to have the infinite space needed to store the clutter of all those facts and figures perfectly.

Use the 80-20 principle.   Consider the concept that when you have a job to do, the majority of it can be accomplished in the initial stages using 20 percent of the time you have available. In fact, when we sit down, buckle up, shut out the world, and start it, we discover that we can get 80 percent of the job done in 20 percent of the time. That's a pretty astounding statistic.

Here's where the perfectionist comes in. She doesn't believe in the 80–20 principle. She doesn't think that most of the work gets done at the beginning. She likes to use 100 percent on every job. She actually enjoys applying that last 80 percent to the remaining 20 percent of the job. She can nitpick, screen, rethink, count, analyze, compare, and rework so that a whopping 80 percent of her time is used to complete the final details. This is not an efficient way to work. It is not pragmatic if you have five jobs of equal priority to do. It's simply not practical—you can't afford such hypervigilance at every turn.

The perfectionist will protest, "But I want the last 20 percent to be perfect. I will check every decimal point, polish every word, double-check every assumption, and withhold this project until it is perfect. This may take up all of the remaining time I have available. But it will be perfect."

If you have five projects to complete and five hours available, don't spend all five hours on the first project. Allow yourself only 20 percent of your time for each project.

For example, Anne and Audrey have each been allotted five hours and given five assignments. If they use only 20 percent of their allotted one hour for each project, they would be spending twelve minutes per project.

Being the perfectionist, Anne spends the whole five hours—all 300 minutes—on the first of the five projects. She gets one project done using all of her time and energy and probably getting it done nearly perfectly. But that leaves her no time to work on the other four projects.

100% of 5 hours = 1 project

All together, Audrey has the same allotment of five hours. She plans ahead and anticipates that there could be problems in Projects 2, 3, and 4. She may have to devote more time to them. Fine, she will do so. She uses 20 percent of one hour for each job. Projects 1 and 5 are easy and she completes them in this amount of time. She uses up an extra 20 percent on Project 3, and perhaps an additional 57 percent on Project 4. Maybe she decides to use a whole hour of the allotted time on Project 2. Audrey ends up with time leftover to clean up and wrap up.

Projects 1–5: 20% each of allotted 1 hour each = 100 minutes used
Project 2: extra 80%   = 48 minutes used
Project 3: extra 20%   = 12 minutes used
Project 4: extra 57%   = 35 minutes used
_____
Total time in hours for five projects: = 195 minutes used

This leaves 105 minutes to spare, or 35 percent of Audrey's time left to clean up, recuperate, celebrate, pick up, put the projects in a FedEx bag, or wrap them up with a big red bow. One project used 100 percent of its allotted hour, one used 40 percent, one 55 percent, and three used 20 percent. Audrey's boss receives five completed jobs. Even though Audrey spent her whole allotted time on the difficult Project 2, she still managed to finish all the jobs within the alloted time.

Anne, on the other hand, got one perfect job done and seemed to ignore the job-sensitive, boss-priority, high-payback item, Project 2.

In Audrey's case, she used 65 percent of her allotted five hours, with time to rest, and she accomplished all five jobs. She used a full hour on Project 2 because she concluded it was a high-payback item for the boss. Do you think her boss was happy?

Poor Anne never even got to Project 2. You do the math.

Watch your priorities, as well as your boss's priorities. Prioritizing your to-do list is your first and most important job. Don't try to check off each project on the list. If you have to confer with the boss, do it. In fact, go in with five to ten projects, prioritize them 1–10, and then ask if the boss agrees with the priorities. Then give your boss a time estimate for each job and ask whether the lowest-priority jobs may be cut off if you do not have enough time allotted to work on them.

We often choose to complete certain projects because we simply like to do them. That is fine if you pace yourself and balance those items with what is imperative to do. You might love cleaning out the supply cabinet. Or you may find filing or counting a relaxing pastime. Or you may enjoy strategizing, conducting meetings, planning events, or solving complex problems. Of course, you need to do some of what you just plain like to do, regardless of the priority.

I am on the Boards of Directors of several nonprofit organizations, not because they are good for my business, but because I love the people and want to be in their presence. I need to rank those Board meetings for my priority list, and then I have to convince my own Board that I deserve time to meet some of my personal needs, too. Here are some examples of effective campaigning for the low-payback but favorite jobs you simply like to do:

> Harry, I want to go to that conference just because I love New Orleans and it will give me the morale boost I need to tackle Gem-Star when I get back.
> Let me do that numbers crunching. It's fun for me.
> You know I love that stuff.
> I need a break from the big-picture work.
> Crunching numbers helps me relax.
> You know that is my favorite project and I'd like to be there when it launches.
> Put me back on the bench for this, coach. I love that problem.
> Just because I want to indulge myself about this…
> I want to play a little with this.
> I get such a kick out of shopping at Office-Maxi-mart.
> I'm passionate about that project.

If You Are a Bully Broad:

You probably cannot afford to be known as a Bully Broad and a perfectionist at the same time, although they often come in the same package. These time-bomb qualities can combine to create a frightening challenge to the insecure, conflict-phobic people who might work with you.

When a person is insecure, he or she will not be comfortable or work well with you if you tend to obsess over things. If that person worries about all of his or her inadequacies, and if you always seem to have something to critique, a sure-fire bet is that he or she will become the quivering employee who fears your every thought, word, and deed. You and the employee lose on every front.

Suppose you really are a forgiving and loving human being who doesn't judge others and is not retaliatory by nature but simply misunderstood. I offer the same advice to the bully and to the person whose reputation has been acquired erroneously. Both of you have work to do to clean up your image. You may not deserve the complaints directed your way, but if someone could possibly believe those things about you, the problem is nevertheless yours to deal with.

If you think you are misunderstood, ask yourself the following questions:

1. Why would someone want to believe this about me?
2. Why would they be afraid to tell me about this?
3. Why would anyone want to believe that I am tough, rude, aggressive?
4. Why would anyone believe that I am a perfectionist?
5. What do I do to demonstrate this perfectionism? What do I say that sounds like a perfectionist?
6. Do I talk about the "right" way?
7. Do I seem to overwork to get a job right?
8. What do I do to perpetuate my reputation?
9. Do I seem to dress perfectly, walk with purpose, stand straight, show rigidity?

If you can answer these questions, you are ready to begin your journey to insight. Stop denying the possibility that people can see the real you, even if you have been trying to hide some parts of yourself. You may even have to compensate with some new behaviors that could dissuade the most resolute enemy. Try some of the following suggestions:

- Show a relaxed response to mistakes.
- Admit your own mistakes in a lighthearted way.
- Learn to equivocate: use words like *almost, sometimes*, and *perhaps*.
- Say, "Well, for the most part, this was good."
- Say, " I am trying not to drill down too far on this."

If nothing else works, sit your colleagues down and give them an explanation. It would actually be quite good for you to try to get others to understand you. You might even get to understand yourself this way, too.

Take responsibility for your own image, whether you deserve it or not. When you begin to share yourself, your own vulnerability will wash away some of the projected behaviors assigned to you. Talk about your dilemma.

Try something like this: "I have been told that I am seen as a perfectionist. I am sorry about this. Of course, I don't see myself this way, so we have a misunderstanding. But I am going to take responsibility for my own reputation and I am starting by asking you to comment when you see me being too careful, too detail-oriented, or too nit-picky about things. I want to learn when and how I turn you off. I promise that I will listen. I do not promise to change everything about myself. I like that I am thorough. But I want people to enjoy working with me, so I am going to have to make some compromises.

"This may all sound strange to you. I am not used to asking for help. You know that. But I am ready to dump this image. I guess it's been hard on you. In the long run, it is also hard on me."

WHEN YOU WORK WITH A BULLY BROAD

It's easy to find fault and get fed up with perfectionists. They have such high profiles. They are not usually mute. Their positions or their personalities just create the megaphone effect. You soon learn about their idealistic values and their strong desire to be accurate and right. In the big picture, of course, these are grand values. The perfectionist just takes her improvement plans too far. She doesn't know it, though. You will have to teach her.

"Oh, phooey," you say. You don't want to be responsible for the person who sometimes makes your life hell. You don't want to fix her. You just want to get away from her. Well, if she won't learn on her own decide to be her tutor. You don't have any other choices, and you might learn something, too. The ultimate reward, of course, will be the gratitude you will receive from her. It might take awhile. Don't expect early results.

Approach gently, but deliver the message.   The message is that you are no longer going to take her overzealous approach to your work or your mistakes. You will remind her that you are just a human being, not a human doing. You will also remind her that microman-agement and scare and humiliation tactics are no longer working. In fact, teach her that you seem to get too anxious when you are worry-ing about her quality control, and that you actually make more mis-takes that way. There are lots of studies that claim that tension in the workplace adds personal pressure and decreases clear thinking ability.

Apply the "clutch your fist" test.   If you close your fist tightly for a few moments, you will begin to feel your fingernails digging into your palm. You will feel the muscles and tendons in your arm start to tighten. Do it now, if you haven't. Notice the ballooning veins in your arm. Does your arm or hand feel stressed? When you relax, do you feel that you have to shake your arm or hand out before you go on with things?

Creating tension in others is not good supervision or teamsman-ship. Teach your perfectionist to guide, teach, and coach, but not to stand with arms folded and nostrils flaring, looking for mistakes.

My two granddaughters play basketball for their high school. They are excellent, hardworking three-point shooters. Each was named most valuable player in her tournament this year. (Uh-oh, is this Bully Broad competitiveness still running in the family?)

Their father used to sit in the stands, hypervigilantly watching for flaws. Sometimes they said they could hear him above the roar of the crowds: "Hands up, follow the ball, watch your fouls, heads up, pass, dig, screen out, box out, don't panic." They could even hear him when he wasn't saying anything. Now, fortunately, they and their mother have coached their dad to loosen up in the stands. He is also a great athlete, so he does know what's up, but sometimes he just has to sit on his hands and keep his mouth closed. Glenn (the grandkid's

Dad) is quiet now, and we are all having more fun. By the way, Shaq O'Neill, the famous National Basketball Association star, claims his father was tough on him in high school, too.

We easily become allergic to criticism and faultfinding. The perfectionist worries that something will go awry, but she will have to control that fear so that it does not spread.

Your job is to get your perfectionist to do some behavior modification. Try this: "Say, Mary, this last job was great for me. You seemed to hang back a little and let me make my own mistakes. That helped so much. I tried to be careful, but I did not feel so intimidated this time, and it was easier to work."

If she hasn't improved, try this: "Say, Mary, I have an idea that can help me improve my mistakes ratio. When you stand behind me, or threaten me, or double-check me at every turn, I become more nervous and then I tend to make more mistakes. I want to improve, and I will work hard at improving my efficiency rate, but I have some ideas for you, too." You can then present her with a list like the following:

Don't grab the report out of my hands.
If you can start with anything positive, that sets the tone.
Don't appear to rush to the minute details.
Don't expect me to work as fast as you can.
Don't contrast my integrity with my error factor.
Believe in me.
Trust that I am doing the best I can.
Don't let some measurements distort my whole working life.
Don't humiliate me in public.
Acknowledge me when you can.
Don't apply my past reputation to my future work.
Don't set impossible expectations; they don't motivate me.

Then, practice what you preach.   If you are expecting your perfectionist to reward you positively for an approximation of success, you must do the same. Offer up something like this: "Gosh, Barb, you seem to be easing up a little on me. I feel the reduced pressure and I actually feel I am working better. I appreciate that you are trying to make things a little easier for me. Your intention about that, and about me, really feels good. I want to improve the quality of my work, and you are helping by ignoring some flaws and only concentrating on the main issues. Now and then, you even throw in a little laugh, and that really relaxes me.

"I am not asking you to treat me like a child. Just don't treat me like a prisoner or someone always on trial. If we can assume that I am doing the best that I can, and your complaints don't actually motivate me, we might see some wonderful, new interchanges between us."

RULE

14 You Can't Control Everything

CASE STUDY

Violet Hobert, managing partner for a large Las Vegas law firm, tried to control every part of her life. She also wanted to control every movement by her staff. With rules and regulations and no room for exceptions, Vi eventually lost most of her team. Many people enjoy the structure of knowing what is expected, but Vi allowed no room for her subordinates' ingenuity and creativity. She was a serious taskmaster. She was also what we call a *Silent Judge* (SJ). She did not waste time or words building rapport or "making nice." There was a job to be done, and she did it.

Women see men getting ahead by taking their work very seriously and proving how well they can do the job. Women do not have many female models in higher places. Certainly Vi did not. Ambitious and talented women take on more and more responsibility. They enjoy the special rewards and perks that hard work brings. Before they know it, they are risking themselves for bigger and grander projects. They fall in love with their own strategies and working styles. They are so infatuated that they sacrifice listening to the ideas of others. They want it all, and they want it all right. They slowly become intolerant of imperfection.

Vi may have begun with a mild allergy to frustration and ambiguity, but with the onset of power and the burden of heavy responsibility, her coping skills were reduced. Her law firm demanded accuracy. She enjoyed having a structured environment and was very much at home with doing things by the book. But add a demanding new boss, organizational change, and stress in her personal life and you have a Bully Broad in high gear. She is a train, heading full force off the tracks. The problem is that the Bully Broad's reaction to the speeding train is to try even harder. She won't allow herself to stop or take care of herself in other ways. She doesn't want to know her limitations.

To Vi and other people like her, being in control means being safe. She does not feel she is being rigid; she thinks she is being appropriate. She doesn't have any sympathy for the employees—including the lawyers—who spend less time on rules and more time on creativity. Vi needs to have order. Without order, Vi begins to disassemble. She becomes frightened and frantic. Of course, rigid controllers rarely admit their behavior is about security and safety. It is even hard to guess this, because they seem so confident that the rigid orders are necessary to get the job done.

>-+◆>-O-<+-+-<

What someone like Vi must learn is that she is in the minority among her coworkers. She believes having policies and procedures for everything only makes sense. She knows that some others don't need these boundaries. What she forgets, though, is that others may feel hemmed in by too much structure. She will stifle those who need to do a little independent thinking. She likes to create enough rules and regulations so that the tasks will require almost mindless participation.

Why do some people need such control? If you feel internally chaotic, you may want the outside to feel orderly.

I had a housekeeper who really wasn't good at cleaning, but she was very good at sorting. She loved to create order. She would stack the canned goods alphabetically. She would sort the clothes in a closet by color. She loved to arrange drawers and organize the garage. What was she doing? She was creating order around her.

This woman's story is significant to her working behavior. As a child, she remembers her dad chasing her mother around the house with a butcher knife. It seems every Saturday night they would both get drunk and Dad would get mean. He would end up screaming and shouting obscenities, running after Mom, threatening to kill her. The little girl could not stop Dad. She could only stay in her room, praying that her mother would survive the night. The screaming and crying and bumping and running around the house were loud. The little girl had to block out the noise. She did so by completely distracting herself.

She told me about the five-gallon pickle jar they had in which her mother kept buttons. There were buttons of every size, color, and shape. She loved the button jar and spent most weekends playing with the buttons. It was comforting and familiar. She would pour all the buttons out on the floor and then she would begin lining them up. All the big red ones would go in one line; the small white ones would go in another line. The glass ones, the big black ones—every button had its place. She would line them up for hours. Sometimes she would leave them like that and fall asleep, knowing that in the morning things would be the same. The row of blue diamond-shaped buttons would still be lined up next to the green apple-shaped buttons.

Is it any wonder that this young woman felt safe and comfortable straightening up my drawers, shelves, and jars? The task was familiar to her, like home. Interestingly, she selected a mate like her father. Chaos was rampant. So creating this kind of order in her daily life was a blessing to her. People like my housekeeper sort, count, and arrange in order to create a peaceful experience. Those who don't do this tend to have a peaceful inside, so the outside doesn't matter as much. Some of us have other ways of obtaining peace.

APPLYING THE RULE

If You Are an Everywoman:

Watch out for your own feelings.   When you are afraid, do you compensate by using rigid control? You may believe that if you are in charge of everything, nothing will fall off the table. Decision making, then, becomes autocratic and rigid. Stop and check in with yourself to reflect. Are things in balance? Am I dominating? Am I blocking creativity? Am I feeling a little challenged so that I have to employ more rules? Am I trusting that others will handle things? Am I tackling my highest priorities? Or am I evaluating everything as being of the utmost importance?

Let go and let others learn.   Accept that the intern will not do nearly as well as you could. Your colleague will never learn if you don't back up and give her a chance. Bite your lip, cross your fingers, and look away.

Five centuries from now we may look back to discover that this twenty-first century was the one in which we changed our management and leadership style in business. We moved from a polarized and adversarial point of view in business decisions to business transactions based on global harmony. The controlling bully will not fit into this kind of a business world.

We will look back, knowing that conflict is always possible, but we will seek executives who can work with conflict, not in an adversarial way, but applying a process whereby both sides can win. With cultural diversity, multiple languages, and changing patterns for workers in play in individual offices, the business world will be looking for leaders who can create alliances, rather than litigate differences. If you are in command-and-control mode, you will be ruling out innovations and differences. The noncontrolling executive will focus on spotting divergence and possible conflict in order to resolve the issues with wins for all sides.

Discover what your adversaries want and need.   Find out how to engage in an exchange with them. Discover ways to comfortably partner with your competitors. If you are a controller, you will no longer be able to mask differences and limit difficult discussions. You will have to look your antagonist right in the eye and ask for agreement, with the willingness to assume mutually beneficial risks. Words that connote blame and fault will be replaced with words that convey peaceful alignment.

If You Are a Bully Broad:

You cannot control the world.   Even if you could control everything, eventually you would topple over with the enormous burden of responsibility. The strain of being in charge of it all can create the common stress symptoms of hypertension and heart disease. Beyond your own physical health, being rigid about everything tends to push away the very people who might want to work with you or love you. Your rules and constraints become bigger than you are.

You need touchstones.   You may feel insatiable because you don't know how to connect with anything beyond your own achievements. Much of your work is invisible. So you may be working to be seen, to receive recognition. Although you already receive high praise, you may crave still more acknowledgment. You may not be able to reach inside for internal support because you have become addicted to those external rewards. Your self-talk is full of lists to do, demands, lectures, guilt, and defensive quips. Surrendering is not about giving up or giving in.

Let go.   Letting go is having the maturity to recognize that you can't control the universe. In the *Have, Be, Do* paradigm, you are always engaged in struggle. If I have enough, I can then *do* enough, and I will *be* happy. The ideal paradigm is to *Be, Do, Have*. It is just the opposite of *Have, Be, Do.* The irony is that we forget that you can *be* enough so that you can *do* enough and you will then *have* enough.

Take a look at your working style. Are you too attached to rules and structure? Are you able to be spontaneous? Can you be creative? The structured worker has a harder time with ambiguity and innovation.

I recently had a session with a woman who tends to be more methodical. The goal assigned to her by her boss was to show more strategic and creative thinking. There was going to be an off-site meeting, and I asked her to think about showing herself as more of a risk taker in this retreat. "It would be a good opportunity for you to flash some of your quick and easy decision-making charms," I chided her.

Her answer was classic: "Okay, I'll plan out what I'm going to do that could be spontaneous!" When I asked her to take the word *plan* out of the sentence, she was panicked. We then talked about how she was going to have to let herself simply try an idea, a statement, or an event for which she had not done methodical planning or premeditated her response. For such women, it is a new and frightening way to conduct themselves. Even if she goofed on something, as long as she tried to be creative and spontaneous, she would be making a start. "You do not have to be good, profound, or brilliant. Just risk your style, and belt out something," I urged. She tried yelling "fried fish!" in the middle of my sentence, just to experience her own feelings when she was out of order. She smiled. She laughed. She liked it!

WHEN YOU WORK WITH A BULLY BROAD

When you work with a Bully Broad keep the following points in mind.

The Bully Broad may feel off balance without structure. Understand that the Bully Broad may not have enough self-esteem to rid herself of the *Have, Do, Be* mode of thinking. She cannot trust others and, when things get sticky, she will resort to being controlling. The more things get out of control, the more she wants to put things back in order. Reassure her that she is and has enough and that she surely has done enough. She will urge you to do more, be more, work harder, and you will have to remind her that you have set your limits and that if she wants the ultimate effort from you, she must respect your boundaries.

Check out her mixed messages.   You only see the tip of the iceberg with the rigid woman. You don't know the maelstrom beneath. You can't determine how deeply her behavior is entrenched below the surface. The Bully Broad is confusing. On the inside she may be a mushball, not wanting to hurt anyone. She might secretly take in stray animals or contribute to the Make A Wish Foundation. Publicly, however, her actions belie those intentions. It may be up to you to begin to translate her actions.

The governing style in the business world is moving away from controlling senior officers, which is the right climate in which to teach Bully Broads that they may still be operating by using tight controls and applying rigid rules. Losing or relinquishing control is very upsetting and unsettling to some. "I am losing everything I value. I am slipping out of control and it is terrifying," your Bully Broad might be thinking.

Be patient and sympathetic with intimidators like this. This is new and slippery ground. Your Bully Broad will not give up the control wheel without a fight. She will shuffle and snort and huff, complaining, "The place is falling apart. There is no order anywhere." Console her and agree with whatever you can agree with. Remind her that you will help her make the adjustments necessary to make your workplace a positive place to be rather than a battlefield.

15 Lead with Vulnerability

CASE STUDY

Gail Farmer, Information Systems Vice President for a Fortune 100 company, just couldn't say she was fired. She had been sharing information about herself with us monthly, but she could not say those fatal words. Two years after it happened, she was finally able to proclaim to the Bully Broads Group that she had been terminated.

Initially, Gail had been stripped of her vice presidency. As a *Sarcastic Aggressive* (SA) Bully Broad, Gail had been very hard on an insecure boss. Gail was a big woman, in stature and voice. She was brilliant, and her resume was incredible. Her dark hair and piercing dark eyes were intimidating, especially when she had strong opinions about things. Her judgment of her boss would slip out in humorous little gibes. She knew how to tell a funny story, but he was often the brunt of it.

Gail was eventually barred from senior staff meetings. Simultaneously, she was contracted to be a consultant for the company. She had submerged these facts so deeply in her subconscious that she could not even tell us about what had really happened. She went into denial, simply declaring that her consultancy job was better than her vice presidency and relieved her of some of the more taxing elements of that position.

Why now? Why did it take two years for Gail to talk about her situation? She had been such a Bully Broad at work that no one dared mention her change of status to her. They may have snickered behind her back, but to her face, denial was the operative strategy. Of course, the boss did talk to her about it, but she got to keep her office and stay on as a consultant, and she made a big deal out of how much stock she got as part of the deal. Her transition took the form of an eventual termination after three years in a consultant's capacity. She received quite a package. Applying the double threat of legal action and her own Bully Broad debating style, Gail got away with it.

The question remains, however, why did it take two years for her to be able to admit what had happened? The answer is twofold.

Someone else had to say it. One of the senior officers from an overseas satellite of Gail's company arrived back in town. On his first sighting of Gail, he roared, "Hey, I heard you got fired." Hearing the words out loud finally got through to Gail. Of course, she could explain that she was still there as a consultant, and that she still had her office, although she chose to work at home a great deal of the time. But hearing the truth blurted out by this innocent friend of hers finally exploded Gail out of denial.

"I had never said it," she revealed to us. "And no one had said it to me, until Franco got to town. I am grateful to him. What a load I was carrying. I smiled all the time, told myself I was happy, and never let on that I was miserable and humiliated. Now I can say it. I was humiliated."

She could say she was right. The second reason that Gail was able to speak out now was that her original information systems plan had been rolled out again and the company was starting to look at the possiblity of using it. What a win for Gail. Even though it was two years later, she could still say, "I told you so." However, being the recovering Bully Broad that she was, she had learned not to rub people's faces in the truth. It was tempting, but she knew that it would not bring back the original job, and that she really had benefited from the whole situation. She now stayed home with her son for part of the day. She learned humility. She was young, and she would have the opportunity to be a VP again. "And I will be so much smarter," she reminded us.

Gail's pride required substantiation that she had been right after all. Once she received that, she was ready to admit to the termination. She had not been able to talk about cultural differences or business model discrepancies between her and the boss. Had she prepared herself, she might have been able to say with more accuracy that she was changing her position within the company. Instead, she tucked in her pain, made up a palatable scenario, and carried her grief in silence for two years.

Being vulnerable is a terrifying experience for some Bully Broads. There are many reasons for this. For some, it is just a first-time experience. They never needed to show their weakness before. Being dependent and vulnerable had never been on their list of aspirations.

For other Bully Broads, being vulnerable was an early common experience. In their childhoods they were victims of abusive parents, siblings, neighbors, clergy, coaches, or teachers. It did not feel good then, and they don't want to repeat the experience.

It is my job to convince these executives that their career life is not a repeat performance of their youth. I have to remind these women that they are capable and strong adults who can hold their own with those who might be in superior positions or of higher rank. They can survive a sadistic colleague who likes to collect victims. These Bully Broads know how to protect themselves, so that when they learn to express a little weakness, in small steps, they also learn that they will not have to feel the pain they experienced during their earlier torture.

Yet another reason that bullies shun vulnerability is that they have seen few role models who could gracefully show their liabilities. Both the bullies and their role models believed that if you showed a weakness, you gave up power. They didn't know how valuable authenticity can be to their colleagues and their organization. They didn't understand that their weakness shows anyway, and talking about it can actually produce sanity around them. When a bully learns that it is actually brave to show her weakness in some settings, she discovers that it is quite tension relieving. Ice Queens don't share their celebrations, so they are surely not going to share the bad news.

Of course, Gail couldn't do it. Her career had been her life. She had an MBA and a Ph.D. and came from a family of overachievers. She had not ever experienced failure and she did not know what to do about it, so she shoved it aside and rationalized her new position— that is, until Franco came to town.

Being in a delicate situation but withholding your weak side tends to make other people crazy. Your colleagues probably know when you have been passed over, rejected, or demoted. They seem to sniff out the derailed executive, but if you never let on that you might be in hot water, you are setting up an incongruence. We all like to think of ourselves as being authentic. The bully who hides her pain is being inauthentic. Those of her coworkers who are not in power gather together, wondering whether the bully realizes she has lost power or she is just plain oblivious. Such a subgroup will coalesce around your inauthenticity.

If people around you see that you are in a jam, why don't they tell you? They are afraid of three things:

- That if they tell you, you will crumble and die—that is, you appear too weak to take it

- That if they tell you, you will violently deny it—that is, you won't accept the information
- That if they tell you, you will shoot the messenger—that is, you will turn on the sender

APPLYING THE RULE

If You Are an Everywoman:

If you find yourself in a precarious position, hiding it can cause a lot of stress. You don't need to blurt out the news or take out an ad in the local paper. But you can try sharing some of it with somebody you trust and feel safe with. Try your best friend, a favorite relative, or the gas station attendant. I try out all my bad news on my gas station attendant. He doesn't really care. Sometimes he doesn't really listen or understand me. Sometimes he simply can't hear me.

Saying the words "I've been rejected" is a big step to take. Men seem to do it better than women, but they certainly don't call it rejection. "I've been terminated. I've been dumped. I lost the job." Men tend to take a more cavalier attitude toward these things, detaching themselves a little and knowing that these things happen. Women work so hard to get where they are that they can lose perspective about the meaning of some of the office maneuvers. They forget that the journey sometimes counts more than the destination. Men are also often in a better position to compartmentalize their lives. Women, on the other hand, expect to do well in everything. They want it all, are very willing to work for it, and can become very disillusioned when they don't win it all.

Now, I have to add a caveat here. I know some men whose wives left them, and they did not tell their colleagues about it for years. One man insisted that his wife go to his office holiday party for three years because he was not ready to talk about the divorce.

Another fellow would not tell his sons or his mother about his termination. He was too humiliated and was afraid he would break down when he told them. Of course, eventually he told everyone, but only when his story was cemented, and he was ready.

Saying so does not make it so.   If you regard yourself as a loser some of the time and you tell some others about your loss, you still may not be perceived as a loser. Just as you are not your position or your company or your children, you are not simply your termination or your humiliation for having failed in a production. One woman made a mistake on an annual report for a major corporation. She crawled to my door one night, preparing for her corporate demise. Humiliated and chagrined, her solution was to go in, 'fess up, and suggest a new audit system for those numbers. She was not a loser. Ultimately, she became a company controller.

You may be surprised that you are still valued.   Losing jobs, raises, promotions, and even relationships happens. How you handle your loss will show your true colors. Can you be strong enough to admit your part in the end, or do you have to claim it was not fair, not right, and sometimes not even legal? People seem to expect you to rise up anyway. They don't brood over your loss. Saying hello to the next opportunity is the best medicine for closing the first one. You need to believe that there is something better waiting for you, even if you think you just lost the job of a lifetime.

If You Are a Bully Broad:

You may not be very good at showing vulnerability at first. Losing is never any fun, and you are a competitor. Find a way to tell the truth, even if you have to take baby steps toward doing so. Gail actually asked for our forgiveness when she confessed her two-year delay. "Well, we had that figured out anyway," one of the more outspoken bullies told her. Others comforted her by saying, "I didn't reveal that my husband had left me for years. I always said we grew apart. Well, he grew to a part down the street!"

Bad news leaks out. Share it early.   Even if you don't want to talk about it, others may know anyway. Either they intuit your discomfort or you are just plain leaking out anger or hurt all over the shop. Say it straight, just the way you would say that you got promoted.

It's not always your fault.   In Gail's case, it really was not all her fault. A new boss had come in and he just did not speak her language. He wanted his own team in place, and her high-profile bully tactics were an excuse to ask her to leave. She may have sabotaged herself with wisecracks about him, and her sarcasm and aggression may have cost her the job, but there was a good chance that the executive would have found another way of forcing her out even if she hadn't exhibited such Bully Broad behavior.

WHEN YOU WORK WITH A BULLY BROAD

The vulnerable bully is like a grieving widow. Some days you can approach her with kind words and a casserole. On other days you need to leave her alone. Advertising a bully's weak spots will not help. She must do it herself. She can distract you from the subject and use protective shields and false information to shelter herself. Her pride is so ironclad that showing a delicate side would be a death blow to such a fiercely guarded woman.

Go slowly.   Ask her if you can help decipher the situation. Explain that you have been there, done that, and then back off. She is likely to shun your sympathy and she will not want to be reminded that she is inadequate. Of course, she is not inadequate, but it may take a while before she is sure of that again. You can't remind her. Let her tend her wounds and then be ready when she wants to talk.

Remember that the flip side of hurt is anger.   Bullies show anger much more easily than they show hurt. So when she is having a temper tantrum or is shouting at you, try to translate that poor behavior as hurt. She just can't show the hurt. It is easier to be mad than sad. Sad could lead to depression, and most Bully Broads run in the other direction. They believe in action, not passivity.

16 Soft Sell Is the Best Sell

CASE STUDY

Carol Collins, executive director of the YMCA, gets the job done. She is a hard sell, however, and everyone knows it. Her persuasive skills are well known in the community, and her staff always knows where she stands.

Carol is perky, highly educated, and charming, and did very well at the local Y level. She was a great fundraiser and she assembled a good board of directors as well as a heavy-duty staff. Her challenge was the national board.

Carol is a *Selectively Quiet* (SQ) type, always ready to make a critical remark. She only shows her high level of expectation from you or her judgment when the occasion demands. Even with the regional board, she managed to escape the reputation she developed at the national level. Why did it happen there? The stakes were higher. Policies affected hundreds of thousands, not just a local YMCA population of several thousand.

In her national-level task force, Carol was challenged because she had only brief time periods to get work done or to get her ideas across, so she had to sell harder and faster. Crises or time urgency brings out the bully in the most selective bullies. All of us turn to our defense habits when times are rocky. Bullies turn to their strong results orientation. The national committees met periodically and for only hours at a time. So Carol's persuasive style could only kick in for short meetings when time was the determining element Carol's method of operation went like this: She liked to set an agenda, then she would foolproof it so no one could change it. Next came the hard sell.

If a bully broad has the persuasive tools and techniques on top of her intimidating ways, a passive person has little chance against her. Carol is an example of someone who has the positional power and the debating skills, so she ran the office according to her own form. The other employees towed the mark. When they heard the first rumblings from the national group, however, they quickly formed a posse and seized the opportunity to convict Carol of the abuse they had felt for years.

"I can't believe they would say such things about me!" Carol exclaimed. "I gave my heart and soul to this Y and I have raised more money than any other single human being in the last twenty years. This is the thanks I get."

The thank-you was a significant investigation in which most of her colleagues and subordinates were queried. Even board members were questioned. The result was a quiet dismissal, a grand severance package, and an invitation to transfer to a lower position, in another, smaller Y across the state. Carol was devastated. She joined the Bully Broads Group in the final days of her relationship with the Y. She had daily sessions for two weeks in which she learned how difficult she had made it for people who did not agree with her. She learned that she was an overpersuader at every turn. She bullied people into doing things her way; she had influence over all brochures and marketing materials. Even program designs bore her distinctive touch. Her persuasion skills had been working overtime.

The good news is that Carol stayed in town, took a six-month sabbatical, and then joined another nonprofit organization. To the new organization, Carol brought the skills of a much more mature administrator. She deliberately planned to allow others to have their way some of the time and she encouraged her colleagues to choose their own products and projects. She even refrained from that "extra sell" she had used for most of her life.

▷─┼◇─•─○─•─◇┼─◁

If you are a Bully Broad and you use the hard sell for everything, people will back away whenever they can. Being discriminating is not usually the bully's long suit. She establishes a style, gets reinforced for using that style for the first part of her life, and then gets complaints about it in the last part of her life. Overselling gets tiresome.

Bully Broads use the following tactics:

- They roll out their ideas—with conviction!
- They don't ask for questions, obstacles, or concerns.
- They dissuade anyone from dealing with objections, using time as a lever.
- They reinforce their ideas with presold advocates.
- They raise their voices if they need to.
- They glare, roll their eyes, and sigh loudly if someone takes another position.
- They show passion for their own point of view.
- They disparage other points of view.
- They ask for agreement only.
- They employ a presumptive close, so that only the strong-willed will object.
- They speak over objections, and speak forcefully.

- They belittle naysayers if they need to.
- They stay silent when opposing views are given unless the opposition persists.
- If they persist, they raise the stakes—and get louder.
- They are persistent.
- They don't take no for an answer.

The hard-sell person loves to influence others. She doesn't seem to mind taking up the time and energy to exert her influence, even on some minute points. The persuader overpersuades. She sells the point even after someone buys it. "I can't say it enough," she will protest. Yes, she can. Each repetition has the potential to detract from the first argument. If she does enough overselling, she could end up with nothing.

The persuader always wants to save others their learning-curve time. "I learned this the hard way. I can help you with it and then you won't have to make the mistakes I made," she argues. It might be true that she could be very helpful, but most of us seem to want to do our own footwork, make our own mistakes, and take the long road because we are not sure of our own destination. The persuader sticks tenaciously to an idea and desperately tries to convince others that it is the right thing to do. Persuaders learned early that they could win an argument with persistence and leverage.

I learned the leverage power of persuasion early. As a child, I had a pony. I could persuade my young friends to do almost anything I wanted in exchange for a pony ride. That was my first experience with leverage. If you learn this early, you feel successful at getting your own way. You discover that by exerting a little more pressure or incentive, you can have more than the next person who may not be aware of the power of these techniques.

The overpersuader will drive for results at all costs. Her concern for due process, team morale, and the values held by others will be dimmed by her own enthusiasm. Two skills necessary for emotional intelligence are the ability to recognize the impact you have on others and the ability to discipline yourself by delaying gratification. If you jump to sell your cause, you are forgetting these two basic requirements for emotional intelligence. The overpersuader goes for the close, not the relationship. Of course, it is possible to have both, but the results-oriented bully does not give much weight to the relationship side of the business.

APPLYING THE RULE

If You Are an Everywoman:

It is human nature to want your own way.   It is also human nature to believe your own rationalizations about things. We talk ourselves into what we think is right, and then we want others to believe it with us.

The victims of the oversell, however, have a weakened system that encourages them to back down in the face of opposition. They do not have the personal self-confidence to buck the tide, to stand alone, to be in the minority. Bullies don't mind that others are in that position. They take advantage of it. The end usually justifies the means, to them. They are good at getting their way—the right way!

A good organization will foster a culture that could stifle the overpersuader.   If you are an overpersuader, pay attention to yourself. If you are always getting the last word or winning every argument, you are losing popularity by the moment. If you are not the hard-sell person, help your colleagues to curb the overpersuader in your midst. Not everyone is brave enough to take her on. You may not always be, either. But naming the problem is a beginning: "Carol, I'm noticing that we are always following your plans. You have great ideas, and you are good at selling them, but I would like to see somebody else offer a suggestion and have us all cooperate with that suggestion."

"Oh, I couldn't say that," you claim. Naming the problem will start the ball rolling. The Bully Broad may still get her way, but you have planted the first seeds. One day another person will speak up or remember what you said and begin the smallest revolution, which can help build a consensus.

If You Are a Bully Broad:

Give someone else a chance.   It is very rewarding to always get your own way. You usually have good ideas and you surely know how to persuade others to use those good ideas. You are a natural cheer-leader for a position in which you believe, and your persuasion skills are considerable. But you are a pain to be around. You stifle creativity in others and you pound the courage out of anyone who might have a different idea.

Stifle yourself.   This means discipline yourself to be quiet. Don't throw out the first suggestion. Allow others to stretch a little. Even if their ideas are not as good as yours, refrain from commenting. Let others experiment and learn, while you take the role of the mature leader. Don't sell your own plans, goals, and values all of the time. Let your teammates figure out what to do for themselves. If you do bring up an idea and someone pushes back, fall over. Succumb to the needs and goals of others. Give in. It is character building and will provide the impetus for others to take on the role of persuader. You are good at it, and while you can play it out on occasion, buckle under and let others preside once in a while as well.

Dissent and commit.   One of the major tenets of the successful Intel Corporation is "dissent and commit." They preach to their employees that it is good to disagree. They suggest that employees speak up and offer opposing views, and that everyone should offer objections. Then, when they finally do settle on a course of action, they put away their own reservations and commit to the decision. This is hard to do. It means giving up whining and ceasing the "I told you so"s. Don't be the spoilsport who just backs away because it is not being done her way. To commit means being in there, doing the job, cooperating, and encouraging, as though it had all been your idea in the first place.

Be sensitive to your audience.   Regardless of the size—be it a ballroom with a thousand people or three of you sitting in the cafeteria—monitor the audience's reaction to you. Are they smiling, laughing, and nodding their heads? Are they mouthing the word *yes* and looking you straight in your eyes? Are you eliciting a positive response? If so, proceed. If not, wait and ask a few more telling questions, such as:

Am I on the right track here?
Are we going in the right direction?
Am I getting my point across to you?

Or:

Am I boring you?
Am I preaching to the choir?
Have I oversold here?
Should I be sitting down?
Would you like me to stop for questions now?

In a one-on-one situation, you might start out with simple statements about yourself, the world, or your business. If that goes well, continue. After at least six sentences, check in with the other person. Balancing a conversation will foster your communication skills. Never, ever, do a monologue! Other people turn their earphones off if you talk too long. Some people really love the sound of their own voices. I rather like my own. But I've learned that I cannot entertain all of the people all of the time. It is imperative that you be cognizant of how folks are feeling about you. Get a reading. If you can't read the audience, come right out and ask people sitting in the first few rows, "How am I doing so far?"

Oh, I know. This takes courage. You might get some bad news. You'd rather proceed along, imagining that you are on the right track. Of course, you would not stop in the middle of a speech to a thousand people and ask how you are doing. (Although I have; it is usually when I'm sure I'm doing a good job.) But if you are not sure you are reading your listeners, and it is appropriate, step off your spot at the podium and ask if you are meeting the needs of the group.

WHEN YOU WORK WITH A BULLY BROAD

It is not easy.   You may have a hard time dissuading your Bully Broad. She is used to having her own way. She likes overpersuading, and she thinks it is worth her effort. She thinks she has all the best ideas and she wants to move forward on them. She actually enjoys trampling on your objections and revels in demolishing the barriers you may set up. She is hard to stop.

Remind her about her habit of overinfluencing.   She doesn't do it on purpose. She is not even conscious that she seems to want to influence you on every aspect of your time together. Listen to her selling a movie or a new restaurant or the next procedure for your organization. She is a professional at it. Point this out to her gently.

Take your turn.   Even though you are may stumble, you are easily discouraged, and you don't like to fight to be heard, show others and your bully that you can speak up to her. Let her know that you might not be as articulate or as impassioned as she is, but that it is just your turn to be able to bring people to your ideas. Admit that you may be inexperienced, and sometimes just lazy, so that it is often easier to let her do it.

Your reputation will not improve if you appear as the long-suffering employee who simply wants security. You will have to make a move once in a while. Risking and failing provide the incentive for winning the next time. Being the good guy will not always get you what you want or need. "Companionship, that's what I want," you say. But if your companions don't respect you, your friendships will be very superficial. When you encounter the consummate Bully Broad who seems to have to make the sale, have her own way, or run right over you, try the following:

"Carol, you seem to need this win. You work so hard to get your way. I sometimes think it is not worth it to me. I say to myself, 'She can have it. She is willing to work for it.' Then I give up. I'm not willing to work so hard. When I weigh my priorities, this is not worth fighting over. This is not good for either of us."

Having that conversation will give Carol something to think about. Others who listen will be enlightened, perhaps even encouraged, to assist you in the battle, and everyone will think you are stunningly courageous. You are. Whenever you can confront the overselling Bully Broad, you are stretching your courage muscles. Good workout!

Manage a bully broad.   Managing creative people with special gifts brings special problems. You may have to protect and buffer this poor woman who does not seem to know her own strength. She may think differently from the rest of us. We know she loves to process out loud. She does not always retreat inward to think things through. She will ask your opinion and then smother it quickly with her own. She is a high-maintenance personality—and you should tell her that, too. "Mary, you are hard to work with. You get a lot done and I love that, but managing the people around your compulsive behavior is getting harder and harder on me. I am getting tired of making excuses for you. I want to protect you from those who don't understand you, but I would rather you start understanding yourself and figuring out why you are so difficult for some people. Mary, get yourself together and learn your impact on others, or you will be working alone, on your own, somewhere else."

17 You Don't Own the Company

CASE STUDY

Nancy Cordova worried and fretted over everything. She took on all the problems of the company. Each employee seemed to be her personal challenge. She was furious when people left the company, and overblown expense accounts were her prime targets for rage. She was a Chief Technical Officer, or CTO, not even Chief Financial Officer, but the way she stomped and fought, you would think she was CEO. Nancy did not pick her battles. *Everything* was a personal battle.

In spite of Nancy's loyalty to the company, she was placed on probation. She had intimidated too many employees and the real CFO was fed up with the complaints about Nancy's abuse. Of course, she didn't see it that way. Here she was, trying to save the company's resources, and all she got back for her fierce loyalty was probation.

One night in the Bully Broads Group, after Nancy's litany of company problems in every area of the organization, out of sheer desperation, I yelled, "But, Nancy, you don't own the company!"

She got it. She finally really understood. She was startled. "Imagine that. It's not really my company!" When she heard those words, especially with such high drama, Nancy Cordova finally understood. All the worry and fear of mistakes and concern about employee fraud were not saving the company or her career. At that moment, she loosened up and decided to do her job without attempting to save the company at every turn.

>–+–<>–O–<>–+–<

Even if you do own the company, you still have to use discretion about your tirades over employee abuse. Even owning the company does not give you permission to micromanage every aspect of the company. The latest Gallup Poll (January 1, 2001) asked 2 million people why they would leave their company. Eighty percent claimed they leave or stay in companies because they believe their immediate managers care about them. So you, as the immediate manager, want to show care for employees at all times.

If you don't own the company, calm down. I am not being a heretic about this. I own my company, but I often tell my most diligent employees not to be so concerned about things that are out of their control. When they become the police, others are offended by their overreaching approach to management. You don't get paid enough to become the moral conscience of the company. And even when management hears me telling an employee this, they do not blanch because they know I am saving the employee from a heart attack, saving others from some pretty vicious attacks from the Bully Broad, and saving the company from polarization and fractioned troops.

Here are some rules for the overextended and hypervigilent Bully Broad.

Remember that people marry people—not companies.   So if a coworker's mate or children take precedence over the company, don't jump on your coworker. He or she is trying to achieve a balanced life, not ruin yours. We have learned that people quit companies because of their immediate boss, not because of pay and company policy. If people work for you, help them enjoy it.

Rule by exceptions.   One size may not fit all for your colleagues. Treat people differently depending on their working styles and personalities. It sounds like a lot of work. It may be, at first, but it becomes easier in the long run and you will be more successful. Some of your employees require a great deal of structure. Others want more free reign. It is your job to know the difference. You will have the "jump on board every idea" type employees (the early adopters), and then the stragglers, who are late to adopt. It all sounds like a lot of work. No more work, though, than trying to ramrod something by each person, no matter his or her working style.

Don't make up your own bottom-line standards for the company.   You may want 25 percent growth, but check it out with the boss or the Chairman of the Board, or your consultants, or your advisory board, because they may be planning on 13 percent. A Bully Broad's goals usually are much more stringent than those of the rest of the crowd.

For example, May and her group were planning a simple trip to the PacBell Giants ballpark for a game. She wanted all of the participants to have company hats and sweatshirts and to get tickets in the luxury seats, but not in the upper deck. She visualized a sunny day and everyone enjoying being near the players. She worked out every detail. Then the catastrophes happened:

1. The seats ended up being box seats. May responded by giving the ticket agent her best tantrum, with threats about her company boycotting the ballpark.
2. She swore at the catering service because they didn't even provide standard hot dogs. They served steak sandwiches, which all enjoyed.

3. She was mad at the procurement office because some of the hats were different colors and the shirts were too large for most sizes.
4. Her secretary screwed up the invitations, so she lashed out at her.
5. James made fun of the whole event, so he got a piece of her mind.
6. She yelled at her boss because he decided not to go at all.

In fact, the group had enjoyed the event. For everyone except May, it had been a big success.

APPLYING THE RULE

If You Are an Everywoman:

Remind yourself on a regular basis to back off. Watch when your loyalty tips over into rigidity or overcommitment. Your good intentions may be translated to mean that you are controlling or grumpy. You are not the owner of your company. Even if you are, you probably still have someone to report to: the Chairman of the Board, the board itself, or your stockholders. Keep your perspective in line with your position. Be positive. Optimism helps everyone.

If you don't know your triggers, you could easily be tripped up. Remember what turns you off and be prepared to discipline yourself when that issue has the potential to arise. Prepare yourself and even prepare others to remember what unsettles you. When May was planning the ballgame event, she lost perspective. When things didn't fall into place, she seemed to flare up at every single disappointment. If she had only reminded herself that no one else really cared, the others would not have faulted her for the upsets that disturbed only her. After all, nobody else would have gotten it all right, either.

Working is a balancing act between the needs of the organizations and the needs of the individuals. In a bully's case, this is all compounded by her own expectations that become bigger than the individuals or the organization.

If You Are a Bully Broad:

You are not in charge of everything.   Bullies seem to take on the responsibility for everything in their organization. They tend to worry about all aspects of the business. They are often superresponsible types, who began early in life to worry about the rent or mortgage payments, their parents' health, and the welfare of the neighborhood. Bully Broads are natural worriers, and when they add to that an aggressive stance, they can be quite a handful to deal with, in spite of their good intentions.

Watch out for stress potential.   When you feel that colleagues are wasting resources or slacking off, approach the appropriate people carefully. Do you want to know more about the expense account liberties you see, or would you rather just have the report? What are your underlying motives?

I got an email today from a client in New York, who wrote, "I don't want to look like a private investigator to these folks, but every time I go to town, I find some big mistakes. How can I work to help them problem solve without their worry that I am the inspector general?" This was a very good question from a recovering bully. She has her antenna up about appearing too conscientious about her staff's troubles.

If you are treated medically for stress, you have actually wasted some company money. Give yourself appropriate leeway to worry, and then go home to relax. Besides, it takes a lot of energy to worry about people or systems beyond your jurisdiction. I have seen many subordinates who worry more about their organizations than their bosses do. And the bosses get paid twice as much. Give it up. Get some sleep.

WHEN YOU WORK WITH A BULLY BROAD

When you work with a Bully Broad keep the following points in mind.

Name the behavior.   Calling the Bully Broad on being hyper-vigilant is easier than calling her on swearing or picking on someone in the office. When Bully Broads act like they own the company, sticking their noses into your business, call them on it, but with understanding: "I know you care what happens to this organization. That's why you are so careful about our supply orders. But I feel anxious when you jump in all the time. Others are probably feeling rebellious because they know you don't own the company."

Plan on a poor response from her at first.   Even when your heart is in the right place, the bully might not hear you. Her response to you might be downright ugly: "Mind your own darned business!" You may have to campaign. Why would you stick your neck out and do this? Because her abuse bothers you, and it is not good for the company. Nor is it good for her. And guess what? It is not good for you, either.

So try giving her feedback. Plan on about ten interventions, during which you simply raise the subject. Either she won't hear what you are really saying the first time or she will hear it and not do anything about it. She might do something about it next time, and then forget about it after that. Maximillan Maltz, one of the fathers of behavioral modification and author of *Psychocybernetics*, suggests that it takes 29 tries to change a particular aspect of behavior. Hard changes need plenty of reinforcement and even more reminders.

Even if it is your boss you are trying to change, you owe it to her and to yourself to make the effort. If you are nervous about this, ask one of your supporters to go to lunch with you after the first confrontation. Or treat yourself to something wonderful. You have taken the first step toward being a highly accountable human being.

Here is a sample persuasive argument you can use:

"I really want to work for you. I want to do the best job I can, too. But sometimes I get hung up on your criticism of me and I can't give you the best of me. If I could give you a signal when I am on overload with your expectations, maybe you will recognize when to back off for a bit. Then, when I can collect myself, I will check with you to see if there is anything more you want to say. This will help me do better work for you."

If you are dealing with a peer, the problem is a little trickier. You have no authority or leverage, and the other person doesn't have any compelling need to change for you. So you could try the following approach:

"You know, we are going to have to work together like this for a long time. Our priorities overlap and sometimes our values conflict. I find you hard to approach, and you may think I am too indecisive or passive. I'd like to have us respect each other, and that might take some talking and some negotiation. If you get uptight and grumpy with me, I feel like walking away, and then we get nowhere. I want to give you my second effort. I'd like you to do that with me, too. So it means we both have to be more patient, and make a second move to get to a compromise some of the time. I know that we test each other. I'd like us to pass."

You may be thinking, "Oh, I could never say that." Our clients make the same protestation on a daily basis. Then we ask them to practice some of the sentences, or we role-play being the bully who will give them a bad time, and, guess what? They come back in the next week or so and report something like the following: "Well, I tried some of that talk. I didn't think I ever would, but the perfect moment came up, and I just spilled it out. She stood there with her mouth open, and when I got through, she said, 'I've never heard you talk like this before. You must be serious. Yes, I'd like to work more cooperatively with you. Maybe we could trade gripes and start over.'"

18 Remember: It's Not Your Money

CASE STUDY

Lucille Romano was Treasurer of a billion-dollar company. She bristled every time she had to write a check. She never smiled and she seemed to loathe vacations. Her sick leave remained untouched; however, the morale in her enormous organization was sick itself, without any sick leave available as a remedy. She was delivered to our consulting service with the report that she was mean-spirited and was driving everyone in the Finance Department crazy.

When we reminded Lucille that it was not her money that she was handling, she was stunned. "Well, of course, I know that," she barked. "But who else would monitor these things if it weren't for me?" It took months to convince Lucille that she was on the brink of career disaster, and if she really cared about the company, she needed to make herself gentler. Then she could stay and continue to mind the company's cash register.

When you write checks that total billions of dollars, I guess you get a little heady. Her signature is not hand-embroidered on each check, I reminded her, but she was slow to give up the control and power of complete responsibility for the company's finances.

The company had many checks and balances, and she actually did not have full responsibility for the financial life of the company. In the long run, the Marketing, Sales, and Engineering Departments affected the bottom line more than she did. She managed the money, but she did not necessarily earn it for the company. That was a hard pill for Lucille to swallow.

Ultimately, she took a long overdue vacation. She even spent a lot of money on the trip. When she returned, she promised to offer one smile every hour. The first day back she complained that her face hurt. Everyone believed the vacation must have fixed her, but it was the smile that fixed her. People smiled back. At first they were wary. When the number of smiles did not decrease, mainly because she was getting so much positive feedback, her colleagues began to trust her. What a success story! She did little other than exercising unused facial muscles, but she managed to turn her career around.

We keep having to remind Lucille that it is not her money, but I believe she is adjusting to the idea. The frown lines in her forehead have been exchanged for crow's feet from smiling so much. She looks fifteen years younger, and the company officers are feeling much more lighthearted around her. Her frowns used to scare them, but now everyone feels they are in safe hands with her. Even Lucille enjoys her relaxed approach to her job. She learned that clenched fists are not easy to use: you can't pick up anything. Her clenched face wasn't very productive either.

>-i-<•>-o-<•>-i-<

If you suspect you might be forgetting that the company's money is not yours, you need to look at the big picture. Are you governing appropriately? Is your level of concern appropriate, or are you the "other shoe" type who worries if she is not worrying? We have learned that the "not enough" people are usually uptight, frustrated, and scared. If you are a "not enough" person, you think that you never have enough of the following:

- Time
- Resources
- Acknowledgment
- Money
- Credit
- Love

BEWARE OF THE VALUES WAR

A Bully Broad is usually in love with her own values. They have been burned into her soul, by parents, teachers, her early bosses, or her own translation of life. You value the values you have acquired. Now, can you begin to value the values others hold? This is a difficult task if their values sharply contrast with yours. Can you at least look at another's values, try to understand them, and then begin to see how the two sets of values incorporate some mutual goals? Capture your own value system on paper and then contrast it with that of your nemesis. This colleague's values might be in startling opposition to yours, but at last take a look.

Sometimes we even confuse values with facts—especially our own values. You might become frustrated when you see that people won't necessarily adopt *your* value system as their guide for dealing with ambition, money, relationships, and all of the other basic principles of the working world.

Anyone who goes into the field of finance will have some basic philosophies that do not bend easily. When your values and those of colleagues and managers clash on the job, you should examine the situation carefully to see whether your win would be worth it. Will you win the battle over the insurance payments and lose the war for your career? Would you belittle someone over something you think is important, only to discover that you would lose your job over it? Understanding the values mismatch is the beginning of a real conversation. Values are what we all want to attach to and are reluctant to detach from. Check out your colleagues' attachment to their own values to try to understand why they are important to them. Understanding their values will be more essential than explaining your own. You get yours. Now, "get" theirs!

The "scarcity" versus "abundance" model may apply here. Do you believe there will be enough, or do you worry that there will never be enough? This model supersedes the relative dollars we are talking about. Or is the problem a basic personality twist? Is your interest in rigid control influencing big-picture decisions? Or is it a little of both? A client just sent me twelve glasses, labeled "half full = optimist" (the top half of the glass) and "half-empty = pessimist" (the bottom half of the glass.) He got it!

Ice Queens make great Chief Financial Officers. They keep all the numbers close to the vest, and, of course, they love the power of making decisions based on their own values. It is hard to tear them away from the spreadsheets, but sometimes they have to expose budgets and actually work with a production team, business team, or sales team to make the company work. Then they must remember that the money they are working with is not their own!

APPLYING THE RULE

If You Are an Everywoman:

Believe there is just enough.   If you are one of those "not enough" people, now is the time for change. You simply decide that there is just enough—of everything. Perhaps you haven't experienced it all yet, but the prospect that there is just enough should remove the load from your shoulders and lighten your step. Enjoy!

If you have a great deal of responsibility, you no doubt take your work quite seriously. The CEOs of most major corporations also have great responsibility, but they know that the more you have on your plate, the more balanced you need to be in order to stay sane. I worked with ten CEOs of companies worth over $100 million. We were at a retreat, and I noticed they did not use their cell phones. They played golf or read or swam between sessions. They looked relaxed. They did not have to prove they were busy. You don't, either. You really need to prove that you have a balanced life and that you can keep the big picture in mind.

If You Are a Bully Broad:

Choose your battles.   Your caring for the organization or your staff sometimes gets misinterpreted. You may seem like the police or a wicked stepmother. Your caring is not always translated as being good intentions; therefore, you have to help translate yourself. "Gosh, I know this isn't my department. I guess I got carried away. I'm sorry to be in your pockets. I love this company and I got overconcerned. Please excuse me for this lapse."

"Oh boy," you say, "I won't talk like that!" Well, not at first. Eventually you will learn to—unless you like changing jobs, being the villain, and having people run in the other direction when you walk toward them. It is not your company and probably not all your money! Ratchet down, my friend, and let others do some of the worrying, too.

Watch your attitude.   Giving up control, especially if you are the company controller, is hard. You don't have to have everything your way. And there will be plenty left for you to control. Above all, you can control your own reactions to situations. Of course, your way is better (you believe), but you can't impose it on everyone. You only get more *attitude* about things, and encourage people to hate you. Set limits or boundaries where you can. Let other things go.

Of course, you can do it better.   But don't! You have to let others learn to manage your company's resources. You have not been asked to do it all yourself. If you have been asked to do this, and you are killing yourself to keep it up, ask for help. Talk to those in power and let them know that your health or your reputation with the staff is at stake, and that, although you could do it all, you are really not serving the company that way. We worked with a major executive for a multi-billion-dollar company who was taking on way too much responsibility. He loved it, but he got tired. He got cranky. He lost perspective. He had a nervous breakdown about the most minor fiscal event.

This superior Vice President was asked to give up several financial projects. He couldn't believe it, and he could not take it. He knew that they were really interwoven projects and it would be much easier to handle them under a single domain. He actually believed that no ten people could handle his projects. And he surely believed that the company could not survive without him.

The truth was that his new role, with less responsibility, would require more communication and cooperation with the other project leaders. He knew he couldn't do that. "It's easier to do it myself" is his refrain. (Is it also yours?) He also claims, "I'm not good at persuasion. If we have to debate my good idea, I just walk away, comply, or ignore the conversation." That is a dangerous statement, and one I have heard in my office hundreds of times. It takes longer to negotiate, compromise, and communicate, but in the long run you may save time by not having to solve the same problems on every single project.

The Vice President was asked to leave. The company survived. He did too, after processing his own shock and then taking a look at his control issues and his wish to be omnipotent. He sailed a boat around the world—not alone. He brought a crew, and he learned to depend on them. "I never slept better in my life. I let go," he said. He is in a wonderful new company and, with his wonderful new attitude, the company is thriving.

WHEN YOU WORK WITH A BULLY BROAD

When you work with a Bully Broad keep the following points in mind.

Teach "letting go."   Remind your nemesis that she is appreciated for her diligence, but that in order to take care of herself, she will need to let some things go unfinished. Teach her that others will have to make their own mistakes to learn a task. Assure her that her subordinates will do the best they can—maybe not as well as she could do the job—but that, ultimately, she will be able to count on them.

Bullies are perfectionists who don't abide by the 80-20 rule, but you can help them learn it by talking about the ultimate efficiency of getting most of the work done in 20 percent of the time. The last 80 percent of each task is accounted for by the perfectionists. They love those last details, and thus, use up the last 80 percent for every job.

The 80-20 principle assumes that the major part of the work takes up the first 20 percent of your time. The final details can take up the last 80 percent of your time. Efficient workers decide how much time to devote to high-payback items. They do not use 100 percent of their time on one project when they have five projects to do. This is hard to grasp for the controller who wants to do every piece of everything and do it all well.

Let her bark.   You know that you won't do it all, even though she may want you to. It is hard to withstand the judgment that you are not as conscientious as your critic, but you will have to talk about working smart and not long, and keeping things simple, sweetheart! Your life is at stake. So is hers. Take care of yours first.

Be sympathetic.   She is the one losing sleep over the situation, not you. If your bully acts like it is her money, try to be sympathetic. Bad quarters, wasteful expenditures, slipping stock prices really do hurt her. You can help her get some insight into her warden-like behavior. You can say something like this: "I know it's hard on you to watch this happening, but your shouting doesn't make it better. It doesn't inspire us to work harder for you, either."

When you make a mistake, own it.   It would be so tempting to avoid confessing to a mistake. The abuse is so out of line, that you can rationalize that it is better to ignore the abuser. You don't think the crime ever fits the punishment, so it is easier to make excuses—blaming the computer, misleading directions, someone else's intervention, or impossible time constraints. You will make things worse in the long run because the Bully Broad will suspect you anyway, and then compound the concern by not believing you. Try something like this:

"I made the error. I am upset and mad at myself about it. So you don't have to be. I know you want to be, though. But the pressure of the consequences from you if I make a mistake has driven me to a state of stress. I am sort of allergic to your reactions, so even if you are easy on me, I'm going to imagine public humiliation, and I just give up. Let's try some new approaches. I will tell the truth. You agree to not have a fit. Until we have some distance from this. Until my allergies have cleared up. Will you give it a try?" And then, the clincher: "Remember, it's not your money, honey!"

19 Down, Girl! You Don't Need to Be Confrontational at All Times

CASE STUDY

Freddie Clancy (we will call her), a Head Basketball Coach in the WNBA, was expected to be tough. Frederica has been a coach all her life. Tall, brunette, richly tanned, and an exquisitely groomed woman, she has the courage of a boxing champion. The Women's National Basketball Association was only a few years old. They started out with mostly women coaches, but they have weeded out a good percentage of them. Why? One of the reasons is that many of the coaches were Bully Broads like Freddie.

Freddie is a typical *Sounding-Off Tyrant* (ST). She had grown up in a family of all boys, except for her. The youngest child, Freddie learned early and well how to take care of herself. She also learned basketball from her brothers. An all-star in high school, she ran her teams. It was only natural that Freddie should run some college teams and then, ultimately, the women's version of the NBA. With stars like Lisa Leslie,

Jennifer Azzi, and Natalie Williams, who wouldn't want the job? Freddie lasted only one season.

The WNBA was preceded by the American Basketball League (ABL). I got to be one of the organizational psychologists who helped out with team dynamics. Finding women coaches then was a delicate job. The league wanted women who could mentor the only professional women basketball players in America. Those women had been playing overseas for decades. So a coach who was used to the techniques for guiding college freshman players at Kentucky had to find the appropriate strategy to pull together a dozen women who had played as professionals all over the world.

Why have Freddie and women like her washed out as coaches? For the same reason that they have washed out in the corporate, arts, music, and nonprofit worlds. They haven't quite made the transition from being in charge and making the charge. Women can't get away with the harsh and command-and-control style that many male coaches and business officers can. Men can't always get away with it either. In professional coaching, the raging tyrant man coach is receding to the end of the bench. But unfortunately, for now, when a woman is a bully, she stands out. We seem to expect that she will be more political than her male counterparts. Although this might be true for some, others simply haven't learned the fine art of rapport building while assuming command.

Bully Broads, for instance, can be tough with the waiters, the doormen, the bus drivers, the other team general managers, and most of the players who play for her. These coaches probably all had winning college teams. The professional players have not been as respectful as the college players. They are used to playing overseas and with some seasoned veteran players and coaches. Nowadays, each year the league drafts more college graduates, but in the beginning of these leagues they had to enlist many American women who had been struggling abroad for so long. An American draftee woman who stayed at my house for an interim time cried, "Oh, my first Thanksgiving at home in seven years!"

These types of bully coaches confront their trainers about their techniques, the stars about their work ethic, and the league about their hiring practices. Some cannot seem to turn off the demanding, entitled style. When they are in their confrontational mood, you'd better watch out.

Near the end of the first season of these new leagues, the players protested and the leagues took notice. Some coaches did not return the second year. What was the problem? These women's basketball techniques were incredible, they worked their heads off, and their public relations were good commercially, but nobody seemed to want to have a meal with them.

Entitlement oozes out of bullies. They think the shoe salesperson or the popcorn vendor should be paying attention when they step up. If they don't pay attention, our bully calls them on it immediately. You don't need to confront at every turn.

Here's how an intervention with this type of bully goes (although I did not use this approach with Freddie). The coaches and the players and any special people gather with a facilitator like me. The point is to engage in team building. Our company does it on a daily basis with high-tech companies. The intervention is really the same for both. With an all-star athletic team, we expected the players to be more forthcoming with the coaches than they actually were. I did interventions with several of the teams, and the patterns seemed to be the same with all of them. No matter how much aggression was displayed on the basketball court, the players would be more timid and docile with the coach. In such situations, the coach becomes strained because she knows she could lose her job and she does not want her power eroded. She doesn't realize that her power is eroded anyway because the team loses respect for her when she berates others so often.

A good coach or a good CEO—or a good leader in any situation—will accept his or her own flaws and allow the players or the workers to talk about the problems of the team. In a classic team intervention, with lots of rules and boundaries, each person is invited to share his or her own pain, offer solutions, and repair the damage with another player or coach. It is a magical process. One of the best outcomes is that a serene, open, insightful leader may emerge. Sometimes they have to show their own vulnerability. Bully Broads and Ice Queens hate to do that. Of course, men hate that part, too. One senior officer in a high-tech company bellowed, "I'm not having other people hear some underling complain about me in public!" Little did he know that everyone knew his failings anyway. He seemed to be the last to know, and he will probably remain so.

I remind coaches and other executives that simply showing disappointment, hurt, or rejection is a human response. We are all subject to those responses once in a while. The anger is hard to take. The crying is also hard to watch, but it elicits entirely different responses.

The Freddie types are good candidates for leadership training. They usually have a wonderful sense of humor, which has helped them through the humiliation of losing games, players, and, perhaps, jobs. Someone like this will remind us, "I am big, good, and strong," And, after some coaching for themselves, they will end with: "And, guess what? I've even learned to show my warts and rough edges now and then. It was hard at first, but I felt that others respected me for doing that. People said I was brave to show some pain. I think I was, too. The paradox is that the more of me I show, the more courageous I appear to be to my team."

>-+<>-O-<+-I-<

APPLYING THE RULE

If You Are an Everywoman:

If you think you deserve special treatment, get out of the line.   You don't. Your outbursts only burst your own reputation. If you think that you have the right to tell everyone what most people won't say, you don't!

One of our Bully Broad clients remarked that in her recovery she had to learn to give up the word *should*. I used to "shoulda" everyone, she proclaimed, but all it did was fan the flames and ruin my reputation. If I took my dog to the dog groomer and he screwed up, I would scream, "What did you *do* to my dog! You should have been listening when I gave you explicit directions."

Automobile service departments have their share of the "should" women who bring in their cars. I was waiting in the first-class line at an airport one morning and had a wonderful talk with the clerk at the rope. I asked her if she had to deal with many tantrums after I had just witnessed her handling one that morning. "Oh, two or three each shift" she grinned. "On good days and on bad days. When planes are late and when they are on time. And the women are the worst!"

When the recovering Bully Broad gave up "shoulds," she had to acquire a whole new vocabulary. She actually brought her dog to the group that night. "Isn't he cute?' she cooed. "One ear is much longer than the other!" This time the groomer had not gotten a lecture.

Press the pause button!   When you are about to deliver one of your "righteous indignation" speeches, hit the pause button. Do you really need to expend the energy to tell off that clerk? Do you need to ruin the day of someone who simply wanted to help? Do you need to turn off a whole team because two people missed a signal? Do you need to elevate your own blood pressure because someone "should" have done something else? No matter your Bully Broad score, it serves all of us to watch our own sense of entitlement. Forgiving incompetence, moving off of your own indignation, letting go—all make for an easier job.

If You Are a Bully Broad:

When you humiliate someone, you have caused severe damage.   Even though you are good at it, don't destroy someone

with fatal words. Give the other a chance for a graceful exit. You don't look good when you are demeaning others. You may be making a point, but you are also making a fool out of yourself.

Turn yourself inside out.   Your inside is often softer and smoother than your rough edges. Reach inside and see if you can conjure up some compassion for that poor thing who just did something inappropriate. He didn't know, she didn't think, he was afraid and acted without planning. She isn't a bad person. He isn't really rude. She isn't always unconscious of the effect of her delivery. He had a bad day. She is intimidated when you come in the room.

Turn your thoughts inside, and let out some of that gentleness you have there. You can even say you are angry without showing it or targeting someone. Try this: "I am so mad I could say something awful now. But this is really not your fault. We are caught up in some circumstances and you are a victim, too. Do what you can about this, and I will try to settle down."

My company was flying to Hawaii with forty-six clients and our whole staff. My elderly mother, my best friend, and my son and his friend were also on board. We all arrived early for group seating, as they did several years ago. Only two of us were not allowed on, because we were the company leaders and could wait, the ticket agent thought. The officers tried to go in and ask others to sell their tickets back. The airline official kept assuring us that we would get on.

The next thing I saw was our plane taxiing away from the airport. I could not believe my eyes. They left the two of us on the ground. We were to meet a cruise ship in Hawaii, so there was more than the plane involved. They never told us they were taking off without us. I can feel livid about this, today, fifteen years later, as I think about it. Did I press the pause button?

Oh, no. I made a fuss—a big fuss. Did they care? Had they heard it all before? Was it really the supervisor's fault? He handed us our compensation checks—big ones—and ushered us to the next building and the next plane. By the time I got to the cruise ship in Hawaii, my throat was sore. Although this was a training class and I was to lecture all week long, my laryngitis kicked in and I couldn't utter a word all week. On top of that, I got seasick and I was in my cabin or the medical cabin all week. I did not hit the pause button early enough.

Your speeches can be deadly to others.   I used to think I was just being passionate. I knew that I didn't mean any harm. I just wanted people to know I was dead serious. I didn't really mean to be deadly.

Getting excited can propel you into saying things you later wish you had not said. We rev ourselves up. You can work yourself into a lather with… "and furthermore, and then this, and then more, and moreover…"

Victims know not to accelerate when you are showing how upset you are. You seem to forget it. If you can remember that you are liable to accelerate your drama as well as your hypertension, try changing the speech to a positive one, or a positively short one! Discipline goes a long way—when you realize that you can stop the tirade, you aren't really getting anywhere, and you might regret your trantrum in thr morning!

WHEN YOU WORK WITH A BULLY BROAD

When you work with a Bully Broad keep the following points in mind.

It is hard to stop the snowball rolling down the hill—so run to the other side.   You see the tirade coming on. Her face is getting red. She looks ready for a fight. This is when you don your imaginary boxing gloves. You can offer her several alternative statements:

1. Stop this right now. I don't want to hear it under any circumstances.
2. We can talk about this later, when you are calmer, and when I am ready.
3. Let me talk first.
4. I want five minutes to explain the situation now.
5. If you raise your voice, I will leave.

6. If you look or sound threatening, I will leave.
7. If you look violent, I will call for emergency help.
8. I don't want to help you accelerate your feelings.
9. Your confrontation style is hard on me.
10. This is not a time for an altercation. It is a time for under-standing.

You may think you can't carry out any of the preceding state-ments. You can try the words in a neutral zone, with your good friends, or even with your bully if there is someone else in your presence. Being able to confront a bully in the midst of the war may be your biggest task. You will be amazed at the results if you will just try it. Of course, the bully won't like it. You will likely not get many of those ten sentences out, but you will be planting some seeds.

I have had people glare at me, knowing that I have uncovered their most precious defensive covers, and they act like they don't accept a word I have said. Then, days or weeks later, they return, quot-ing me almost verbatim.

To start out, you can even stammer: "Uh, Susie, this is kind of hard for me. I'm not going to be good at this, but…" Another possibility is to ask your Bully Broad to listen to you recite these options when she is not mad about something. The best time to catch her is when she is open to arbitration. Start with, "You know, yesterday when you were so mad because the report was missing, well, right now, I'd like to tell you what I wanted to say yesterday, but I was too 'chicken.' May I say some of it now, just for practice?"

Let her know when she is feeling mellow how difficult her con-frontations are on you. Give her time to think about it. Don't back down. Don't let her talk you out of using the list the next time she acts out. Don't let her pooh-pooh this. Don't let her distract you. Remember, this is serious business, deadly serious. People have strokes and heart attacks in moments of strain. Relationships wither and die. Marriages crack. Careers break. Cool it!

20 Avoid All-or-Nothing Thinking

CASE STUDY

Camille Kawasaki, founding officer, received the news last Friday. Of course, the idea for the company had been hers. She handpicked her partners. She marched through the venture capital world, ending with a multi-million-dollar round and the very team who were asking her to leave last Friday. She had started out the company in her house, while she employed three alternating nannies to keep the twins and the baby out of her hair. Her husband was livid at first, and he was greatly relieved when the office team moved to another site, miles away from home. This meant long commute hours for Camille, who could not break away from her product sooner than ten or twelve hours later each day.

Camille loved her product—a device that would help wire in home electronics—without wires, of course. She had a great engineering team and the developers were rabid about the possibilities. She had fifteen years of experience with a blue-chip company and had recruited these brilliant minds for her own endeavor.

Camille had given her life's blood to the company. She had sacrificed her home life, and had nursed and pumped and done whatever was necessary to have a new baby and a new company at the same time. The baby was good. Sometimes she nursed her in the car while the nanny drove, and then the nanny would bring the baby back home again. Fortunately, Camille needed little sleep, because little she got. But she was a happy woman, doing what she loved, while still having what she loved at home.

What will happen to Camille now? The partners will give her some alternatives: a severance package or another position working under the new CEO. If I know Camille, she will opt to stay, wanting to ride the wave the whole way, even if not at the top position. Will that work? Will she be able to take orders from someone else who is brought in without the vested interest Camille brought to the project? My short answer, now, is that it will be very hard on Camille.

This CEO was the typical Bully Broad. Fast-talking, fast-walking, hypervigilant, Camille was in charge wherever she went. She liked being in charge. There was no hesitancy in this woman. But she had a flaw—a fatal flaw: all-or-nothing thinking. When we tested her on one of our decision-making inventories, she tested as an idealist. She believed there was one right way, and it was only right to take that right way.

Entrepreneurs must have some pragmatism in them. They must be able to allow "quick and dirty" jobs now and then. They have to look aside and let some products go out the door, knowing they will be reruns or returns later.

The practical, big-picture side of a leader in a company needs to know when to cut and paste and when to go for 100 percent perfection. If she doesn't have the stomach for shoddy output sometimes, she will be killing herself and her staff; of course, she will be killing herself anyway over every error and every miss. We preach excellence. Quality Assurance Departments look for flaws and squawk about them. But the truth is, especially in a start-up mode, you sometimes have to do what is practical to move the project along.

When an entrepreneur starts a project, she must also realize that she can't have things go her way all the time. Camille was actually better off when she first worked out of her home, with one or two of her compadres at her side. Then she had her hands on everything and could monitor the direction of the development. As time wore on and the staff grew, Camille was not able to be in all places at one time. Decisions were made, tasks accomplished, resources purchased without Camille's authorization.

As the product evolved, the level of decision making became exponential, and Camille became more controlling. She wanted all or nothing in all arenas. One of her most creative software programmers left his work unattended for a weekend to go to Las Vegas. She fired him upon his return. "If Olaf doesn't know enough to protect his work, instead of leaving it around for anyone to see, I don't want him." She didn't want him in the company at all. All-or-nothing folks believe that life is black and white. They use the words *always*, *never*, and *absolutely*. With them, you are in or you are out. There is no gray area, no capitulation, and no compromise.

Camille's partners actually talked Olaf back to the company. She had a fit and vetoed the proposition. An all-or-nothing person does not back down easily. It does not fit into the pattern. The compulsion toward go or no go avoids that messy yellow caution position, which makes some people nervous.

Camille missed the boat when she concentrated on product development without any attention to marketing and to revenue stream production. The truth is that her brain could not hold any more data and she would not trust any of her staff to strategize without her input. When she did have to send financial data in for accounting, she would work night and day, breaking her back, only to discover, sometimes, that she had missed reporting a big piece of spending about which she had been unaware. You can imagine the noise when that data was uncovered.

Speaking of noise, Camille had a loud voice. Her personality did not fit her name at all. "Sergeant" might have been more appropriate. She seemed to relish raising her voice. She had no trouble redressing someone who was not practicing the all-or-nothing philosophy.

Camille's future is dark. She will probably get involved in another start-up. She is brilliant, and if she keeps herself lean and mean, she may have a chance. She has learned a few things, too.

"I wish I had used a broader view of the company. I was dogged about the product, but I kept forgetting that we would have to do something with the darned thing when we were through," she said.

"I also did not want to sell premature products," she continued. I didn't understand that I had to be showing income potential. I could have let a few things out. They were not great, not in our main plan, but I could have squeezed out something so that we could show our financial reliability. Drake kept urging me to start selling to the customers who were beginning to beg us, but I did not want to look slipshod to companies like Motorola. I guess my strategy was stodgy for the times."

Camille knows she made severe mistakes, but her biggest mistake was not hiring Fadi Eisnerberg. Fadi was an icon, and he was willing to work for Camille. He wanted a one-year-only contract, and he wanted to work out of his home, three plane hours away. Camille wanted all of him or nothing. She got nothing. The board members heard that she had missed out on this guru, and they were angry. She also lost quite a stuffy traditionalist who had a great resume and could have connected her with some superior customers. "He was too old, too fat, and didn't know our product," she said. Aside from the legal implications that would have ensued if she had revealed that sentence to anyone who might have quoted it publicly, she simply missed out on the man who could have helped position the company appropriately.

>-+>-O-<+-+-<

Bully Broads who apply all-or-nothing thinking have never been introduced to Martin Seligman's *Learned Optimism* theory. Seligman believes that optimism and pessimism can be learned. Habits start early and we can learn pessimism from our parents, teachers, and early work experience. The essence of pessimism is three ways we translate bad news: (1) we *personalize* it, (2) we attribute *pervasiveness* to it, or (3) we grant *permanence* to it.

Although Camille and some other all-or-nothing types don't always personalize bad news (by saying, "It must have been my fault"), Bully Broads do apply the last two strategies. For example, a Bully Broad might apply *pervasiveness* to bad news by saying, "If I am weak in some areas today, I could mess up in all of them. If I had an argument with my mate this morning, I will probably be impatient in the sales meeting." *Permanence* is the big problem for the all-or-nothing thinker, resulting in statements like, "If he screwed up at Apple, he will probably screw up in the next company" or, "If I am not good at math in high school, I will never be good in math." Camille and others like her don't allow for shifts in perspective, life changes, new motivation, or the ability to learn from past mistakes.

APPLYING THE RULE

If You Are an Everywoman:

Watch out for idealism.   "Perfect" doesn't happen often. Loosen up your requirements and be open to the beauty of the chaos theory. If you are an all-or-nothing thinker, you will close yourself to all the shades of gray and other colors available to you.

As a child, I was fascinated that Crayola could make 64 colors from the original eight. With a box of 132 crayons, the decision-making process becomes more complicated. What if we had planned on using only the first eight? Well, it might have been easier, but the result would be much less beautiful. Now there are hundreds of shades derived from those original eight. All-or-nothing people want to restrict the decision-making process. They are afraid of risk, and they don't want too many decisions to confound them; but if they confine the risks, they may miss out on some beautiful options.

Allow for multitasking and multiple decisions.   Learn to use a decision tree. The art of distinguishing the important from the urgent will help. Prioritizing will be your major source of aid if you are an all-or-nothing kind of person. You can't do everything. Some things will have to fall off the table, although you may be cringing at the thought of it. If you try to tackle everything on your table, you might not be using your time or energy well. Prioritize!

If You Are a Bully Broad:

Being overdefinite is dangerous.   Give up saying *always* and *never*, and adhering to the extreme positions, which have earmarked your behaviors in the past. Also watch your "right" and "wrong" habits. Sometimes there are two sets of "rights."

You may believe that you are always true to your own convictions. You probably are, but there are times when you can't afford your own convictions. This is a world of teams, collaboration, and marching to someone else's drumbeat. It will not be easy for you to stop talking and thinking in absolutes. You may need to become an equivocator—the very personality you hate. Remember, though, that this is not all of the time!

Pick the times when you need to convey a more compromising approach.   If you have some difficult meetings with an organization or people who see you demonstrating a rigid approach, make compromise your goal for the next meeting with these people. This means that you may need to employ the equivocator's vocabulary:

Sometimes
Maybe
Probably
Perhaps
Might
Could
Possibly
I guess
I think
In all fairness
I'm not sure.
I don't know.
You could be right.
I am trying to see your side of things.
Let's look at all the angles.

A bully in transition can be uncomfortable to look at.   She is very awkward. She doesn't know which way to turn and she feels betrayed by all those people who did not have the courage to tell her the truth about herself. She misses the confidence she used to have, and she doesn't know whom to trust at first. She is awkward with the aforementioned words and phrases of equivocation, and she misses her old absolutism. She wants definite, specific, concrete decisions— and she wants them now.

Most serious aggressors hate the idea of showing dependence or weakness. The key to eliciting honest responses is to show vulnerability and to ask for gentle feedback. Watching other strong women doing this can motivate some Bully Broads to give it a try.

It goes like this: "Bob, I've been such a tyrant with you. I want to give that up. I am going through a class (or I read a book, or I had a nightmare), and I am changing my ways. I want to be more delicate with you, watching for your reactions to me, and trying to communicate in some new ways with you.

"I know you will not be able to trust me at first. You may see this as pure manipulation because I am in trouble right now. But I think over time you will see that I am sincere and I am making an honest effort to overcome my aggressive reputation. Will you help me, then? Will you give me honest feedback about myself? When I slip and act in my old ways, will you remind me? Will you signal me when you see I am starting out again to be a hard-nosed extremist?

"As you know, I love the right answer. I have been an overdefinite person who has believed there is always the one right answer. I am trying to give up that notion and become someone open to gray areas. I want to get comfortable with ambiguity and uncertainty when it is necessary. Of course, when it is appropriate, I will go into my favored style. But I probably won't always know when the appropriate time really is. I will usually use 'my time' instead of the 'appropriate time.' I will slip and sound like the old me when I should be trying to be the new me.

"When I do something well, and I demonstrate a more compromising style, or show empathy for others, or concern for you, or attention to the feelings of those around me, will you let me know? I will need the feedback, and, of course, I'll need the reinforcement when I start to sound like a regular person again. Can I count on you for this?"

Showing vulnerability is hard on the Bully Broad, but it is also hard on the people who were used to the tiger. When your colleagues see you in a state of uncertainty, or perhaps as a scared little girl, they may feel bewildered. Reassure them that you are in a state of growth, and that your behavior may be confusing for a while.

I heard a key leader share this with her staff the other day: "I am trying to hold back. It is really hard. It is boring, too. You know I used to have something to say about every subject, and I loved to lay the law down when I felt my ethics were being disturbed. Now I am trying to accommodate you, the whole team, and it is rough. I feel so bored and I get distracted and want to butt in there and scream at you all. So when you see me slipping away, or you feel an impatient energy surge from me, prepare yourself. I don't know how long I can be good at this."

WHEN YOU WORK WITH A BULLY BROAD

When you work with a Bully Broad keep the following points in mind.

Make your own changes.   Change in a system can begin from either side—the victim or the bully. Either the bully can initiate the repair or the victim can start it.

The victim would begin like this: "You know, Mary, I think I may have you figured out. You often see only one side or the other. You are passionate about the right side, and you wish we would see it, too. You think compromise is yielding, and your sturdy nature wants to prove to us that you are quite willing to make all the decisions.

"You really want to motivate us. You appear to think that yelling and screaming and jumping up and down may scare us into action. Instead it makes me just more stubborn. I want to get away, and I sure don't want to cooperate with you. So you get just the opposite effect from what you want.

"I'd like to stop this silly game. I want to be able to stand up to you or push back when necessary. I want to be courageous enough to do this because I'm tired of this nonteam stuff that we do to each other. Would you help me out by backing off a little when I say 'time out'? Or would you just take a breath when I say, 'Down, girl!'?

"I really want to work with you and I am sure proud of knowing you and the work you have accomplished. I want us to be a team. We'll both slip. You won't back down. I will slink away sometimes. But I hope one of us has the guts to pull the other back and start over again. Okay?"

21 Remember That Your Persona Scares People

CASE STUDY

Margaret Ruba, a Director at a very successful computer components corporation, was quite surprised when her timid peer, Bill, was promoted to Vice President right over her, especially as they had both been Directors for about the same amount of time. Even though Margaret had done the majority of the work on their most recent project, it was Bill, the slow and indecisive colleague, who was given the promotion. Margaret knew that she could run circles around Bill, and decided that she needed to take some extra steps to make the distinction between them more obvious to upper management.

As Margaret took on more and more responsibility for her teams, she took every opportunity to comment on Bill's apparent lack of production. They were expected to lead together, she grabbed the reins, tearing down his every idea and criticizing every move. And when Bill went on vacation, she undid his decisions and inserted her own because, she rationalized, he was not following the plans.

Margaret never considered that voicing her resentment about Bill's promotion could backfire on her. Although she could be an awesome leader and a great team player, when she consciously decided to outmaneuver Bill she did not realize that many people in the company witnessed her devaluing and undercutting behavior. Her righteous indignation superceded her good judgment.

What does retaliatory behavior do? One consequence in this case was that even people who trusted Margaret—her friends and allies—now became wary of her, believing that she was capable of doing the same kind of damage to them if they got in her way. People tend to rally behind underdogs, especially if there seem to be some moral principles that have been violated. Bully Broads do not rally around underdogs. They usually despise them. But remember that Bully Broads are usually in the minority in any given population.

When Margaret became more dramatically overt in her attempts to dominate, especially in Bill's absence, people saw her in a negative light and Bill as the innocent, well-intentioned bystander.

Margaret's persona did not match her intentions. Her intent was to stand out as someone who got things done, someone who deserved a promotion. Instead, she was seen as vicious and unforgiving, one who would not maintain loyalty. She forgot—or had never learned—that working with people was part of working. She didn't know when to back off about Bill's leadership. She didn't realize that she was developing a reputation as a woman with retribution in mind, which undercut her otherwise good image.

Margaret was a combination of several of the bully descriptions, but perhaps her most pronounced characteristics fell within the category of the *Sarcastic Aggressive* (SA) Bully

Broad. When combined with her tendency toward retaliation, this lowered her character in the eyes of her peers as well as subordinates. She seemed to lose perspective about Bill. Watching this, her colleagues feared for their own situations.

This befuddled and hardworking woman ended up in a crisis because her own people were afraid to work with her. The irony of it all is that the behavior Margaret employed in reaction to this situation was probably the very behavior that had become the obstacle to her getting the promotion in the first place.

⤞•⤜•○•⤛•⤝

The Bully Broad's persona, the image she presents to the world, what she shows in meetings, walking down the hall, in crisis situations—that's what precedes her behavior. It seems to make more of a lasting imprint than deeds done.

The reputation for being ruthless and out for number one is hard to succeed with, especially once Margaret's character fell under suspicion. As her reputation evolved, it could be summed up like this: "Margaret goes out for her goals and steps all over people if she has to." This image will not hold up well when a consensus is called for around her. The perception that "she's going to keep her cards close to her vest" will not help her reputation when she is assigned a facilitator position.

Bully Broads and others like them are always surprised when they are accused of behavior their Bully Broad attitudes have suggested. They cannot understand why anyone would believe that they could be the kind of person who would commit a real offense in the office. I usually tell them, "Yes, I believe you did not do such a thing. But, there is a much larger problem here. *That anyone could believe that you did* is the problem. Your job is to figure out what you do that would lead people to believe you could do this."

Another way of gathering insight is to imagine that others are drawing a picture of you. What would they draw? What else would be in the picture? If you don't know how others perceive you, you are missing a great opportunity to learn about your image, and to change it if you choose to.

Your persona may not match what you think you are showing.   Most of us have come to rationalize our behavior so that we believe our public face matches the person we think we are inside. Well, let me hand you a mirror. Your public persona depends on the perception others have of your personality and actions, not the image you *wish* to convey.

THE IMPOSTER SYNDROME

Unlike those of us who enjoy fooling ourselves that we are better than we are, the imposter syndrome describes people who think they are not as good as they appear to be. The imposter is always on the verge of being discovered—she thinks! She worries that people will find out how inadequate she really is.

In spite of her Ph.D., she will probably make a math error. In spite of public speaking training, she "knows" she is not a good presenter. In spite of her Phi Beta Kappa key or her numerous promotions, she believes that any moment someone will find out who she really is— an incompetent, inadequate, and unqualified imposter.

If your persona is based on the imposter syndrome, get some confidence-building help ASAP. You are damaging your career and wasting every day with worries that may be unjustified. The imposter must come to believe that *everyone* makes mistakes and *everyone* has flaws and everyone worries that he or she will be discovered some of the time. When you decide it is normal to worry a little, and you can decide to take some risks and fail, you will have arrived. Failures produce success. No failures produce blank slates. Count your failures and you will begin to mark your personal milestones toward success.

It is interesting to note that Bully Broads and Ice Queens can fall into either category: too much confidence or too little confidence (the imposter syndrome). In our intimidating woman, both categories manifest in bluff: "I am omnipotent, ferocious, and undaunted. I am also right."

APPLYING THE RULE

If You Are an Everywoman:

You may be bigger than your job description.   Be aware that your authority in a job requires responsible care for other people, above you, below you, and across your company. Your actions and attitudes, your words and expressions carry more weight than your position. People are influenced, affected, and moved by your judgments of others. When a bully puts energy into devaluing another, all eyes will eventually fall on her. People don't care as much about the truth as they care about their own perception of you. Idealists hate this notion. They believe that actions speak louder than words. Perceived intentions speak even louder, my friend. So watch how others may be perceiving your intentions with regard to those precious actions.

People need to believe that you are fair-minded and caring, and that you will act respectfully despite someone's handicaps.   Your colleagues will devalue you if their expectations are not met. They may be idealistic about you. One sentence, one act, can throw you from grace. It is your job to be mending any emotional gaps you may have created.

If you have been overcompensating, due to imposter syndrome or some other cause, you will need an accurate reading of yourself. Does your walk match your walking plans? Does your talk match the way you talk to yourself about you? Are you a phony who is teasing herself with rationalizations, or are you on the track your persona deserves?

"Mending emotional gaps? That's too much work," you bellow. No, it is not. When you learn to watch others and check your impact on them, you will get a continuous and useful reading back about how people perceive you. If you have a skewed view of yourself, ask your colleagues to give you a reading. It might go like this: "I'm just not sure how I am perceived in those coordinator's meetings. Do you think I have overcome some of my aggressive tendencies in there? Have you noticed me interrogating anyone lately? How am I doing about Fred lately?"

If You Are a Bully Broad:

Your persona scares people.   If you have a tough side that doesn't allow for weakness in others, people will pick up on this in a variety of ways. One response is fear. Another is passive aggression. Learn about your own vulnerabilities and use the four-step approach when handling people with less than superstar qualities. Manage your own thinking about what is happening, and put a positive, more compassionate spin on it.

> **Step One:** Identify your own insecurities. Example: "I need to accept the parts of me that feel weak. Everybody has some."
> **Step Two:** Look at the big picture. Example: "I value the company. The company values Bill's contribution, and therefore, I need to see his contribution and value to the company. I must work for overall results, not just my own agenda."
> **Step Three:** Watch out for judgments. The bully realizes that the goal of monitoring her own approval/disapproval process is to help make her persona less frightening, thus helping to accomplish the bigger goals and results.
> **Step Four:** Repair misunderstandings and conflict. Example: "I want to work better with you. I know we both have to make some compromises. I will be starting with my part."

Remember that your intimidation reputation is a handicap.
Keep in mind that you are being judged on past performance—not just current acts. Try to overlay some positive feelings on your formerly perceived judgmental style. You may have to work hard to remind people that you are not the nasty person your reputation advertises. Let people know that you are hurt by the judgment, and that you want to improve your image. Explain that your reputation is a bit bigger than the acts for which you were falsely accused.

Then, every time you have an opportunity to campaign for the new you, try it. This campaign may take twice as much time as the period in which your bad habits started. If you have been the bad guy for ten months now, you will need twenty months of campaigning. This is just an estimate, based on the 6000 executives we are working with. Of course, you don't want to feel that you are always coming from behind, but if you are the arrogant type who always feels entitled, it won't hurt you one bit to try a little humility building.

WHEN YOU WORK WITH A BULLY BROAD

When you work with a Bully Broad keep the following points in mind.

Reset your bully's belief system. You and others will play the role of mirroring the bully's faulty belief systems. Stop taking her message personally and let her know the impact on her relationships, her team, or her career. Say something like this: "Margaret, I know you wouldn't want to be seen as noncollaborative, but when you redirect Bill's team to all of your ideas it might negatively impact both teams. Could you consider your tone and your language when you jump to conclusions like this?"

Examine your own personality and behaviors on the job. Check out your own persona. Are you big enough to make necessary changes? Are you patient enough to coach and not get much back in exchange? Are you seen as the meek peer who will never stand up for herself? Or the nonmanaging manager who ducks out of conflict? The bully is poised to fight back and she is better at it than you are, so you will need some practice rounds. Try this: "You know, you are better at this than I am. I don't want to get discouraged, though. You will try to defend yourself. That is a natural instinct. You will also want to discredit me. That is a natural instinct. I won't let you, though. I will try to be brave. You can help out by noticing when I seem to want to pull back and away from you."

Then remind your abuser that her reputation may precede her behavior. You can try saying things like this: "This must be hard on you. After all, you are innocent and have not done anything untoward. It's just that you are known for these antics, and even though you are innocent now, you will still be judged from past behavior. I will help you into the new era, however. Together we will clean up your reputation for you. I want to help. You may even want to thank me one day."

22 Don't Judge— Enjoy

CASE STUDY

Rhonda Redding, an attorney, volunteered herself for our program. She had a friend who had successfully graduated and been promoted, so Rhonda thought she would give us a try. She started with a visit to the Bully Broads Group, where she realized immediately that she was not the typical bully woman. In fact, the participants instantly intimidated her.

Rhonda is a classic example of the *Silent Judge* (SJ). She was very pleasant when she came in to our office. She had a nice smile and said the right things. But I immediately registered some strong expectations from Rhonda, and I felt like I was going to have to work extra hard to please her.

Rhonda and her friend were both already Vice Presidents at their fiber-optics company, but each felt she had not become the kind of executive she wanted to be. Each wanted more, of herself, her position, her boss, and her subordinates.

Rhonda was a textbook case of the judge. She critiqued every-thing, and nothing quite made the grade. Of course, this all started when she was about four years old and attempting to please her hypercritical parents who saw their main job as giving her the feedback no one else would. "Only a mother can tell you this" or "Only your dad knows your true potential and must push you into the next level," they would tell her.

Rhonda's parents really did their job on her. From age four on, she remembers having to do things right. Hold her fork right. Put on her socks right. Smile right. Write right! A good student, in the family tradition, Rhonda went on doing things right for the next 40 years. Well, almost right. She was left-handed, a little nearsighted, poor in physical competition, and unable to distinguish one melodic tone from another. With all these "handicaps," and being shy to boot, Rhonda thought that she had a lot upon which to be judged. She was very hard on herself and could not take a compliment without a disqualifier, which she voiced or said silently to herself.

Rhonda was not fun to be around; she was always worry-ing, second-guessing, and wondering what else she should be doing. On road trips, when the whole company would relax and unwind, she would be in her hotel room, going over the next day's events. The rest of the team was pretty happy about that.

But, worse than that, Rhonda was hard on her colleagues. She did not mean to be, but she was used to checking every-thing, so when she quizzed the marketing manager on his materials he assumed she did not like them. When she asked the speechwriter for the CEO to make sure he included some local material, he freaked. After the CEO finished delivering his speech and before he stepped down from the lectern, she even cautioned him to watch his step. Then she stopped him to remind him that he needed to catch the Microsoft man in case his last remark had offended him. Rhonda was always in critique mode.

When Rhonda was considered for the Senior V.P. job, everyone groaned. They knew she was a good employee and worked hard, but each person had had his or her own individual editing done by Rhonda, and each wanted no more of it. "She is a wet blanket; nothing is ever enough, and she's always raising the bar. That could be good. She is a standard-bearer. But then why do we all feel so bad?" the CEO said to the others.

When Rhonda did not get the new crown, she decided to do something about it. In her visit to the Bully Broads Group, she realized that most of them were just saying out loud what she was usually thinking: "He is a slimeball and not worth my time." Or: "She really doesn't know her job, and I am not going to enable her inadequacies any longer." Such sentences resonated with her, but she knew she could never talk that way. In fact, she was terrified to speak at all in the group, for fear they would jump on her. It would be very easy, too, since she felt she was so inadequate at so many things.

Rhonda hung in there for the first few sessions and she soon learned a good lesson. These people took feedback from each other very well. She didn't even seem to mind when one member remarked, "Rhonda, we like you, but we really don't seem to be getting to know you. You are holding back, so it makes us wonder if you are judging that we are too silly or too bold or just not up to your standards. You help us to feel bad about ourselves. And we don't like it."

Rhonda got it right away. "My silence is as loud as their judgments. I had better step up and reveal something quickly, because I am looking as bad to them as they were sounding to me in the beginning."

Rhonda started just throwing out whatever came up. It was liberating. No one seemed offended. No one judged her harshly, even when she talked about her own faults. They actually seemed sympathetic. "Imagine. I can say what I want and not feel judged!" she thought to herself.

Of course, Rhonda believed this could happen only in a group like this where no one was afraid of being criticized and they all understood each other. Back at the office, she feared she couldn't talk this way. "Try it," the group members pleaded, "but with kid gloves." That soft touch—that's what made the difference. Not the content. Not the intent. The delivery made the difference. When you give feedback, you need to begin a process that feels participatory to other people. If they sense the possibility for judgment or confrontation, they often close down before you have begun your sermon.

Giving yourself away first puts the other person at ease. "You know me, Harry, always worrying about the details." Then offer your complaint or criticism.

Convincing others that you are not imagining the worst or that you don't believe a fatal error has been committed can soften the approach. Rhonda tried this at work and was instantly relieved and pleased about how easily people took her remarks. A side effect is that her colleagues seemed to sense a relaxed tone, and the uptight Rhonda disappeared from sight and sound. What a relief to her and to her company.

In our program, Rhonda allowed herself to apply new and more realistic standards to herself. It was amazing to her that the lower she set the bar, the higher became the quality and quantity of work that got accomplished. Her staff began to trust her intentions. "Lighten up" was her mantra, and with the lightness a sense of humor appeared.

For a homework assignment, we asked Rhonda to spend the next week trying to humiliate herself. She blanched. "Are you kidding? I have tried to save myself my whole life from ridicule and humiliation. Why would I want to do that?"

We explained that just trying to accumulate such an experience would free her up to revealing more, taking more risks, and then to be seen as someone with a lighter touch. It was a paradoxical experiment, but our intentions were to encourage

Rhonda to come out of herself a little more—with the proviso that if she did do something really stupid, she could always use us, her leadership class, as an excuse for her bizarre actions.

Well, Rhonda flunked that assignment. "I didn't get humiliated or ridiculed. It was weird. I really tried. I said some way-out things. I risked a lot. I even did a little dance in the middle of the meeting. People laughed. They led me to believe it was appropriate for what we were talking about. I'm pathetic. I can't even do this assignment."

Rhonda finally did get the message. She started recalling that same day about how many people had been talking about her lighter approach to things. They all thought she seemed so much more relaxed. "And, I am!" she chortled. When she stopped judging herself, she felt better, and then she did not have to continue to find fault in others just to stay equal. What a relief to her and to her staff.

>—+—◆>—◇—<◆+—<

Rhonda's compulsivity sometimes displaced emotional balance and texture. In such cases, sacrifice and denial become surrogates for nurturing and being nurtured. Emotional armor designed to provide invincibility hides a core that is fragile, vulnerable, incomplete, and unfulfilled. If the Bully Broad doesn't learn to channel all this energy more productively, she can self-destruct.

In the early stages, Rhonda and her comrades in the group just seemed oblivious to their effect on others. They were stunned and hurt when they learned the truth of what people thought about them. The tough exterior began to soften when they applied the principles and the program we have designed. They were able to examine the insecurities and lack of self-esteem that kept them stuck.

One of our 360 questions is about "appropriate use of humor." So many derailed executives get low marks in this category. Rhonda, naturally, got low scores there too. Since she was so sensitive about herself, we asked her, as homework, to start concentrating on how funny her own little idiosyncrasies were. She started laughing to herself, and eventually she could describe some of her own peculiarities to others. That "light touch" loosened the icy exterior. The thawing-out process was good for everyone.

APPLYING THE RULE

If You Are an Everywoman:

If you had the misfortune of having to be judged early in life, give it up now. Declare yourself okay as of right now. You can't afford to be so hard on yourself. Your parents, or your teachers, or your first boss meant well. They were probably all taught that to be a good authority figure, you were supposed to find fault. I still do it myself as a mother. I forget myself and begin to believe again that it is my job to simply point out any danger that my forty-year-old children might run into, and save them from it. If you were taught to stand guard, always try to please, and always do it right, you have some work to do. Give in a little. Ease up. Don't be so hard on yourself.

Curb your instinct to be judging others at all times.   You will have to do quality control some of the time, but only when it is appropriate. Don't sit there listening to a speech while finding every mistake the speaker makes. Don't look for flaws in your peer's report. Don't jump to conclusions about what is wrong. You—and your reputation—can't afford it. You are too rigid by nature to add such fault-finding to your repertoire.

People want your approval some of the time.   They want you to give them the benefit of the doubt. They want an "atta boy" even when you see some of the negative areas of the issue or event. Forget the constructive criticism. Cool it, lady.

If You Are a Bully Broad:

Cut out the scorekeeping.   We know you are good at it. You have probably done it all your life. You are even keeping score on yourself, but nobody cares much about that. They just don't want you keeping score on them. Even if you are the supervisor, you are going to need to handle the critical evaluation and feedback in a new way. We want you to tell the truth. We want you to give poor grades when necessary and show constructive solutions for people who depend on you. But watch your presentation style. Use the sandwich method. Just as a sandwich is arranged:

Bread
Sliced turkey
Bread

your constructive solutions should be arranged

Positive
Negative
Positive

If you can't think of anything positive, at least try, "I believe you might have been trying to make these adjustments. Unfortunately, they are not apparent to me yet."

For a while, until your own image is readjusted, you will have to compensate for the reputation you have.   While that is happening, in public forums, ask others to comment on something you would ordinarily have addressed. This will take discipline. You will not get the satisfaction of making the point.

Let others do the critique.   Even if you can do it better, let someone else do it. You can't afford to complain one more time about your favorite issue. You be the cheerleader for when things go right. Ask another to watch for the pitfalls and spills that you usually watch for. Ask them to call someone on the action because people are tired of you making the complaints. In fact, they are so used to you having an opinion that they don't even listen to you. They will not be as vigilant as you are. Just plan on that.

Accentuate the positive whenever you can.   At first, people will look at you funny. They will wonder what is wrong. They will be expecting bad news, or wondering if you have had a bad biopsy report. In actuality, undesirable biopsy results tend to make a difference in the managerial and supervisory approaches of those who receive them. Suddenly everything looks different. Big things turn small. Priorities shift, and, believe it or not, the person becomes a better manager. Don't wait for the biopsy.

Determine the high-payback items.   Comment on those. Pick your battles. You will need to determine which really are the high-payback items for you, your subordinates, and the company. Then, to a subordinate, explain why this is so important. Present to this subordinate the underlying assumptions, the consequences, and the rewards that go with the task, and get the person's buy-in that indicates that he or she at least understands the importance of the quality of the job. If the person gets it and you later determine that he or she has slipped again, talk about it. Remind the person that slips happen. Don't rely on the "shame on me" adage. It may be a good one, but not for you, not now, and not until you have smoothed out those rough edges.

Don't hit below the belt.   You are very good at assessing your own power plays. Don't always use them. Don't get in the last word, win the argument, or win—period. I seem to be asking you to give up all your fun. Not really, and not in all situations. Fun at the expense of another is never fruitful. Public humiliation of another at your hands only makes you look bad. You may be used to directing public sarcasm at others. People laugh. It can be funny. Give it up anyway. In the long run, you can't afford it.

I asked an executive to give up sarcastic humor in board meetings and he replied, "Hey, that's all I've got." This was true, up to that moment. But he learned to add a few more assets to his act. He learned to honor other people's efforts and speak to that. Some of the sardonic behavior had come from boredom, so he learned to amuse himself with useful acts such as taking notes.

Learn to experience enjoyment. This may be a big job for the serious-minded, no-nonsense kind of person you are. This is not to say that you should become the clown. You may just want to show some enthusiasm, some spirit, some light-heartedness. You will have to fake it a little, but few will notice that you are faking. In fact, few will notice your changes at all. That is why you need to upgrade your techniques as you get more comfortable. In twelve-step substance abuse programs, participants are often reminded, "Fake it until you make it!" This is an important practice. You always have a way out by telling the truth, which will double your score points. "I was kinda clumsy just then with Stewart; I'm sorry. I am trying not to appear so sarcastic, and I miss my nasty old sense of humor, and a little of the old stuff just leaked out." There you are apologizing, but you are also showing your vulnerability, which is exactly what you want to be doing whenever you can.

It is time for Bully Broads to see the handwriting on the corporate wall. In the new management era, collaboration is a fact of organizational life. People skills are priceless. Companies have to be capable of quickly merging with other companies. Databases have to be blended and operations coordinated. If required, managers have to adjust to radically different corporate cultures, align with former competitors, and seamlessly integrate disparate operations. As intelligent and capable as they may be, some female dynamos don't always get it. They simply can no longer afford to be a one-woman team.

WHEN YOU WORK WITH A BULLY BROAD

If you are already particularly sensitive to being attacked or judged, the Bully Broad will easily trigger you. Recently I dealt with a man who had been totally broken by a statement his boss had made about him indicating that he was not of the educated caliber he needed to be for a promising promotion that everyone seemed to want. His feelings of inadequacy were triggered by the boss's comment about his credentials. That was *his* baggage. The boss was just stating the facts about his qualifications. In the long run, the lack of an MBA would not be his distinguishing feature.

This man had quit school at age sixteen, but he was brilliant, got a GED certificate, took a year of college, was bored, and then was drafted for a good position in an incredible company by the owner and founder of a nationally known institution. This man was good, but he had allowed himself to be destroyed by the judgment of the already designated bully boss.

Check yourself out.   Are you being too sensitive, as a result of your own insecurities, so that you are just waiting to be stomped upon? If you are on the reactive side, take ownership of your part in the process. Then say to the bully, "You know, I am a little sensitive in that one area, so I am trying not to overreact. Still, I wish you had come to me about this deficiency so we could talk about it calmly. I know I haven't really justified myself to you, and some of this is even my own stuff again. I try to test people to see if they will realize how brilliant I am, even if I haven't given them any reason or room to find out about my accomplishments. I may have done that with you. That's not fair to you."

Train the bully.   Let her know where your tender spots are, and let her know when she is stepping on them. Teach her that you can do a better job for her when you feel her confidence in you. Do some coaching. Remember, if she jumps back at you defensively, that's her insecurity showing. If she seems too busy for your coaching, simply mention to her, "I'm going to let you know about this later on down the road. I can see this is not the right moment, but it is important to me, and this is something we need to understand together. I want to help you to work better with me. I know you want a lot out of me. I want to give a lot, too. So I need to express to you what might be the barriers to this successful end."

Don't persist in internalizing the remarks.   If you are automatically going to internalize the bad stuff, you are going to have to work very hard to buffer some of the complaints. If you can't speak up for yourself, you are really being a masochist. Even writing a three-sentence memo is sometimes better than swallowing it forever, contaminating your body with that acidic response to conflict.

The Bully Broad phenomenon isn't unique to Silicon Valley or to the business world. Your minister, your librarian, your neighbor may all incorporate that internal judge who looks for flaws first. Remember that she must be playing the judge because she was trained to do so, and because no one has had the courage to tell her that it is no longer working. If you have a visceral response to her aggressiveness, I can promise that others do, too. So, muster up some courage and see if you can find a way to remind her about her abrupt and critical style.

Expect a poor response the first few times. Both you and the Bully Broad will be surprised and disarmed when you comment on her behavior the first or second time. She won't like it. And what does she do when she doesn't like something? She lashes out and makes a fuss. She wants to teach you never to do that again. Most of her response will be subconscious. She isn't fully aware that you hurt her badly enough for her to scream at you. And she doesn't even realize that she is screaming at you.

In our practice, we have actually videotaped some hot discussions, and the person who is acting out is always surprised to see how vicious she has appeared. The one who holds in her response, by the way, is likewise surprised at what a milquetoast she has appeared to be. She was hanging in there, the adrenaline was rushing, she was contemplating what to say or do, and she felt brave just standing in front of the howling banshee, but it didn't look that good on tape. Her appearance did not belie those feelings. Rather, she looked calm and collected and not bothered at all by the Bully Broad's outburst. Our outsides and our insides are not always congruent.

Enjoy your life. Enjoy some of these moments, even though they can be challenging. Try to reframe the situation by telling yourself the following:

I told off the bully.
She turned on me.
I was a wimp.
I learned something.
I lived through it.
I made an attempt to coach her.
She knows I don't run away.
I will do better next time.
There will be a next time.

Enjoy your growth. Make fun of yourself: "Boy, I am slow to get it. Maybe I can pull a speech out of my pocket. Naw, I've got to get it together. I can. I have a long time to learn it, after all. Maybe another five or ten years! That may be time enough!

RULE 23

Success Starts Inside

CASE STUDY

Rene Sanders was young, startlingly beautiful, and a gross-talking, single-focused wild woman when she felt she had been mistreated or misunderstood. She was a prototypical *Sounding-Off Tyrant* (ST). She was a time bomb, exploding whenever she could. There were four ways you could always get her going: (1) *interfere* with her plans, (2) i*nterrupt* her discussion, (3) *injure* her with a slight of some kind, or (4) *insult* her by misquoting her or misreading her intentions. These triggers of Type A behavior are labeled the "Four I's" and are attributed to some folks by Milton Friedman. Rene seemed to use every excuse to show how far her voice would carry, how abused she could feel, and how mad she could get.

Rene worked in a family-owned business that sold security systems, fire extinguishers, and other protective devices. Unfortunately, she was one of the family members; nevertheless, she could rise up at the patriarch as easily as against anyone else. She had no particular favorites. She seemed to always be testing how far her voice could carry. She could feel affronted by any-one—staff, vendor, or customer. That meant a reactive response.

As with all Bully Broads who deserve the appellation, she went too far. She told off the company's best customer, who sent the CEO a detailed letter about why he was cutting off all business, now and forever.

Dad finally blew the whistle, and sent Rene to us.

Rene was furious about having to start a coaching pro-gram. The Sounding-Off Tyrant part of her was in full bloom when she entered our building. She had a rationale for her behavior. She felt that her Dad had enabled this customer for years and she was proud of herself for putting a stop to it. She couldn't see the big picture—that the company was now in a very fractured state, nearly out of business. Fortunately, the business climate was good and there had been a waiting list of prospective customers. But would she eventually find fault with other customers as well? Probably. And if not with them, with the vendor of the critical equipment they needed. Or with the stock clerk. Or with the mayor. Sounding-Off Tyrants don't enjoy introspection. They like evidence, action, making things happen. Getting Rene to look inside herself was the hardest job we have ever had.

Bully Broads, Ice Queens, and other Ms. Understoods love to turn their frustration on to other people. They always look to the other person as being the source of the problem. If they own a piece of the problem, believe me, it is always a very small piece. They are not introspective, so the problem maker is always perceived by them to be sitting across the way, or at the other end of the phone, or down the hall.

There were so many good reasons to look outside:

• Her father's sniveling ways
• Her brother's laziness

- A sister's incompetence and dishonesty
- Sales team members who got away with murder
- The controller who stole from the company
- Another relative or two who manipulated her father and mother
- The Engineering Department, which held up every order with nitpicking changes
- Customers who were demanding and rude or changed schedules
- Banks that held back
- Her own nuclear family that used her and burdened her
- The government
- The city council, city planning commission, and city manager
- The police and fire department
- Her dog, who howled at night
- Her neighbor, who parked in front of her house
- Her allergies, her hives, her PMS, her headaches, her mother

Yes, poor Rene had lots to distract her from her own behavior. She had grand stories about all of these transgressors, which could justify whichever tirade she happened to be throwing. Once, we had five executive coaches in the room with her: two counselors, a note taker, a timekeeper, and a facilitator. She really loved taking us all on. She especially liked all the attention. It was only when we threatened to quit the job that she straightened up for a few moments.

At that time we preached to her: "We don't care about the circumstances that prompted your temper tantrums. They are abnormally frequent and furious. We are sure you can stop them, but you have not disciplined yourself to do so. You have not disciplined yourself to do so because you have not looked at your underlying belief system behind the behavior. You haven't looked because you are too busy getting attention for acting out."

Getting inside meant hearing the reasons she carried along as her beliefs. It was an internal dialogue that kept her ravings as positive responses in her own mind. Here is her list of reasons. They were not congruent as the basis for her beliefs, and we had to prioritize them for her, because she used them interchangeably.

I deserve everything I want.
I am entitled.
If I fuss enough, I get it.
Nobody will say "no" to me if I act up.
Everyone but me is incompetent, lazy, dishonest, or stupid.
Nobody but me will call people on their antics.
If they refuse to cooperate, I can get rid of them.
I have a lot to do.
I have to do everything.
I have the whole burden of this company.
I have the whole burden of my family at home.
I am in charge of everything.
I don't have enough time to do it all, so I have to scream to get attention.
Screaming gets attention.

We worked with her on every belief. We asked her if she would put aside some of them. We helped her to see that she felt so frazzled and got no collaboration from everyone else because she saw them as so inadequate. We showed her that she tended to render her victims defenseless, defeated, and finally, quite uncooperative.

She cried. She revealed childhood, school days, and first-job traumas. Each new ordeal had taught her not to trust others and reinforced to her that it paid off to make a lot of noise when she wanted something. We helped her to see that she did not have to do that anymore. She was no longer a child, no longer a schoolgirl, and no longer in a new job. She could make decisions, be in control, and get a lot of what she needed without the display of anger.

The most important thing we taught Rene, as we teach every Bully Broad (and they hate it)—is that the flip side of anger is hurt. We helped Rene to recognize when she was hurt instead of angry. We asked her to talk about being hurt, disappointed, betrayed, sabotaged, and rejected. She didn't like it. Bully Broads do not like being associated with being a victim. When someone feels weakened by hurt, they feel out of control. They become victims, under the control of the perpetrator. Rene hated feeling weakened.

Rene much preferred the perpetrator role. We convinced her that she knew that role too well. She was one-dimensional, stuck in the position, and had turned off everyone around her. Even her husband was ready to leave her. She knew that, but because denial was her major defense mechanism, she could put aside her husband's threats, just like she could disregard her father's threats. Rene was quite a project.

Slowly, she began to give up some of the notions that ran her life. We walked her to the far end of the worst possibilities—leaving the company or leaving her husband. She discovered she could probably make it whatever she chose to do with her professional life. She also realized that she might even be good relationship material if she could make some real trade-offs.

As she shed some of her damaging beliefs, she was able to decide to change her behavior. That meant moving into a vulnerable space now and then and telling the truth about her hurt feelings rather than focusing on her angry feelings.

The "inside work" included giving herself some room to make mistakes and some encouragement for growth. She redefined success for the present time. She memorized our "Given the givens" mantra, and she had her own version of comforting herself. She had to jettison her indulgence of temper as something bad for her instead of something that gives her what she wants. She learned that temper is only a temporary reward, and that she would have to pay later for these tantrums.

Rene learned just how high a price she paid. She ended up alone. She would have to do more than her share of the work because she pushed away everyone else. She didn't feel so good about herself. She felt lonely. She knew that others talked about her. She knew that she was in trouble, and that she made trouble. She knew that she was also taxing her body, with the strain and stress and the lack of peaceful communication. She also had no out-of-the-office relationships because, of course, she was very hard on friendships. She was married, but her husband had his own reasons for putting up with the abuse.

Within a year, Rene came around. She mended all the broken relationships and even recovered the customer who was so incensed by her. She met with him several times. She concluded that she had to jump through some hoops to get him to trust her again. She brought him and his partner to a session with her at our office. She had to suffer his wrath, which had been building up over the years, for several sessions without fighting back. She learned to discipline herself not to get the last word. Oh, what agony to hold back, to refrain, to bite her tongue, to smile and tolerate another's perception of an event when it did not match her own interpretation—but she did it determinedly, and the customer resumed doing business with the company.

>─┤◆─O─◆├─<

Rene was the kind of Bully Broad who is very good to subordinates because she delegates fiercely and wants the work done. She sticks up for her team because they are almost part of her body. She needs them—the way she needs her right arm and leg. Subordinates often see through this kind of manipulation and, unless the care is authentic, they find passive-aggressive ways to attack back. When the caring is authentic only sporadically, subordinates become unsure about the motives of the Bully Broad. Rene's staff had mixed reactions to her care of them. They did not trust her. Just one of her tantrums could erase years of sweet gestures from her.

Bullies have extremely high expectations of their bosses, and this places a heavy burden on those who must manage them. With her mixed reactions to her father, Rene was continuing in her usual response to authority figures unless he was opinionated and openly aggressive. When the bully registers a boss as incompetent, she has a difficult time offering any respect. She will skip meetings because she believes the boss is unworthy of her attendance. At some point, she has to learn who is really in charge, and what she can learn or get from her boss if she offers a little respect.

No matter what their responsibilities outside of work, many exceptional women are "lifers" at work. Rene was no exception. Her self-esteem was tied to her job. She actually may have lots of other wonderful things going on in her life, but a Bully Broad personally measures herself by her career success. Not getting a promotion, a raise, or a special privilege can be devastating. Rene actually had to learn how important it was to get some of her needs met away from the office and to find happiness and fulfillment in places other than work.

These exceptional women need to find new ways to feel comfortable at home—with children, mates, in-laws, friends, and neighbors. They actually need the same listening skills they use at work. Bully Broads really need to learn the extra and special responses called for in intimate relationships where more emotional connection is needed and where fewer boundaries are available to protect them from stepping over the line.

"Her white-heat tantrums finally got to me," Rene's husband explained. "I used to think they were kind of cute. Now I detest how she puts down waiters or ushers or even neighbors. She always has a rationalization, but she never seems to notice how others look at her while she is ranting and raving. I don't want it anymore."

Of course, her husband loved Rene's new and improved style. She didn't let loose at home the way she used to. She disciplined her impulse to vent. We often hurt the ones dearest to us. "My temper scared even me sometimes," she admitted. Anger outbursts, overdefiniteness, and judgmental criticism became her indulgences, but Rene now has a complete handbook of other ways to indulge herself. Interestingly, she also admitted she no longer felt so burdened and as a result needed to justify herself far less often.

APPLYING THE RULE

If You Are an Everywoman:

If you are having a hard time with yourself and the world outside of you, perhaps an "inside job" is required.   Going within for insight, and checking out your biases and trigger points will help. Examining your own part in all of your dilemmas and talking to others about your responsibility for the situation might clear up some things for you. We don't really want the truth if it hurts. It is so much harder to look into the mirror than at the inadequacies all around us. We cannot see what is showing on our face if our hand is covering it. So pull your hand away and take a peek.

Ask your friends and colleagues for feedback.   We are asked to teach that feedback class more than any other in our field. Even though most forward-thinking companies use written and oral appraisals, and even though the 360-degree evaluations are popular, employees still don't seem to know how to give and take critical feedback.

Feedback can't be just an annual or quarterly event. It may have to be a daily event. When you can't give it well, or take it well—oh, well, we have a mess. So tell your confidantes that you might not be good at giving or taking feedback, but we all had better get started. If you are aware of your impact on others, you may not be too surprised by the feedback you receive.

When you do get negative feedback, consider the idea of projection.   Was that person simply imposing his own ideas on you, based on false premises or rumor or an initial impression? Is the feedback accurate? If there is a kernel of truth in it, use that and investigate further. Ask others for help.

Your personal internal dialogue will help you evaluate your feedback. If you are too hard on yourself, you better not listen. If you are too self-indulgent, you might do selective listening and hear only parts of the message. The best practice is to check out your own interpretation with a number of other people, and if their translation of you matches the feedback, start talking to yourself!

If You Are a Bully Broad:

Success is an inside job. You can do it. Read yourself and your impact on others and make the internal changes necessary for growth. Categorically, our Bully Broads talk too much about other people. We want to introduce you, the exceptional woman, to the rest of your life. We want to help you celebrate the easier and gentler life that will replace all the aggression and stress you've been living with. You will have fewer enemies, fewer lawsuits, better appraisals, and a whole lot more fun. We do, however, want to remind you to prepare for the inevitable downturns and crises that can tailspin you into old forms of behavior.

Get your own feedback system. To maintain the new look and feel, you need a feedback loop that catches you when you stray. Old habits are comfortable, and you'll be tempted to reach for them in emergencies. Bully Broads attract emergencies, because they are so willing to take full responsibility for events. So when crises arise, your new awareness needs to come forward and protect you from your old ways. If it doesn't, you need to depend on others to remind you: "Sue, it's happening again. You are embarrassing Howard in a public meeting and we are all uncomfortable."

Train someone to talk to you this way—preferably in private, but you can build in hand signals in case a public situation turns really ugly. It will happen—you are, after all, still just a human being.

Stop nagging yourself. Quit the nagging, frightening voice within that calls you to work beyond your capacity because you have scared yourself into action. Be mindful of your new voice that shouts, "Be quiet, critic. Leave me alone. I am doing the best I can."

Stop nagging others, too.   Your inner judge needs a break. Your colleagues need a break. They may also need to discover a few things on their own. Your peers and subordinates and even your boss can't always hear you anyway. Take a period of time for all of them to detach themselves from the notion that you are out to get them.

With new insight, you will no longer enjoy the indulgence of temper tantrums or venting on colleagues or friends who can't take it. Oh, you will often feel out of your own skin, a little disoriented, and sometimes downright phony. As you get more feedback from others, however, and as you get more comfortable with expressing vulnerability, you will begin to relax. As a recovering Bully Broad said recently, "I still do most of the things I used to do to be successful, but I feel better, don't create events, and people just plain like me now."

Take a leap of faith. Others will see the change in you.   I want to reassure you, the new woman, that you are on the right track. I want to prepare you to be proactive with all the opportunities ahead—now that people are not scheming to trip you up. These opportunities are limitless. You can now reveal the new woman with the softened edges. You will probably discover a profound success by being the authentic women you used to hide.

Our Bully Broads Group reports on an ongoing basis that relationships at home improve when they learn to look at themselves. Stop yelling at your mate, your kids, your parents. Keep showing them the other side of anger—hurt. People will handle your hurt so much better than your anger. They won't feel attacked. They will be able to feel sympathy for you. They will not be so frightened. They will want to help. "Oh, dear, do I have to cry to get my husband's attention?" screamed an abusing wife. No, she won't get it this way, either. Try the calm approach. That is why writing a letter sometimes helps. But, if you read it to him, read with a calm and steady voice.

You will backslide.   Apologize. Plead with him to accept your own faith that your new insight is the beginning step. Remind him that you have given up using denial as a defense mechanism, that you will move into a proactive rather than a reactive state, and that you believe you might even be worth the adjustment.

WHEN YOU WORK WITH A BULLY BROAD

When you work with a Bully Broad keep the following points in mind.

When you have to work with the bully who is not aware of herself, your job will be to help her out. I know—you hate that. It really should be her job. Yes, but if she won't do it, hasn't tested new insight, can't look inward, you may have to be patient. While you are waiting, remember that the bully isn't really a raging bull but a wounded animal who does not know how to express her own pain appropriately.

Sometimes you will simply have to set boundaries and limits. Say, for example, "Marian, I cannot have your loud voice in my office. If you want to talk that way, go outside. I won't be there, though, because I can't really hear you when you are screaming. I have a limited tolerance for your ranting about Paul. I don't want to hear about it. You fix it with him. And don't come into my office without knocking. And, while you are at it, when you do come in, would you please ask me if this is a good time for the interruption?"

Then you will have to help her off the floor while explaining, "I realize I have not set these boundaries before. This is new for me, and you may wonder what happened to me, but I finally realized that you have overrun my tolerance scale, and I am now going to take some action. In the long run, you will approve, and you will probably even respect me. It has not felt like a coequal relationship yet, and I want that for us."

Your inside job is to understand your own hesitation. You probably know why you used to be intimidated. You can decide you are a grown-up human being now, and you probably don't have to be afraid of conflict any more. If you are afraid, just the possibility of it can be so debilitating that you are sabotaging yourself. You are handicapping yourself if you are always waiting to step on a land mine. If you do hit one, it will not blow your foot off, so wait a minute, and then proceed. It may not be pleasant and you won't be good at it yet, but you will live through the perceived deadly conflict. Try just naming the situation: "Oh, I can see that I've triggered something in you about this. I sure wish I hadn't, but since I did, let's try to handle it."

Remind her of your lack of experience. Say to your Bully Broad, "I'm not so good at this, so give me a little slack. You are very good at having hard debates. I am no match for you yet. But I am going to get better. I insist that you get better, too. Don't hit below my belt, give me time to answer, and don't interrupt me. I will be slower to respond, and I may look scared, but I'm hanging in there, and we have quite a bit to work on together."

Victims become tiresome if they don't take a stand. Rene's father finally took one. He threatened to fire her, and he meant it. Sometimes we have to work with the victims who need some mentoring about how to make the intervention. It is a new experience for some people to make that call. Some would rather change jobs, leave the company, or slither away like they didn't hear what was going on. Rene's dad was ready; the customer led the way. Sometimes we need assistance. If you had broken your leg, you would ask for crutches. Don't hesitate to get the help that you need to deal with your Bully Broad.

24 They Won't Believe Your Changes at First

CASE STUDY

Hillary Clinton, our former first lady, was judged for her eager jump into her husband's presidency. She ramped up a medical plan that few dared to try. She was known for her action, her risk-taking ability, and her desire to make a difference. This really scared a lot of people. Was she a Bully Broad, an abusive woman who pushed her ideas through without reflection or consensus? Perhaps. In any case, the first reaction to Hillary was mixed and mainly negative.

She seemed to do a grand job over the next years of being an exemplary first lady. But people wrote and talked more about her hairstyle changes than her work behind the scenes for the world.

Then, her husband's indiscretion put Hillary in the victim role. Bill Clinton certainly did not do this on purpose to help Hillary's image. And she did not perform like a victim. She steadied her course and kept her chin up. She didn't show her vulnerability. But the American people placed that victim's mantle upon her. People around the world projected onto her a vulnerable state. We could all relate to her because of the plight she was in—her husband's unfaithfulness, the public humiliation, and the stresses of protecting their child from the tawdry accusations about the daughter's beloved father.

We don't know the inside story. We may never know. But when Hillary ran for the New York State Senate seat, she had the sympathy of much of the nation. We projected onto her the image of the suffering wife, but we yielded power to the woman who could get the work done. Hillary had us back.

Perhaps Hillary Clinton made no internal changes at all. She did not conduct herself like a victim. But we, the American people, imagined her vulnerability so that we could relate to her. Anyone who had ever felt betrayed about anything felt a new appreciation for Hillary. Perhaps the press and the rest of us just projected onto her these roles and the feelings of betrayal. In any case, she won our hearts and her Senate election.

>━◆>━O━◆━<

The dramatic twists of Hillary's transformation were unusual. When you make changes of any kind, your friends, colleagues, and relatives will be slow to hear or see these changes unless they unfold within a drama like Hillary's. We average folks usually do not have our courage or victimhood placed for public scrutiny. Hillary was a great public example. We got a chance to see the best of her in the long run. In the beginning, we could have just projected the Bully Broad style on her. It is hard to really know when and if people change. All we can do is put one foot in front of the other and hope someone notices that we have begun walking the straight line.

If your reputation is really bad, you will have to work double time to improve it. Others may still be hesitant about you. They are holding their breath, waiting for you to make the same mistake again. They can't believe you are really going to change permanently. Then, of course, if you do make a slip, you will slide a long way backward, amid cries of "I knew she couldn't do it!"

Don't be discouraged if you don't get pats on the back. Sometimes your great discipline and wincing control will not even be noticed. This hurts. It is like losing the first five pounds when you still have fifty more to lose. No one notices. You may have starved yourself and experienced all kinds of deprivation, but it may be only the last ten or twenty pounds that will draw attention.

Waiting for rewards for diligent change is fruitless. We train people in our programs to announce their changes. Even if you have not altered your behavior one bit, announce that you plan to change. That will score points. In the long run, a negative image may take a very long campaign to revise.

One Executive Vice President called his staff together and distributed his latest review from his boss to his staff. It was quite a scathing review, but he was willing to risk the judgment of others as a trade-off for those who would notice when he did change. It was an effective ploy. Showing his poor review to his direct reports was a strong demonstration of his intention to change. In that company, reviews were very private and confidential. His personal exposure heightened everyone's awareness of his goals for change. That's what I call campaigning.

Ask your colleagues if they notice any changes in your work. Keep your improvement fresh in their minds. Your reputation has been imprinted deeply, so don't give up when your colleagues choose to see you in the same old bully way. You can't count on the outside dimension our first lady was accorded without her lifting a finger. Her decorum did help her. That is probably the attribute we can place on her. Our company talks a lot about decorum to our participants. The act, the deed, the dilemma often do not count as much as how one accepts the situation.

If you have a little setback, of course, all of you will have to go back five spaces and start again. It is hard to keep up new behavior. When you slip, admit it. Say so out loud or even put it in writing. It helps. But be careful of adopting a defensive tone. That comes naturally to the Bully Broad, you know.

DON'T GIVE UP RIGHT AWAY

Don't give up after trying three times—or two timse, or four times. There is no charmed number of efforts you must make to change. You may have to ask for feedback many times. Here's why:

- Your reputation was cemented in the minds of your colleagues.
- Although they seem big to you, your changes are actually minute and are barely noticeable.
- People are still mad at you due to your past behavior.
- Some have learned to hate you and don't want to give that up.
- You have become a comfortable target.
- It will take a change of thinking to see you in a new light.
- You may not have been charming when you asked for feedback.
- Nobody feels he or she owes you a favor.
- You have been serving as a wonderful and obvious scapegoat for someone.

These reasons may seem overwhelming and impossible to combat. You will need to develop a strong philosophical stance against such responses. Tell yourself, "I have to rebuild my reputation. It may be a long haul, but it will be worth it. I can do it. I am worth it. I will have to continue to look at the other person's point of view. This may take a while. I have a while."

With each rejection you may feel less motivated to try again. You will need to remember that the request itself will count for positive points, even though you don't receive an answer. For example: "John, maybe you can't answer this right now, but I am hoping you will give me some feedback about how I am conducting this meeting. In the past, I have been told that I was dogmatic and abusive to some team members and without regard for the Engineering Department at all. Since I am trying to retool myself, have you noticed any slight difference in me?"

Then you have to help John to answer by supplying some suggestions. "I have been attempting not to interrupt or finish people's sentences for them. Have you noticed any instances of that lately?" If he hasn't noticed, just move on.

"Well, do I seem less focused on the final goal and more interested in getting consensus by pulling people into the conversation?" If he hasn't noticed, just move on.

"Well, do you see that I am not raising my voice to the engineering guys? I am not being sarcastic either. I am actually trying to listen to them. Have you noticed this at all? If he hasn't noticed, just move on.

After your final attempt, close with, "Thanks for listening. I am hoping I've kind of raised your awareness about my wanting to change. I really need the feedback. I may not deserve it from you, but I am working on being a new person, and I need your input. Please think about it."

Now, you may be thinking, "I'm not going to grovel like that!" This is not groveling. Groveling sounds like this: "Oh, please, please, I will die if you don't tell me I am better. I am trying so hard, and I really need you to support me while I make these dreadful changes. I can't do it without you. You are my only hope."

So, with neutrality and perseverance, attempt to create a feedback loop without getting discouraged on your first few tries. Don't take resistance in others personally. Remember that resistance is normal, not abnormal. Also try to keep in mind the notion that most innovations fail, most proposals fail, and some sincere efforts to change people fail in the beginning, so you may have a wary audience.

CHOOSE THE RIGHT BATTLE

Don't approach your worst enemies. Start with the easiest people. When you get to an archrival, don't start out with your largest disagreement. Start small. "Charlie, I know we can't talk about the Z10A project. We are both too heated about that. But can you give me a little feedback about some other things? We will get to our stalemate dilemma, but I'd rather start with more minor areas. Did you think my last email was a bit more conciliatory than I used to be? If you didn't read it, or you've forgotten it, let me remind you. I tried to present all sides, which is rather new for me. I am really trying to change my commandeering style. I hope you will get to notice that."

APPLYING THE RULE

If You Are an Everywoman:

Make a list. Send a note.   Unless you inform your staff about the subtle changes you make, you will not be hearing from them. Remind them that you do want recognition for improvement, and would also welcome reminders about your slip-ups.

You may not be in marketing, but you need to start your own marketing campaign. We receive a lot of resistance to this idea from many candidates. They retort, "If they can't see my changes, the heck with them!" This is not the attitude you will need to get people to notice your transformation. Of course they don't really notice your 3 percent change—they are remembering you the way you were. You still dress the same, you are still the same height, and you may still even be doing and saying the same old things. Although you are aware of the difference, you are still worrying that the nuances of your change will not be recognized and you will not get the reinforcement you need.

So start your campaign.   Develop your slogan, your logo, and your strategy. If you were a withholding kind of a person and that got you into trouble, try the slogan "I can't wait to tell you," and use the logo of an open book. Your strategy will be to help remind people that you are trying to stop being a withholder who kept everything too close to the vest. Actually say these words: "I used to withhold something like this, but with my new image, I want to share it with you. I have nothing to hide. Hiding was my old habit, and I don't want to do that any more."

Now suppose you were a ranting and raving tyrant. If you use the campaign slogan "I can give up the noise!" and the logo of sealed lips, you will start your strategic interventions by telling your colleagues, "You are going to notice some changes in me. I don't intend to have a big temper tantrum again. I may regress, but my intention is to give up some of my noise. I want to seal my lips and let others talk more. I may look a little out of it at first, because, as you know, it is hard for me not to express an opinion, especially if I am angry about something. But I am intending to show a more disciplined approach to all of you and this business, and I hope you will begin to notice it. Please tell me if you see I am doing it. I have been quite unconscious of my impact on others, so I will need you all to teach me when I am doing things well.

"I appreciate your indulgence and I really need this feedback. No, I didn't fall on my head last night. I have just finally come to the realization that I was looking darned immature and my aggressive scenes were not getting the job done anyway. They were just alienating you from me, and I want that to cease. I want to be part of the solution, not another problem."

No matter the form of change, colleagues need reminders.
Even to say, "I sure bit my tongue on that one," is a hint and helps. If you are just observing the perpetrator and the victim, be willing to step in and call the players—"May, you were pretty hard on Dee just now."

When you see improvement, comment on that: "Say, May, you and Dee seem to be on a more even keel right now. We have all stopped being tense around you two, and it feels great."

If You Are a Bully Broad:

Talk about your problems out loud.   This will be one of your more difficult tasks. Here's a sequence of excuses you might have been using all your life to maintain your old behaviors:

1. First, you don't really think you have any problems.
2. Then, if you did, you might not want to admit them.
3. If you admitted them, you might not want to talk about them.
4. Then, if you did talk about them, you wouldn't want to have to ask for help.

5. You surely would not want to have people noticing when you are becoming more vulnerable, soft, gentle and, oh yuk, approachable!

So your new steps toward recovery are:

1. Admit it is possible for you to have a problem.
2. Accept and name your problem to yourself.
3. Tell someone about it.
4. Ask for help.
5. Let others note when you are being vulnerable.

Bully Broads usually hate the last step.   Why do we have to be vulnerable? Because this will compensate or turn around or decrease the image that you are impenetrable. People are uncomfortable with other people who appear to be robots, with no chinks in their armor. You are not a robot. Your chinks sometimes show, whether you will admit them or not.

Don't expect miracles.   Teach others not to expect them of you, either. Just break out of your pride and tell folks what you are up to. They will be pleased and may even give you some constructive feedback. They will not laugh at you or belittle you. They will know that you are finally brave enough to talk about some of the hard habits you want to break. Try small moves here and there, asking for affirmation. "I think I was easier on Jed in this review period. Do you?"

If you have had the habit of speaking negatively in front of one person about another, and you attempt to change this, you will be tested! It is so easy to fall into the trap again. Others will even seduce you into doing so. Someone, for example, might tempt you by saying, "I think Malcolm is after the Grady project again." How you would love to remind them about the last time Malcolm did that, and how deceitful Malcolm is, and how he triangulates people in situations like this!

But, the New You will have to catch yourself as soon as that diatribe gets underway. Simply stop in the middle of a whatever you're saying, with, "Oh, heck, I am trying not to talk about people behind their backs. It is very tempting, but I have to stop this. Maybe Malcolm has a good reason to want that Grady project. I will talk to him about it. There may be something you and I don't know about this."

WHEN YOU WORK WITH A BULLY BROAD

When you work with a Bully Broad keep the following points in mind.

Remember, she doesn't change easily.   She probably hasn't been able to depend on anyone for a long time. Even if she has an enabling, helpful husband or family at home, she may have the belief system that at work you can't trust anyone. Her old thinking is that you can never show your back. She may believe being weak is giving up power. If you understand how hard it is for some people to be dependent, you may muster up a little sympathy. Being vulnerable feels like being weak and impotent. Bullies are terrified of crying in public, of having to be needy, and of not being in control of their emotions. The fear of being out of control with no power is terrifying to the power-hungry person who believes that being in control is a survival skill.

Help the bully along.   Let her know how courageous you think she is when she can talk about her concerns. Appeal to her integrity when she shows what you are probably imagining anyway. Her bravery in showing feelings or sharing unpleasant news, or just her willingness to admit a liability might be her best work yet.

Reinforce an approximation of success.   Even if you see only a slight change, reinforce an approximation of success. She needs some encouragement. The only way unmotivated folks change is with reinforcement for small successes. Here are some examples:

> "Jane, yes, I noticed that you were speaking more softly, even when you got agitated."

"Donna, you did not call on Bob today, even though you knew
he was late. That made us all feel better. When you jump on
Bob, we all get uncomfortable."

"Sarah, the first half of the meeting went very well."

Don't worry about the bully's reaction to your feedback. Just be
honest. Try to reach into that back pocket and pull out anything that
can be the slightest bit of encouragement. When she slips, remind her
of it. When she seems too out of character and manipulative, say so.
When she has apologized too many times, and is not making the
changes fast enough, tell her that you are getting discouraged about
her progress. This proclamation may surprise her; it may even disap-
point her, but it is an honest response—something you may all be trying to model.

The final call can be something like this: "Claire, I know you are
trying. That is great. Maybe we couldn't see it at all today, but I now
believe that you are making an effort, and that's what counts. We are all
watching and pulling for you."

RULE

25 You Are Not Joan of Arc

CASE STUDY

You are the case study here. In order to be successful, resourceful, healthy, and powerful, you may need to give up some of the dictatorial, controlling, and combative habits you have seen in others—former bosses, men, your mother, your sister, Barbra Streisand, Eleanor Roosevelt, or others who represent independence and success. Each of us has used our inner resources to get where we are. You may need to use new tools to get where you want to go.

Carly Fiorina, CEO and President of Hewlett-Packard—the first woman to hold that legendary position—seemed to rule like a man in the beginning of her tenure. She made dramatic changes. She appeared indefatigable. She roared, and things happened. Then she seemed to begin to rule like a woman. She encouraged strategic alliances and seemed to be a team builder. However, when this courageous woman experienced crisis in her company, with economic downturns and slipping stock prices, Carly seemed to be ruling like a man again, and she was not as popular as during her early honeymoon days with the company. All of this is projection. We don't know what she really did; we only read the press and hear the employee scuttlebutt. She is an interesting leader to watch. Few women have held her kind of job without the eventual torment from her critics.

Carly has had few women role models to guide her. She may have learned that she could not quite get away with as many power plays as her male counterparts in other companies. Women have to find their our own style. They need to watch for the treacherous label of being an intimidator. They can't afford the bully label, even though their male predecessors could. Intimidation seems to show up more dramatically in women. If this is not so, why do we only get intimidators as our referrals in our consultancy for women? For men, the symptoms are all over the map. The business world can't seem to cope yet with the aggressive woman the way it can with the aggressive man.

Carly Fiorina made the front page of *Business Week* on February 19, 2000. The eight-page feature worried that Carly had taken on too much at HP. The author, Peter Burrows, believed that Carly and her nine-person strategy team were trying to change an institution in the middle of an economic whirlpool. Carly believes that if this is not done in all segments of the business, HP will fail and have to rebuild itself in the way IBM did ten years earlier and Xerox is doing now.

She seems to have the right strategy, but taking on the monster of one of the largest and most prestigious, well-known, and respected organizations in the world is a big task, even for a Bully Broad. Her strategic decisions and business judgment may not determine her legacy. *Her own personality may determine where she sits at the end of this cycle.*

Whether Ms. Fiorina becomes the heroine or is tossed aside as a rebel will depend partly on whether she makes the right moves, on global opportunities, and on the Chairman of the Federal Reserve, Alan Greenspan. But a piece of her history will depend on Carly herself. Will she anger the press, impose her will on the analysts, or distrust her colleagues? Will she be harsh with her staff, or maintain such a tight rein that division chiefs lose respect for her? Will she demand respect and not earn it? Will she be too aggressive, for a woman? One passage in that feature article stated, "Fiorina gets frosty at the notion that her restructuring is hitting snags." Is this kind of statement the first sign of a testy Carly?

Or is Carly just protecting her vision? "She's playing CEO, visionary and COO, and that's too hard to do," says Sanford C. Bernstein analyst Toni Sacconaghi.

An iron-clad ego will be required to withstand the world's second-guessing of the commander in chief of this venerable institution. HP has always had the gentle leadership culture— with caring for employees and caring for the world as a set of values. I remember doing a training there a few years ago. I had never been in a room with as many really "nice" conscientious, conservative people in my career. I understand that the culture is shifting some, not at Carly's doing, but because business must be nimble, using very learning-agile employees.

No matter the outside influences, being CEO of HP would be a Herculean job for anyone. I wish I were her coach. She needs several coaches, just to do what she must do in the months and perhaps years ahead. We will all faithfully watch her, worrying for her and wondering whether she can make the goal without giving up her crown.

At some point in your career you will have the incredible burden of your life plopped on your shoulders. No, you may not be selected to run a billion-dollar company. You may become head of your department or be put in charge of the deli counter. Even if you chose the goal and you are thrilled with the opportunity, how will you handle it? Or, in hindsight, how did you handle the opportunity of your lifetime?

Does the pressure of a big job or a new enterprise bring out the rigid, controlling part of you? Does the tense environment of crisis spin you into your more hysterical mode? How do you stay calm and centered and present when everything you ever cared about is at stake?

You, the subject of this case study, will ultimately have to be a multitasker, collaborator, nurturer, and pragmatist all at the same time. Those roles come automatically and naturally to most women—thank goodness! But governing organizations, companies, and nations is something that we have not been doing for very long—we are still trying out new leadership roles.

Many of you are successful in your new positions. Some of you are a bit uncomfortable. Others are very uncomfortable in their roles, perhaps because they have become authoritarian, perfectionistic, and intimidating. It might have been the only way they knew how to get the job done. They want to run their own organizations like the women they want to be. Sometimes they are not even conscious of sounding like a first boss or their father.

You are not Joan of Arc. Give yourself a break. Look at all the people who work for you, around you, or over you. What habits do you possess that might possibly hinder their jobs? What slip-ups on your part could be hurting others? What personality traits in you will others find difficult? Since this book has concentrated on abusive and aggressive qualities, what do you do that could intimidate others?

Don't forget that Bully Broads come in four forms. The *Sounding-Off Tyrant* is easy to spot. You usually even recognize her in yourself. The remaining three are more subjective and elusive. If you are a *Sarcastic Aggressive* type, you may have trouble giving up the laughter when you cut someone with your wit. You can transform your sarcasm into just plain humor, so don't worry about giving up your most significant character trait.

The *Selectively Quiet* type and the *Silent Judge* are very hard on others. They and the Ice Queens only articulate a small part of their judgments about and expectations of others. The face, body language, and sometimes verbal language they use are our only clues as to what they are really thinking.

Ice Queens don't reveal much. They listen well, usually with their eyes raised up and a frown on their faces as they contemplate what you are saying. They don't mean to look cold and unyielding. They are not judging; they just appear to be. So the Ice Queen needs to learn to listen and keep her eyes focused on the speaker, to apologize if she digests the information without any engagement, and to express what the speaker has said in her own words. She will no longer merely say, "I heard you" or "I understand."

She also must give up listening by interrogation. She will not ask you the kinds of questions that make you feel you must prove your statements to her. She will not even ask for examples, because that also will make you feel the same way. She will say something like, "I think I heard you say that the environment here is not conducive to good work and that you are sick and tired of my excuses about this place."

For all of you, then, Bullies, Ice Queens, and Other Ms. Understoods: Make two lists: a list of *My Goals* and a list of *Their Goals*. The list of your goals comprises your own personal objectives and dreams. The list of their goals includes those that your teammates might be wanting from you. Your boss may have goals for you that he or she has not elaborated upon, but if you do some real soul-searching you can make your own list for all of your subordinates, peers, and managers.

Their goals list might be about habits they wish you would break, traits you demonstrate that are hard on others, and pesky little aspects of your personality that discourage others from working with you effectively. If you can't think of anything, start collecting answers from your colleagues—especially those whom you don't believe understand you. Don't be self-centered about their goals list. These are really the backbone of the work you will need to do to have a productive working relationship with others.

Following are sample lists of My Goals and Their Goals:

My Goals List

1. Get transferred to New York.
2. Talk to my boss about a promotion.
3. Have Ted and Mary know who I am.
4. Get appointed to the president's task force.
5. Finish my MBA.

Their Goals List

1. Have a special one-on-one with each member of my team.
2. Learn the company story and then teach it to others.
3. Get to know my peers.
4. Collaborate with Jake about the special task force.
5. Find a way to repair the situation with Allen.

Now that you have made the two lists, diligently work on Their Goals list first. Not until you have accomplished the majority of their goals can you work on My Goals list. You will be amazed at how much more easily your goals can be met if you take care of the needs of your colleagues first.

>-·->-·-O-·<-·-·-<

APPLYING THE RULE

If You Are an Everywoman:

Be patient with yourself.   Give yourself some time. You have been waiting a long time for these decision-making opportunities. We women have not worked out all the life balance issues. We may love being home and mothering, and some of us even love being the little woman. We also love being in the world—we love work, challenge, and learning.

You have been watching men manage and lead seemingly forever. You are still fairly inexperienced. Some women, however, are natural leaders in the professional arena and love it. Some want to manage; others want to lead. Some want to do neither. Some want to do both.

Being a Bully Broad won't work in the long run.   The tyrannical, sarcastic, and insensitive women eventually get theirs. Someone will trip them up. So for your part in the system, be patient with the transition. It could take another hundred years to find the exact and comfortable leadership niche that fits our female culture and our personal attributes. I am not asking you to wait one hundred years. I am asking you to have faith that your own needs can be met, with time, with perseverance, and with understanding of the bully/victim syndrome. I have no idea what our final leadership style will look like. I have a hunch it will not be gender specific. We know the Bully Broad style will not work. We will have softened that role, found a way to be direct, honest, and straightforward without being intimidating. One day we will not be talking about the differences in the way men and women manage or lead.

Enjoy the journey.   Will we be happy, overworked, and running everything, or will we find the parity we need with the ability to choose our lifestyle and career style, depending on our career moments?

While you are waiting, enjoy the trip. We are going where our grandmothers never even dreamed, much less traveled. We are doing things our mothers never did. Our daughters will be in another era— probably having more, doing more, leading more.

If You Are a Bully Broad:

Don't rush the trip.   You have plenty of time. It will not be a perfect trip. You will experience detours. Even men take professional detours. Allow for your own. Remember: Given the givens—who your mother and father were, what your biology was, what your chemistry was, your learning disabilities (we all have them), who your first boss was—you are doing the best you can!

The eight stages in recovery are listed here to remind you that this is not an instant fix. Some of you will not progress sequentially, and others of you will miss some of the stages completely.

1. **Leverage.** The reason to change may not be very romantic or idealistic. It may be because the boss says so, termination is looming, you are on probation, or there are attrition problems. At this stage, you figure out the reasons to change and the price of not changing.

2. **Feedback.** You are starting to take feedback without defensiveness. You are moving out of denial and think there might be something to this stuff. You are looking for the kernel of truth about yourself.

3. **Motivation/inspiration.** You are getting to the point where you want to change. You realize that you haven't been as happy or successful as you claim. You are looking forward to change.

4. **Insight.** You are learning about yourself and you like it. It is a relief to know why you behave as you do and what you can do about it. You are reevaluating some faulty belief systems that may have been holding you back.

5. **Practice.** You are practicing new behaviors and trying on exercises that are hard.

6. **Vulnerability.** You realize it is courageous to show vulnerability and you are actually expressing fears, pain, and disappointment.

7. **Feedback loops.** You are equipping friends and colleagues with ways to remind you when you slip and encourage you when you make improvements.

8. **Celebration.** You are advertising your new tools and celebrating when others notice and when you handle hard things the easy way. You are celebrating inside and inviting others to recognize and celebrate your changes with you.

Bully Broads are the exceptional women in our midst. They are wonderful, exciting creatures. They are not dinosaurs or monsters. They are beautiful human beings who can stop hiding their liabilities and start appropriately accentuating their assets.

You do not have to save the world, your company, or your department. You may want to. You may be quite good at it. But if you still have controlling, abusive tendencies, the parade behind you will be quite short. You may have wonderful ideas and grand intentions, but be sure that you are expressing those plans and ideas in a way that others can hear you.

WHEN YOU WORK WITH A BULLY BROAD

When you work with a Bully Broad keep the following points in mind.

Be grateful for the bully women who stir things up. They have the courage to be outraged, and they make you look pretty good a lot of the time. Help those colleagues to overcome the Bully Broad stage when you can. Help those who are in it to move swiftly and gracefully beyond being the intimidating woman.

Check yourself out. Are you a quiet, passive-aggressive person who attracts bullies? Or are you the well-adjusted person we hope you are? The stages of leadership are complex. The phases of success and power are elusive and sometimes dangerous. One day, the gender leadership traits will blend completely and then we will just be looking at the behavior of individuals on the job.

The leverage you have over the Bully Broad might actually surprise you. Your pain, of course, depends on your own self-esteem and emotional courage. It does not depend on the positional power of the bully or even on your own positional power.

The more repressed you are, the stronger the bully becomes. She doesn't have ultimate power over you. You do. You can protect yourself. You can learn to anticipate the triggers that set off your bully.

Then you can begin to understand when you need to do something and what you need to do to circumvent the disaster.

Your biggest challenge is to stop avoiding conflict. When you can look it in the face, expect an eruption, and plan for the disagreement, you are home free. To do this, keep your own protective limitations in your back pocket so they are easily accessible if you need them. Here are some of the possibilities:

- Setting time limits
- Calling for noise limits
- Creating time-outs
- Omission of certain topics at certain times
- Making boundaries about space
- Being able to state your position, intention, or perception
- Expecting that the better you are at taking care of yourself, the worse the bully will feel—in the beginning
- Going round two, three, four, and more…

Another important job for you is to help the bully express her vulnerability. Put words in her mouth. Do a lot of guessing. An example of something you might say is this: "You could be feeling discounted right now, especially when you did most of the work on the project." Don't forget to reward an approximation of success. "Gee, Ruth, you handled that very well. Bob almost changed his mind. I believe it was because you were so mellow with him."

The reward: new self-respect!   By taking up the battle, you will begin to sense a great and new respect for yourself. But here is the flaw in your expectations. Your Bully Broad may not give you anything back for your efforts. She may even redicule you at first.

Don't work with your bully conditionally. When you decide to be the good sport and tell her what you see is going on, don't expect repayment from her. I am sorry to say that many of these women are completely unconscious of their behaviors, so the feedback or the intervention may fall on deaf ears at first.

If she is in recovery and is really learning to read the impact she has on others, she may salute you. Just don't set yourself up to expect it. You may believe that life should be reciprocal—"if I help her, she will want to help me back"—that's not necessarily the case. Your bully may not be ready for such give-and-take. Don't forget, however, that when you start conducting yourself like a confident person who expects to be treated well by others, you will have gained new respect from your colleagues. You will also earn your own self-respect if you can be open to the possibility that you are not Joan of Arc.

Joan of Arc gave her life for her ideals. You don't have to. Just do the best you can, coaching whenever possible, changing the situation when you can, and enjoying your own journey. It is exciting to be a woman in this world.

For Men: Much of what I have said here also applies to men, so readers can feel free to pass this book on to a man. Some men will understand the message and be able to improve themselves. Others will scoff that women should get no special treatment in this department. We are not talking about the kind of abusive woman who will need an eventual jail sentence. We are talking about the average, everyday woman who can scare the wits out of some people some of the time. Some men may say they never see discrimination directed at an intimidating woman. Share the book anyway. Some men will find liberation from the tyranny they have lived under by coming to understand this aggressive woman.

Unfortunately, the powerful and strong woman is still a relatively new phenomenon in our time. We want her to be accepted, respected, and heralded as the kind of leader and team player who makes our world go around successfully. Every woman, Bully Broad and victim alike, has the opportunity to change her life set in a minute. It can start with a new mindset. It can start with one new sentence. I have given you a wide range of sample sentences in this book. Are you ready to begin?

For Women: Thanks for being who we are. And thanks for being willing to change. The trip will be an exciting one!

Test for Bullies and Those Who Have to Deal with Them

Circle the numbers that seem true for you *most* of the time.

1. I hold back reactions, but I know when someone is wrong.
2. If I'm right I say it straight out.
3. I make a joke and use puns to make a point.
4. People seem to want more from me.
5. I tend to avoid conflict.
6. My humor seems to scare some people.
7. People tend to think I am more judgmental than I am.
8. I can't seem to protect myself when someone is irate.
9. When it is deserved, I am willing to make a public demonstration.
10. People laugh at my dark humor when I'm trying to get someone.
11. People squirm when I am giving someone a piece of my mind.
12. I shy away from aggressive people.

13. Although reserved, people know I may be catching their mistakes.

14. When I am silent, others seem uncomfortable with me.

15. I refrain from volunteering if I know things are going to escalate.

16. Others ask me, "What are you thinking?"

17. I don't point out all the errors that I usually see.

18. I don't speak up until I am sure; then I will pounce.

19. I give honest feedback even if it hurts someone.

20. It's fun to pick on someone as long as I am being funny.

21. I can tell off a rude clerk or administrator.

22. I feel intimidated by certain types of people.

23. People who talk too much don't have anything profound to say.

24. I hold back when someone is going down the wrong path.

25. People get uptight when I am just being humorously honest.

Give one point to each circled answer.

Add up circled 2, 9, 11, 19, 21   = ST, Sounding-Off Tyrant
Add up circled 3, 6, 10, 20, 25   = SA, Sarcastic Aggressive
Add up circled 1, 13, 17, 23, 24   = SQ, Selectively Quiet
Add up circled 4, 7, 14, 16, 18   = SJ, Silent Judge
                                        (Could also be Ice Queen)
Add up circled 5, 8, 12, 15, 22   = V, Victim

Look for the category in which you scored the highest. Does this label fit you? Don't worry about your score. Finishing this book could change some of these scores anyway.

A total of 3 points in **any** category = **the label fits you!**

A total of 3 points from all categories = you can teach this course.

A total of 4–7 points from all categories = you are neutral.

A total of 8–14 = keep reading! You have some work to do.

A total of 15+ = Call the paramedics; you are too intimidating and/or too scared.

Remember, even a Bully Broad can be a victim of another Bully Broad!

Bully Broads, Ice Queens, and Other Ms. Understoods: Watch Your Fatal Responses to Feedback

It takes courage to give feedback. Most people have an easier time talking *about* you than talking *to* you. When people sit and discuss matters, eye to eye, that terrible behavior they were wailing about last week seems suddenly less offensive.

When others do have the courage to give you information about your working style, behavior, personality, or any other habit that may be disturbing to them, take it like a man, or a woman, and don't fight back. Your first response needs to affirm what you heard, from the other's point of view. When you receive feedback about areas you are prickly about, please do not respond with the denial or reactive responses listed below:

Blamer: "If you could answer me more precisely and quickly, I wouldn't have to jump on you that way."

Denial: "I can't believe you are saying this. I've never done that; I don't have that trait."

Excuser: "Yes. I was off the mark. But my sister is in town, and the boss is on my case!"

Flight to Health: "Oh, I understand my shortcomings. I'm better about that old tic now."

Intellectualization: "I recently saw a description in the *Wall Street Journal* about my behavior and I understand it completely now."

Pessimistic: "I know. But I can never fix that about myself. I am doomed to be this way."

Pontification: "If you understood the big-picture demands of my career, you might not suggest this at all! It's important for you to look at the big picture, not just this outburst."

Rationalization, Part 1: "I only do that response when I know it's justified. He deserved that tirade."

Rationalization, Part 2: "I am too busy to stop and think about how I treat my subordinates."

Rationalization, Part 3: "My job demands micromanaging tactics or we would never launch."

Rationalization, Part 4: "I have been doing this my whole career and I am very successful."

Scorekeeper: "Well, you missed our appointment last week. That made us even."

Slap Back: "You have a nerve talking about me when you have your own bad habits."

B Quick Checklist of Red Ink Behavior

THE POSSIBLE CONSEQUENCES OF AMBITIOUS CONSCIENTIOUS LEADERSHIP

Many brilliant, talented, and hard-working prospective and practicing leaders demonstrate some of the traits below that can derail or slow progress for the high-potential executive or senior leader. Often he or she is unaware of the blind spots that can inhibit the success this executive strives for and deserves.

PROBLEM AREAS

- Anger management
- Arrogance
- Attacking others or benign situations
- Authenticity: Does not perceive impact on others
- Barriers: Creates them unnecessarily and at will

- Collaboration: Seems unable to cooperate or engender collaborative experiences
- Coaching: Cannot motivate, delegate. or reinforce others
- Communication: Inhibits productive dialogue
- Conflict management: Avoids acceleratation without resolution
- Consensus: Ignores the possibility of its merit
- Contradictory
- Controlling: Micromanagement
- Crisis-oriented
- Criticizes publicly or inappropriately
- Defensive
- Dictatorial: Not inclusive when in decision-making process
- Empathy: Does not show appropriate care for or about others
- Evasive when data or action required
- Feedback: Does not give or take feedback constructively
- Flexibility: Does not adapt to changes in direction easily
- High maintenance: Something always needs attention
- Impatient
- Inflammatory: Escalates difficult situations
- Inhibits creativity in others
- Inspiration: Inability to motivate others
- Listening: Does not reflect back, listens selectively, wants only to be listened to
- Mentoring: Seems unable to accept mentoring for self or provide mentoring to others
- Organizationally scattered
- Politically naive
- Power: Does not appear to empower others to use own power appropriately
- Priority: Does not assess well
- Procrastinates decisions and tasks
- Reactionary: Too quick to act
- Reading others: Seems unable to identify effect on others
- Reality check: Often seems alone in his or her steadfast convictions

- Repair ability: Can't mend difficult situations
- Resistant to new ideas or difficult feedback
- Rigid: Does not stay open to options
- Sarcastic: Uses cryptic and cynical humor
- Strategy: Does not use big picture concepts
- Stress: A stress manifestor or "carrier"
- Team play: Can't create or work as a team member
- Time-urgency predominates: Unable to manage time
- Tolerance: Seems impatient under specific conditions
- Trust: Unable to engender
- Vulnerability: Does not express personal or professional fragility
- Uncooperative: Does not manage up, down, or with peers
- Unempowered: Does not demonstrate motivational leadership
- Withholds information

The preceding personality and working style characteristics can be enhanced with a program that assesses for severity, presents opportunities for insight through belief and value systems identification, and provides intervening tools for change.

NOTES AND COMMENTS:

_____

_____

_____

_____

_____

C Phases of Leadership

Most Bully Broads want to be leaders in their group, team, department, or company. But leadership is a mysterious set of characteristics. A good leader is one who has the qualities that allow others to trust her, follow her, and feel empowered by her. I can spot a leader at almost any phase of her career. She shows the appropriate maturity and awareness of others. She listens and empowers others and she doesn't back away from conflict. The list of traits grows as she grows.

The following leadership phases are not necessarily sequential. Some leaders bloom very slowly, some very late, and some never make it past phase one.

PHASE ONE: "I WANT IT MY WAY"

This phase can begin at age two, and blossoms at age seven.

At this critical juncture she receives encouragement to get what she wants. Her self-esteem is nurtured by environments that reward risk taking. These people and places provide enough structure and limits that she knows she is not in control, nor is she completely out of control.

She realizes she can't have everything she wants. She has to learn to be patient. She doesn't have to test others over everything. She trusts the leadership of those around her.

PHASE TWO: "I CAN HAVE IT MY WAY IF I'M WILLING TO TAKE RESPONSIBILITY"

This phase takes place roughly from age seven to fourteen—sometimes much later in a career path!

She learns to shape her authority with concern for others and the operating mores around her. She's willing to be confrontational when necessary. She realizes what she can and cannot do. She is just beginning to enjoy leadership in school, club environments, or work collaborations.

She's willing to do what it takes to get the job done. She knows she can't always count on others. She doesn't complain because she works harder than some of her colleagues do.

PHASE THREE: "I WILL TAKE THE NECESSARY RISKS"

This phase covers from age fifteen to twenty-seven—and much later in the careers of some.

She stands out because her opinions are sound. Her mature and rational approach excels in educational and institutional surroundings. She measures the level of danger against the possible rewards and she chooses accordingly.

She prioritizes and scrutinizes; if the payoff is good, she is willing to face the challenge.

PHASE FOUR: "I AM WILLING TO STAND OUT IN A CROWD"

This phase takes place from age twenty-seven to fifty-two—and for some, much later.

Her profile attracts attention. She is noticed for her ideas and ability to make decisions. She doesn't back away from conflict. She pushes the process.

She is at the height of leadership ability, and she knows it. She stands up for solid issues that she thinks have merit and a chance for support. She doesn't stand out to be rebellious or to get attention or to retaliate. She isn't afraid of disagreement.

PHASE FIVE: "I MAKE THE TEAM"

This phase can happen at any chronological age.

She's willing to play on the team. She sacrifices rewards to pass to other team players. She encourages collaboration, believes in "group think," and hands off opportunities to others.

She doesn't hog the ball and only takes appropriate credit when necessary. She knows others must feel good, too. She wants to shift some of the responsibility. She is not a do-it-yourselfer.

PHASE SIX: "I CAN STAND BACK"

This phase covers from age fifty-two to eighty.

She mentors, coaches, and supports others. When she needs to lead, she will. She teaches what she knows, and she shows others by walking the talk. She doesn't need the encouragement or adoration upon which she used to thrive.

She is not addicted to the limelight. She wants others to try things. She likes developing others and revels in their achievements. She doesn't need to stand alone at the top.

PHASE SEVEN: "I AM ACTIVE AND PRODUCTIVE AND PEACEFUL"

This phase can cover from age sixty-five to one hundred and five.

She has what she wants and does what she wants. Her leadership is demonstrated in her sponsorship of people and ideas. She is content, but not dead. She still thinks, solves problems, debates, and roars about the positive things around her.

She doesn't fall back on saying, "Ain't it awful?" or "When I was there…" or "In the good old days." The good days for her are happening now.

In which leadership phase do you find yourself? Don't be discouraged if you are still in an early phase. You are in a growth spurt, you know—just by reading this book!

D Group-Building Exercise

We were conducting our favorite big group exercise at a high-tech company. It was a two-day off-site engagement at a wonderful beach resort in California. Everyone was upbeat, but the problem was that everyone was very territorial about his or her products and job description. The President wanted more cooperation between the troops and less of a silo effect between departments. We tried several interventions as well as the roles and responsibilities game, but nothing seemed to jiggle people out of their respective departments. They would all sit together, lunch together, and go out in the evenings on excursions together.

We asked people to go to one of eight groups based on a number each person was assigned. We (the staff) carefully crafted the groups so that each department had no more than two representatives together in a group. Then we asked them to nominate a leader for each group. The leader of each group was given a big brown paper bag, which contained the following twelve items:

- A shoe
- An orange
- A small shovel
- A big ball
- A baseball cap
- A book
- A hairbrush
- A bottle of mouthwash
- A small fuzzy bear
- A compass
- A shawl
- An apron

The following instructions were given to each leader:

Take your group to a remote place so no other group will hear you. Give up your leadership role as soon as you have found the destination.

These instructions were given to the group as a whole:

Produce a play.
Make it funny!
Make it profound!
The play can be about your company, or about anything you choose.
But it must be funny and profound.
Each member must have a line in the play.
Each member must use one of the props in the bag.
Each group has twenty minutes to produce the play.

Then each group performs their play in front of the entire audience. The entire gathering votes for the play they think should win the "Academy Award." The award itself is pre-selected by the company and represents something the organization produces that symbolizes the company. Sometimes these awards are funny, and sometimes they are profound.

We created a stage and an amphitheater environment. As the plays begin, these eight or so people, who may never have worked together before, come forward with creative, charming, funny, and inspirational messages. It is an amazing phenomenon because many folks had never been in the same room together before, much less cooperated on a creative endeavor. The team camaraderie is exciting. While the groups are preparing for their productions, we observe the interpersonal dynamics of each group. We watch for those who:

- Really participate
- Tend to just watch, even though they have a line and a prop to use
- Seem to enjoy the game
- Are willing to risk looking undignified
- Become the motivators
- Are willing to direct
- Emotionally drop out

If you put a Bully Broad, Ice Queen, or other Ms. Understood into a group like this, she may take several turns of:

- Trying to run the show
- Getting the lead role
- Making up the best lines
- Backing away if she doesn't get support
- Instructing others to perform the role under her direction
- Walking away from the group if she does not get cooperation

Some of these exceptional women immediately grasp the reason for the exercise and pitch in. Those quick learners usually comprehend what they need to do academically, and will perform appropriately. With enough time, they learn that group think beats solo think.

Everyone seems to put heart and soul into this intervention. People who have never been supervisors play boss roles, often with great vigor. Teetotalers play drunks, and straight-laced folks try being flirtatious. Quiet workers take on boisterous and silly roles.

The point of all of this is to show a disparate group of people that they can work together with all the complications of:

- Changing leadership
- Fixed resources
- Time limitations
- The need to use everyone
- The mandate to be creative
- The need to show their product

We usually give twice the amount of time we instructed the participants to prepare the plays. The real team building happens in the last few moments when we go around and ask the groups to block out the stage directions and practice their roles. They improvise, get creative, and start laughing a lot.

They sit together in the theater, whispering and twittering, and end their plays with arms virtually locked and a sense of competitive and creative adventure. They learn to address people's roles and responsibilities while getting the job done.

INDEX